The Continuing Imperialism of Free Trade

> 'The changing fortunes of free trade in the [illegible] political economic turmoil make assessing the relevance of Gallagher's and Robinson's free-trade imperialism thesis crucial. This rich and insightful collection is a valuable aid in this task."
>
> **Lucia Pradella**, *King's College London*, UK

In 1953, John Gallagher and Ronald Robinson shook the foundations of imperial history with their essay 'The Imperialism of Free Trade'. They reshaped how historians saw the British Empire, focusing not on the 'red bits on the map' and the wishes of policymakers in London, but rather on British economic and political influence globally. Expanding on this analysis, this volume provides an examination of imperialism which brings the reader right up to the present.

This book offers an innovative assessment and analysis of the history and contemporary status of imperial control. It does so in four parts, examining the historical emergence and traditions of imperialism; the relationships between the periphery and the metropolitan; the role of supranational agencies in the extension of imperial control; and how these connect to financialisation and international political economy. The book provides a dynamic and unique perspective on imperialism by bringing together a range of contributors – both established and up-and-coming scholars, activists, and those from industry – from a wide range of disciplines and backgrounds. In providing these authors a space to apply their insights, this engaging volume sheds light on the practical implications of imperialism for the contemporary world.

With a broad chronological and geographical sweep, this book provides theoretical and empirical engagements with the nature of imperialism and its effects upon societies. It will be of great interest to a broad range of disciplines across the humanities and social sciences, especially those working in History, Politics, and Management and Organisation Studies.

Jo Grady is Senior Lecturer in Employment Relations at the University of Sheffield Management School, UK. Her research focuses on pensions, neoliberalism, asymmetries of power in the employment relationship, gender, intersectionality and inequality, political economy, trade unions, and labour organisation.

Chris Grocott is Lecturer in Management and Economic History at the University of Leicester School of Business, UK. His research focuses on the history of economic thought and political economy. Having trained as a historian, he still retains a significant research interest in British imperialism, not least all the history of British Gibraltar from 1704 to the present.

Routledge Frontiers of Political Economy

243. Economics, Ethics and Power
From Behavioural Rules to Global Structures
Hasse Ekstedt

244. Supranational Political Economy
The Globalisation of the State-Market Relationship
Guido Montani

245. Free Cash, Capital Accumulation and Inequality
Craig Allan Medlen

246. The Continuing Imperialism of Free Trade
Developments, Trends and the Role of Supranational Agents
Edited by Jo Grady and Chris Grocott

247. The Problem of Political Trust
A Conceptual Reformulation
Grant Duncan

248. Ethics and Economic Theory
Khalid Mir

249. Economics for an Information Age
Money-Bargaining, Support-Bargaining and the Information Interface
Patrick Spread

250. The Pedagogy of Economic, Political and Social Crises
Dynamics, Construals and Lessons
Edited by Bob Jessop and Karim Knio

251. Commodity
The Global Commodity System in the 21st Century
Photis Lysandrou

For more information about this series, please visit: www.routledge.com/books/series/SE0345

The Continuing Imperialism of Free Trade

Developments, Trends and the Role of Supranational Agents

Edited by
Jo Grady and Chris Grocott

Routledge
Taylor & Francis Group
LONDON AND NEW YORK

First published 2019
by Routledge
2 Park Square, Milton Park, Abingdon, Oxon OX14 4RN

and by Routledge
52 Vanderbilt Avenue, New York, NY 10017

First issued in paperback 2020

Routledge is an imprint of the Taylor & Francis Group, an informa business

British Library Cataloguing-in-Publication Data
A catalogue record for this book is available from the British Library

Library of Congress Cataloging-in-Publication Data
Names: Grady, Jo, 1984- editor. | Grocott, Chris, editor.
Title: The continuing imperialism of free trade developments, trends and the role of supranational agents / edited by Jo Grady and Chris Grocott.
Description: Abingdon, Oxon ; New York, NY : Routledge, 2019. | Series: Routledge frontiers of political economy ; 246 | Includes bibliographical references and index.
Identifiers: LCCN 2018023125 (print) | LCCN 2018025756 (ebook) | ISBN 9780203732809 (Ebook) | ISBN 9781138301085 (hardback : alk. paper)
Subjects: LCSH: Free trade–Political aspects–Developing countries. | Imperialism–Economic aspects. | International relations. | International economic relations.
Classification: LCC HF2580.9 (ebook) | LCC HF2580.9 .C66 2019 (print) | DDC 382/.71091724–dc23
LC record available at https://lccn.loc.gov/2018023125

ISBN 13: 978-0-36-758527-3 (pbk)
ISBN 13: 978-1-138-30108-5 (hbk)

Typeset in Bembo
by Taylor & Francis Books

Contents

List of illustrations vii
List of contributors viii
Acknowledgements xiii

Introduction: the continuing imperialism of free trade 1
JO GRADY AND CHRIS GROCOTT

PART I
The imperialism of free trade in historical context **19**

1 Gladstone, Suakin and the imperialism of British liberalism 23
JAMES FARGHER

2 Spain and Britain's informal empire 34
NICK SHARMAN

3 Economic imperialism in Cuba, 1898–2017: hegemony and embargo 47
ADAM BURNS

PART II
Periphery-metropolitan relationships **57**

4 Imperialism and the military-peasantry complex 59
GIBSON BURRELL

5 The Good Friday Agreement and Britain's 'deep state': Britain's long goodbye and speedy return 72
PAUL STEWART AND TOMMY MCKEARNEY

PART III
Supranational agents of imperialism **87**

6 Policy as a tool of economic imperialism? 91
MARTIN QUINN

7 The role of the Troika in the Greek economic crisis and its social and political consequences 101
COSTAS ELEFTHERIOU AND ORESTIS PAPADOPOULOS

8 Lessons from Marikana? South Africa's sub-imperialism and the rise of Blockadia 113
JASPER FINKELDEY

9 Chile's trade policies in the context of US contemporary imperialism: the free trade agenda and the loss of national autonomy 125
JOSÉ MIGUEL AHUMADA

PART IV
The continuing imperialism of free trade **137**

10 Imperialism, dirty money centres and the financial elite 139
MATTHEW HIGGINS, VERONICA MORINO AND NIGEL IYER

11 Commissioning imperialism: EU trade deals under neoliberalism 152
MARK DEARN

References 166
Index 185

Illustrations

Figure

5.1 'Collusion = state murder' 79

Tables

9.1 Chile and the WTO: impact on policies 132
9.2 Chile and the United States: interest in signing a FTA 134
9.3 State sovereignty after trade agreements 134

Contributors

Editors

Jo Grady

University of Sheffield

Jo Grady is Senior Lecturer in Employment Relations at the University of Sheffield Management School, UK. Her research focuses on pensions, neoliberalism, asymmetries of power in the employment relationship, gender, intersectionality and inequality, political economy, trade unions, and labour organisation.

Chris Grocott

University of Leicester

Chris Grocott is Lecturer in Management and Economic History at the University of Leicester School of Business, UK. His research focuses on the history of economic thought and political economy. Having trained as a historian, he still retains a significant research interest in British imperialism, not least all the history of British Gibraltar from 1704 to the present.

Contributors

José Miguel Ahumada

Department of Political Science and International Relations, Universidad Alberto Hurtado

José Miguel holds a PhD in Development Studies from the University of Cambridge and teaches international economic relations at the Department of Political Science and International Relations, Universidad Alberto Hurtado, Chile.

Dr Adam Burns
University of Leicester

Adam Burns is Senior Lecturer in History at the University of Wolverhampton. His first book, *American Imperialism: The Territorial Expansion of the United States, 1783–2013*, was published by Edinburgh University Press in 2017, and he has previously published on US history in journals such as *Comparative American Studies, American Nineteenth Century History*, and *Philippine Studies*.

Professor Gibson Burrell
University of Leicester

Gibson Burrell is Emeritus Professor of Organisation Theory at the University of Leicester.

Mark Dearn
War on Want

Mark Dearn holds a BA (Hons) in Geography from King's College, University of London, and an MSc (with distinction) in Asian Politics from the School of Oriental and African Studies, University of London. He is a Senior Trade Campaigner for War on Want and also a board member of the Trade Justice Movement, UK, and coordinating group member of the Seattle to Brussels Network.

Dr Costas Eleftheriou
University of Athens

Costas Eleftheriou holds a PhD in Political Science from the University of Athens. His area of expertise is in party politics with a focus on European radical left parties. He co-authored a monograph on Greek social democracy, and his research has been published in academic journals such as *South European Society and Politics* and *Greek Political Science Review*.

James Fargher
King's College London, University of London

James Fargher is a doctoral candidate in the Department of War Studies, King's College London, specialising in naval and imperial history. His research examines the impact of naval technology and strategy in the late nineteenth century on the expansion of the British Empire. Specifically, his work explores how efforts to craft an imperial defence policy in the 1870s and 1880s shaped British imperialism in north-eastern Africa.

Jasper Finkeldey
University of Essex

Jasper Finkeldey is a PhD researcher at the University of Essex. For his research into grass-roots mobilisation against the extractive industries, he was hosted at the Centre for Civil Society in Durban between 2016 and 2017. Jasper taught on organisational behaviour at Essex and on resource conflicts and social movements at Freie Universität Berlin.

Matthew Higgins
University of Leicester

After a dalliance with a legal career, Matthew trained as a sociologist just at the time when British government policy saw the closure of many leading Sociology departments. Needing to pay the bills, Matthew worked in the dark arts of marketing, eventually bringing together his interests in social theory, ethics and marketing through his PhD thesis. Since joining the University of Leicester in 1999, Matthew has written extensively on critical approaches to marketing and undertaken research and consultancy with SMEs, social enterprises, charities and public sector organisations.

Nigel Iyer
University of Leicester

Nigel Iyer has over 20 years' experience investigating and detecting fraud and corruption. A computer scientist and qualified chartered accountant, Nigel soon found that his true passion lay in rooting out corruption and fraud. Nigel is also today a qualified dramatist and has written a number of films and plays based on his experiences, many of which are used in teaching worldwide. He has written several books and papers, and he teaches widely on how to defend organisations against the 'commercial dark arts'. He is also a fellow of the University of Leicester School of Business.

Tommy McKearney
Independent Workers Union

Tommy McKearney is a socialist and a republican who currently acts as northern area representative of the Independent Workers Union while also holding a seat on the National Executive of the IWU. Tommy was a member of the IRA during the 1970s and 1980s, spending 53 days on hunger strike in 1980, and he is also the author of *The Provisional IRA. From Insurrection to Parliament.* He now lives in Monaghan in the Republic of Ireland, and he recently acted as a spokesperson for the anti-Household Charge initiative and was also active in the campaign against water charges.

Veronica Morino
University of Leicester

Veronica Morino has over 15 years' experience investigating, finding and training others on how to prevent and manage fraud and corruption around the world. A sociologist of work and economics with a Master's in Organisational Science, she has developed holistic desktop investigative research and analysis tools to explore organisations, business partners, suppliers, customers and key individuals in order to discover what is really going on, using a fraction of the resources normally associated with investigation. Veronica has also worked for several years in the assessment of the effectiveness of organisations' anti-fraud and corruption programmes and is currently completing a PhD on that subject at the University of Leicester School of Business.

Dr Orestis Papadopoulos
Keele University

Orestis Papadopoulos holds a PhD from Warwick University. He is currently Lecturer in Human Resource Management and Industrial Relations at Keele University. His area of expertise is in industrial relations with a focus on youth unemployment, trade unions and social policy. His research has been recently published in academic journals such as *Economic and Industrial Democracy* and *European Journal of Industrial Relations.*

Dr Martin Quinn
University of Leicester

Dr Martin Quinn is Lecturer in Regional Development at the School of Business, University of Leicester.

Nick Sharman
University of Nottingham

Nick Sharman is a PhD student in the School of Cultures, Languages and Area Studies at the University of Nottingham. He holds a BA (Hons) in Economics and Politics from Trinity College Dublin; an MPhil in Urban Planning from University College London; an MBA from Henley Management College; and an MA (Research) in History from Royal Holloway, University of London.

Paul Stewart
University of Strathclyde

Paul Stewart is Professor of the Sociology of Work and Employment and was coordinator of the international Marie Curie ITN Changing Employment programme 2012–2016. He is a member of Cairde Teo in Armagh City in the north of Ireland, a social economy organisation working in the medium of the Irish language. He is member of the Independent Workers Union and UNITE. For over 20 years he worked with shop floor trade unionists in the Auto Workers' Research Network at Cowley and Ellesmere Port, researching the impact of lean production on workers' lives. Recently he co-authored *We Sell Our Time No More*. He is currently working on a book titled *Protestant Women in the Insurgency in the North of Ireland from 1969*.

Acknowledgements

The editors would like to thank the University of Leicester School of Business for providing funds which allowed us to hold a one-day symposium examining the themes of this edited collection, and we would also like to thank all those who took part for their very valuable insights and contributions.

Introduction

The continuing imperialism of free trade

Jo Grady and Chris Grocott

In 1953, John Gallagher and Ronald Robinson published a short, well-crafted and scandalously provocative article entitled 'The Imperialism of Free Trade' (Gallagher and Robinson, 1953). The essay reshaped understandings of the nature of imperialism. It argued that economic coercion was crucial to securing British interests in the global economy. They offered a definition of imperialism that focused not on the annexation of territory, but rather upon the ways in which states undertook the global projection of political and economic power. They offered forward the idea that 'imperialism … [is] a sufficient political function of the process of integrating new regions into the expanding economy' (Gallagher and Robinson, 1953: 5). This process was designed to maximise the opportunities for British capital overseas at minimal cost to the British state. For Gallagher and Robinson, then, the real history of the British Empire was informal imperialism whereby Britain secured trading advantages at the frontier through the reconfiguration of peripheral economies by imposition of policy prescriptions favourable to British trade. To do so, the British looked for willing collaborators overseas and worked through them to achieve their goals. In this vision of imperialism, free trade became coercive; British policy objectives were consistent and unwavering; formal annexation of territories was a last resort; and decisions as to how to create an empire were made not in the metropolitan but at the periphery.

In 15 pages, Gallagher and Robinson had turned the history of British imperialism on its head. The debate as to whether or not they were right rages on within the historical discipline. In 2014, the editors of this collection offered forward a development of Gallagher and Robinson's concepts (Grocott and Grady, 2014). The social sciences have dedicated tremendous efforts to the theorisation of imperialism (Kiely, 2010). But we wanted to offer something forward that was both empirical and theoretical. Gallagher and Robinson's ideas provided us with a perfect opportunity to do so. What appealed to us was the way in which ideas of informal imperialism, continuity of imperial purpose and collaboration at the frontier could be applied not only to Britain but also to analyses of other growing economies searching to integrate new regions into their expanding economies. We demonstrated that Gallagher and Robinson's analysis of the British Empire could be easily translated to the experience of the development of capitalism in the United States. And we speculated that the methods of British imperialism were beginning to be used by China in the twenty-first century too. We charted how these concepts had been adapted in the years since Gallagher and Robinson had first written 'The Imperialism of Free Trade', and we even broadened out the scope of these concepts to include supranational organisations. In sum, we mapped out how expanding economies make use of both formal and informal methods to secure their interests and the frontier.

This present volume presents 11 essays addressing themes raised by Gallagher and Robinson and which also help to give empirical examples of the broader theoretical sweep we offered in our 2014 work. We revisit the arguments of Gallagher and Robinson in this introduction and demonstrate the ways in which conceptually their ideas can be broadened out. We look at the objections to traditional analyses of imperialism which Gallagher and Robinson offered forward. Then we look at their concepts of continuity of imperial purpose, formal and informal imperialism, and collaboration, updating these as we go along to demonstrate how they remain extant in the operation of expanding economies. With this sketch completed, the contributors to this volume offer forward both historical and contemporary analyses of the ongoing 'imperialism of free trade'.

Traditional analyses of empire: Gallagher and Robinson's objections

Throughout the nineteenth and into the twentieth century, Conservatives had generally been protectionist in their economic outlook. But from Adam Smith onwards, within economics, British mainstream political economists and, within politics, a good section of the Liberal left had seen free trade as a force for good, not one of imperial domination. In 1846 the defeat of the Corn Laws, which had protected domestic agriculture with tariffs, was both a practical and symbolic victory for a certain vision of the British economy, one based upon industry over agriculture; entrepreneurs over landowners; and a global approach to economic growth over mercantilist protectionism. Of course, the reality was less clear-cut. But Britain's perception of itself as a global trading power was nevertheless matched by reality. The workshop of the world drew in raw cotton from the US Deep South and, later, India, whilst cotton textiles were sold the world over. Towns such as Manchester grew into cities as labour was drawn in to work in the cotton mills. Elsewhere, coal mining, steel manufacture, and a range of new industries rapidly urbanised substantial areas of the country. The industrial revolution propelled Britain to the position of the first global economic superpower. And at the heart of this global economy lay the principle of free trade. Britain worked tirelessly to break down tariff barriers and other protectionist policies so that it could trade with the world. The process was reciprocal, if albeit often unequal, as *quid pro quo* the rest of the world could access British goods and markets.

It was not only in economics that Britons held to the belief that free trade was about openness and reciprocity. In addition, the finest political economists of the era gave moral support to the principles of a liberal economic system. Writing at the time of the American Revolution, Adam Smith made the case for the operation of the free market, with the invisible hand of the market being preferred to the visible hand of the state. Critics of classical and neoclassical economics see Smith's advocacy of an economic system based upon a small state and upon the needs of the individual as being central to the problems of contemporary economic theory underpinning broader neoliberal political economy (Harvey, 2005). Yet at the time he was writing, Smith was making a case for individualism and the free market as liberatory devices. Whilst the absolute rule of kings, breaking down amidst the French and American revolutions, had been characterised by centuries of stagnant economic growth and continued poverty, Smith saw the new age of industry and commerce as a golden one. Through an unfettered global market, the creation of wealth would benefit not only entrepreneurs but society as a whole. As the wealth of entrepreneurs grew, the knock-on effect of investment, the creation of employment and of new markets and investment opportunities would, Smith envisaged, lead to a trickle down of wealth. Whilst there would be inequality still, Smith's economics reflected the metaphor that all boats rise with the tide.

What was, in the eyes of Smith, good for Britain was also good for the world. Not long after Smith, David Ricardo extolled the virtues of comparative advantage. When two countries traded with each other and focused their efforts on producing those goods which they were best placed to produce, both would enjoy increased prosperity. Thus, Ricardo gave the example, if Portugal could produce port wine more efficiently than Britain, whilst Britain could produce cotton manufactures more efficiently than port wine, free trade between the two maximised the efficient production of goods for the people of both countries to enjoy (see Yuen, 2018: 46–49). For Ricardo, the key to such prosperity was free trade, and his advocacy of that policy was crucial to the eventual defeat of the Corn Laws.

Yet the coercive power of Britain's free trade empire was for Gallagher and Robinson central to an understanding of British imperialism. Informal imperialism, which exerted control over areas of the world not depicted on the map in red, was extant where political leverage was used in order to ensure economic power was deployed. If empire evoked images of coercion and force, for Gallagher and Robinson to place it alongside free trade was shocking to political economists, politicians and sections of the public who were steeped in the classical and neoclassical view of liberalism and free trade, what we might broadly term the Whig view of British history. Nevertheless, Gallagher and Robinson were unequivocal: 'refusals to annex [were] no proof of reluctance to control' (1953: 3).

For critics of imperialism, who saw British economic power as a force for subverting economies at the periphery, Gallagher and Robinson's swipe at free trade might well have been a source for satisfaction. Nevertheless, Gallagher and Robinson had criticism to level at various scholars who had tried to understand the existence of the British Empire in terms of the empire being a necessity for British global trade. As much as they took a swipe at the Whig view of history, Gallagher and Robinson were also challenging Marxian interpretations of the history of British Empire.

John Hobson (2005), for example, argues that the scramble for Africa at the end of the nineteenth century was driven by Britain's desire to secure new markets. Yet, as Gallagher and Robinson pointed out, the enigma of the British Empire, requiring explanation, was that British capital investment overseas and indeed British emigration went by and large outside of the empire. As such, a vision of the empire as a necessity for sustaining British capitalism could not be held to. Likewise, Gallagher and Robinson took issue with Lenin's assertion that imperialism represented the highest stage of capitalism. Central to Gallagher and Robinson's assessment of British imperialism, as we shall see, was a concept of continuity. For Lenin, British imperialism developed from mid-century indifference to full-blooded thirst for empire at the turn of the century. Yet Gallagher and Robinson pointed out that in this early era of so-called indifference, significant annexations were taking place. New Zealand, for example, provides an example of a significant annexation in this period.

Others took up similar themes either at the time, but not in English, or later, after the publication of 'The Imperialism of Free Trade'. But even if they had access to these works, Gallagher and Robinson's objections to them are pretty obvious. Rosa Luxemburg's focus on investment in the British Empire misses the objection that British capital tended to flow outside of the empire (for both Lenin and Luxemburg see Kiely, 2010). Hilferding's (1981[1910]) focus on empire as a development of capitalism would have been rejected on the same grounds as Lenin's argument was rejected. The argument that empire tended towards protectionism would also have been rejected given that British imperial might was often deployed to open up markets rather than to close them off. In sum, neither the Whig liberal view nor Marxian analyses of empire convinced Gallagher and Robinson. Their objections rested on safe ground. Having rejected so much of the received wisdom of theories of empire, clearly new concepts were required. We turn now to examine these.

Gallagher and Robinson: the concepts

Three key concepts that arose from Gallagher and Robinson's work run throughout the chapters in this volume. First is the idea of continuity of imperial purpose. By this Gallagher and Robinson set out to challenge the idea that government policy was shaped by waxing and waning enthusiasm, or indifference, to empire on the part of the public and politicians. They pointed out that during the nineteenth century several annexations took place during periods of imperial antipathy, whilst in some moments of enthusiasm annexations were sparse. Second is the idea that informal empire was to be preferred to formal annexation. This helped to overcome Gallagher and Robinson's critique of Marxist understandings of imperialism, which failed to account for the substantial amount of investment and migration which took place outside of the British

Empire. Third is that the nature of imperialism – formal or informal – rested upon collaboration at the frontier. If collaboration broke down, then new collaborators, perhaps installed through formal means, would be required. In this way, Gallagher and Robinson challenged the idea that decisions about imperial government rested solely upon the desires of the metropolitan power and, rather, suggested they owed much to the situation at the periphery.

We map out these ideas here and expand the scope of their application beyond the British Empire to other economic powers, in particular the United States of America, and to supranational organisations which have served to further the economic strength of their members. In order to expand the original analysis of 'The Imperialism of Free Trade', we need to also employ some conceptual frameworks that were not available to Gallagher and Robinson and which help us to understand events after the publication of their original essay, and we explore these alongside Gallagher and Robinson's original concepts.

Continuity of imperial purpose

Gallagher and Robinson developed their original ideas in relation to the British Empire. Nevertheless, at the time they were writing, 1953, there were clear signs that other dominant economies, seeking to consolidate the frontiers of their economies, were looking to employ similar tactics to those which Gallagher and Robinson outlined in 'The Imperialism of Free Trade'. After all, the immediate post-war period saw the passing of the global economic superpower baton from Britain to the United States.

US pre-eminence had been demonstrated at the Bretton Woods negotiations of 1944. Held with the intention of shaping post-war global economic architecture, the agreements reached there demonstrated Britain's diminishing economic power. Even with Lord Keynes, the greatest economist of the day, in charge of the British Treasury delegation, Britain's ability to bend to its interests global trade institutions proved insufficient (Steil, 2013). Keynes proposed that a new global system, overseen by a supranational organisation, should be established where an international unit of account, the Bancor, would be created in order to allow for the operation of a mechanism that would smooth out international trade balances and surpluses. By happy coincidence, Keynes's proposals would have been beneficial for Britain, which was running enormous trade deficits due to wartime conditions. Tellingly, the American delegation at the negotiations point blank refused to entertain the proposal, signalling the new predominance of the United States in the global economic system. Like Britain before it, the United States was now intent on ensuring an international system that suited its interests.

When Gallagher and Robinson discussed the idea of imperial continuity of purpose, they did so within the context of the British Empire. To this end, they pointed out that whilst there had been times in which British politicians, whether followed or led by the public, had professed indifference to empire, there had nevertheless been significant annexations of territory into the empire. Likewise, there were moments when seeming enthusiasm for empire was accompanied by relative inaction. For Gallagher and Robinson, the contradiction was explained by the presence of two forms of imperial expansion, formal (annexation) and informal (influence), of which more below. Thus, focusing upon formal expansion and the public sentiments attributed to it was missing the point and was merely examining, as they put it, only the tip of the iceberg. Nevertheless, as they were developing and committing to paper their ideas on the continuity of British imperial purpose, this continuity of purpose was altering and becoming not so much one within the British Empire, but rather a continuity of tactics, with the United States now taking up Britain's preference for 'informal means if possible, or by formal means if necessary' (Gallagher and Robinson, 1953: 3).

In the immediate post-war era, formal control in a number of regions was indeed necessary in order for the United States to successfully counter the establishment of new communist governments and Soviet client states. West Germany was occupied, albeit with the responsibilities for doing so divided between the United States, Britain and France. Located in East Germany, Berlin, divided into four zones, was a symbol of resistance to the advance of the Soviet Union. Elsewhere in the immediate post-war era, the United States set out to support economically those states which backed its efforts to contain the spread of communist regimes. And whilst the United States professed an anti-imperial agenda, seeming to fully support the United Nations in its efforts to decolonise countries occupied by the crumbling European empires, behind the scenes matters were somewhat murkier. British decolonisation in Africa proceeded slowly after the Second World War (in contrast to the rapid timescale in which India was decolonised). One of the reasons for this was US insistence that Britain retain areas of economic or strategic importance rather than leave a vacuum into which the Soviet Union could move.

It was not just US support for the slow decolonisation of the British Empire which demonstrated a continuity of imperial purpose across the eras of British and US global economic dominance. At the same time as pressing anti-imperialist policies at the United Nations, the United States was not above informal interventions in regions where collaboration with local elites had broken down and where it was deemed that only a change in collaborators would safeguard US economic interests. Upon occasion, the intervention was more surgical in nature, with local militaries co-opted to provide military assistance and negating the need to deploy significant ground troops beyond specialists and intelligence officers. Two well-documented cases where local collaboration was reinstalled by co-option of national militaries, representatives of local capital and right-wing politicians are those of Guatemala in the 1950s (see Litvin, 2003) and Chile in the 1970s (Harvey, 2005). Others have made extensive case studies of the events which saw new governments installed in these countries with the support of the United States, but it is worth drawing out here some crucial elements of US intervention in Guatemala and Chile. The latter is given specific treatment in chapter 9 of this volume.

In the case of both Guatemala and Chile, the immediate cause of US intervention was government-threatened expropriation of US business interests. In Guatemala, the democratically elected government of Jacobo Árbenz drew the ire of the US company United Fruit with proposals for the expropriation of land and its redistribution to peasants. The Árbenz government was moderate in its policies in comparison to those of many of Guatemala's neighbours. Indeed, land reform was a necessary part of dissolving the somewhat feudal legacy of the Spanish Latin American empire and its successor states and was in keeping with the Republic of Guatemala's attempt to develop a liberal capitalist economy. But the precedent set by this redistribution threatened United Fruit's extensive landholding interests. Moreover, reforms of labour laws were designed to free workers from oppressive conditions and threatened to increase costs in United Fruit's operations. United Fruit lobbied the US government in regard to these reforms, portraying the government in Guatemala as being not many steps away from facilitating a communist revolution. In response, the CIA worked with an exiled member of the Guatemalan military, Carlos Castillo Armas, to train and equip a rebel armed force to overthrow the government. In June 1954, this force launched its bid to seize power from Castillo Armas's place of exile, Honduras. Despite the somewhat ramshackle nature of this coup, support from the United States in the form of a radio station to transmit propaganda (and the blocking of government transmissions) combined with bombing raids on the capital city forced the government to concede defeat.

As with Guatemala, likewise in Chile. The government of Salvador Allende, admittedly distinctly more radical than the Árbenz government in Guatemala, was working towards a social democratic economy. This involved the breaking up of large monopolies and the creation of trading blocs based around agreements with other Latin American countries. In particular, the firms in the largely US-owned copper industry, along with the telecommunications company ATT, had good reason to believe that the Allende government, democratically elected in 1970, would expropriate their businesses (we see in chapters 2 and 7 other examples of extractive industries agitating against troublesome governments). Once again, the CIA worked with dissatisfied individuals and organisations to undertake a coup against the government. For military support, the United States found a willing collaborator in the form of General Augusto Pinochet. Pinochet was not only willing to undertake a coup, but to implement neoliberal economic policies in its aftermath. Such policies suited representatives of Chilean business who likewise backed the coup, offering support during its conception and promising continued support and a sympathetic approach to US interests post coup. The coup was a more highly polished affair than that in Guatemala. The outcome was nevertheless the same; a dictatorship was installed, in this case under Pinochet, with concessions made to US capital and social democratic ideas being proscribed. In the cases of both Guatemala and Chile, an important point to pick out is not only that the United States was prepared to make strategic informal interventions to secure its economic interests but also that it then supported those regimes which followed. Military action undertaken by collaborating forces within peripheral countries followed by a leveraging of new governments so that they adopted policies favourable to US capitalism smoothed the passage to a return of informal control.

Part of the point of Gallagher and Robinson's analysis of a continuity of purpose was that the use of either formal or informal control did not represent waxing and waning support for imperial objectives, merely a change in methods which was dictated at the frontier by the willingness of local elites to collaborate with the imperial power. Perhaps mischievously, Gallagher and Robinson cited India as an example of this. They argued that the sequence of moving from informal control under the East India Company to formal control in 1858, which occurred in the aftermath of the Indian Mutiny/First War of Independence of 1857, followed 90 years later by independence in 1947 represented a willingness to shift methods but not purpose. Gallagher and Robinson no doubt overplayed that particular part of their argument, but a broader point still stood; informal control was preferred to formal annexation, and formal annexation would be shifted to informal control as quickly as possible. Doing so did not signal a desire to weaken the metropolitan's economic advantages. We return shortly to the methods by which states have made the transition from formal to informal control with increased ease in recent years.

Formal and informal intervention to counter the breakdown of collaboration at the periphery represented a continuous policy of ensuring the frontiers of the US economy were secure. Where, for example, elites might be looking to collaborate with the Soviet Union or other states holding undesirable positions of political economy and ideology, or where policies that were detrimental to US interests where explored, action was taken, demonstrating not only a continuity of purpose with US overseas policy but also with British imperial methods prior to 1945.

Locating the iceberg

As we have seen, Gallagher and Robinson argued that imperial action was taken by Britain regardless of whether or not there was a professed support or disdain for imperial action. Likewise with the United States (Grocott and Grady, 2014). Over the long run, Britain and the United States demonstrated a willingness to operate both formal and informal imperial means to achieve their goals of securing and maintaining economic opportunities at the frontier. When we consider the scale of US formal interventions in Korea, Vietnam and Iraq, we might imagine that formal control (or attempts to control) formed the mainstay of imperial policy. Similarly, the intimidating span of red which coloured the world map at the height of the British Empire might give rise to the appearance of a preference for formal control. Yet these formal manifestations of imperial control were for Gallagher and Robinson the tip of the iceberg, with the informal empire forming the much greater mass below the waterline. We proceed by examining here the formal tip of the iceberg, returning to the informal empire soon.

For Gallagher and Robinson, the existence of suitable collaborators at the frontier was essential. Territories with sufficiently amenable collaborators could be moved towards informal empire at a rate suitable to local conditions. But where such collaborators did not exist, formal intervention was required. In early nineteenth-century New Zealand, for example, the indigenous Maori population initially proved open to trade with British merchants, in particular for guns, tobacco and alcohol (a trade which was for the Maori themselves disastrous, exacerbating warfare between Maori tribes and facilitating widespread chronic alcoholism; see Crosby, 2004). But this did not translate into willing incorporation into the wider British economy, and the lingering threat that France might establish a colony in New Zealand pressed the British government into action, annexing the territory in 1840 and establishing it as a colony in its own right in 1842. Frequent wars against the Maori throughout the nineteenth century precluded a move to informal empire in the short term. Yet, as we will see below, the annexation of territories such as New Zealand was followed by European migration, which subsequently facilitated a move to informal empire.

Elsewhere – for example, in African colonies in the late nineteenth and twentieth centuries – local collaborators were hard to come by. Whilst formal imperialism was costly in such places, it was necessary, or else perceived as necessary, to ensure British economic interests. In the latter part of the twentieth century, it was Western powers' fear that local elites in Africa could easily work with other polities seeking to exert imperial control – namely, the Soviet Union – that delayed decolonisation in these areas. Similarly, where collaboration broke down, either because a set of elites struggled to maintain its legitimacy with the indigenous population or, more dramatically, turned against imperial rule, a pivot from informal to formal empire was required. India presented such a situation with the mutiny/First War of Independence of 1857 resulting in formal annexation and the creation of the India Office in 1858.

By contrast to colonies such as New Zealand after its influx of European settlers, in some colonies there might not have been collaborators who the British felt could be trusted, thus requiring extended formal control and direct rule. In the fortress colonies of Malta, Gibraltar and Bermuda, local elites were prosperous, and in the case of Malta and Gibraltar, European; but they were not trusted with internal self-government until very late in the day. For example, the first elections in Gibraltar took place as late as 1921 and then only to a city council with an elected minority (Grocott and Stockey, 2012). In Hong Kong, where military concerns were equally paramount but where the local population was not European and was therefore treated with even greater suspicion, it was as late as 1995 when the colony's legislative council was comprised of wholly elected members – and only then to preface the transfer of sovereignty to China in the hopes of maintaining favourable conditions within the territory following the British withdrawal.

For other imperial powers, formal annexation also followed the logic of a paucity of collaborators, or else of the 'right type' of collaborator. But such formal imperialism might well take place in the form of an 'internal imperialism'. For example, within the Austro-Hungarian and Russian empires disparate peoples were brought together under a united polity, with various regions reconfigured around the pull of a metropolitan centre (and in the Russian case, with Russians only accounting for a small proportion of the overall population). For the United

States, the situation was something of a hybrid between the experience of the land-based and the British empires. In 1776, the United States occupied only the area of the 13 colonies on the eastern seaboard. Over the course of the late eighteenth and nineteenth century, it expanded ever westward to the west coast (the end date of this process is contested, though Frederick Jackson Turner somewhat (in)famously put it at 1898). At first, annexation of these territories was achieved through financial means; for example, with the purchase of Louisiana in 1802. Other purchases, and wars with European powers, brought Florida and Oregon into the United States. The war with Mexico in 1848 completed the rough process of mapping out the limits of the United States in the north and the south of the North American continent. However, it was in the west, unclaimed by European powers, where the process of switching from informal control to formal annexation was pursued most vigorously. A series of successive treaties was made with Native American peoples who inhabited the west. Yet, ultimately, these peoples resisted integration into the US capitalist system, and formal annexation followed, with one of the last battles of this struggle occurring at Wounded Knee in 1890.

Whilst the United States had occupied most of the north American land mass south of Canada by growing steadily westward, there were still divergent interests internally that required formal action. After all, with an agricultural economy providing cotton for British cotton mills, the American south was economically locked into the British economy. Just as much as the American Civil War brought an end to slavery in the United States, the end of slavery also reconfigured the US economy in such a way as to make the north the dominant economic force over the south (and, by default, causing a recession in Britain, forcing it to look to India for serious quantities of cotton, somewhat underscoring the importance of formal annexation less than ten years before). And just as the United States secured its own frontiers through formal methods, it secured from the Spanish, amongst others, Cuba in 1898. As we will see in chapter 3, in Cuba a constant battle to move to informal control was being fought in the face of struggles to find suitable collaborators, a battle which was lost with the Cuban Revolution of 1953.

During the nineteenth century, the United States had exerted formal control over its expanding western frontier. At the same time, the principles of the Monroe Doctrine warded off European powers from destabilising its interests of the wider North and South American continents. The post-1945 world called for the United States, as the leading global economic power, to exert formal control elsewhere. Within Europe, post-Second World War Germany posed an immediate problem. With no obvious satisfactory collaborators available, formal occupation was necessary given the external threat to West Germany from the Soviet Union and the fragmented nature of German society. Only after a period of de-Nazification could the move to a looser form of control, somewhat akin to indirect rule, be contemplated. Even after the fall of the Berlin Wall and the collapse of the Soviet Union the year after, Britain's Prime Minister, Margaret Thatcher, counselled against the unification of Germany, fearing that a united

Germany would not offer forth leadership that would line up with the wishes of Britain or the United States. Yet despite this historically introverted analysis, the reality was the German state was integrated well into the Western economy. Indeed by the end of the twentieth century it was a leader within global capitalism and a boon to US interests rather than a threat. Indeed, rather than offering a threat to US-led international interventions, since 1990 Germany has contributed troops to NATO forces in, for example, campaigns in Afghanistan and Iraq.

If immediately after the Second World War collaborators were difficult to come by in Germany, the problem was thornier still in other parts of the world where countries shifted their ideological outlook radically towards Soviet-style communism. In Vietnam, the withdrawal of French troops from its empire in Indo-China created a vacuum that required action to prevent a communist government emerging; though, of course, in this case formal intervention by the United States was ultimately unsuccessful. In the case of Korea, the deployment of the combined forces of the United Nations boded well for the United States's interests. After all, the sharing of the responsibility for ensuring that further countries were not drawn into the communist orbit dispersed the costs amongst several powers. But the commander of the UN forces, General MacArthur, had ideas as to how to prosecute the war that differed from those of US President Truman. Moreover, the mixed nationalities of the forces under his overall command meant that MacArthur was able to play various governments off against Truman, whose strategy in Korea he disagreed with. MacArthur was recalled, but Truman's decision to do so was controversial and MacArthur subsequently toured the United States criticising Truman, gaining some popularity and even threatening a run at the presidency.

Yet despite the failure to prevent the establishment of a regime hostile to US capitalism in North Korea, and the difficulties with MacArthur's command, the experience in Korea signalled a new internationalisation of formal imperialism. The experience of Korea scotched the United States's desire to participate in operations undertaken under the aegis of the United Nations. Instead, the North Atlantic Treaty Organization (NATO) and other *ad hoc* military alliances allowed the United States to coordinate internationally the operation of formal imperialism. A significant example of this was the invasion of Iraq in 2003.

The 1990 invasion of Kuwait, which formed the backdrop to the 2003 invasion against the government of Saddam Hussain, signalled the beginning of a collapse of collaboration between the United States and Hussain. Such collaboration had been strong in the era of the Iran-Iraq War, in which the United States had supported the Iraqi government. But the invasion of Kuwait threatened US oil supplies, and the counter-attack by Allied forces demonstrated where the priorities of the United States lay. In the Iraqi retreat from Kuwait, the burning of oil fields by troops signalled that the Iraqi government would, if pushed, prefer to burn oil than lose control of it. This proved to be a dangerous message for the Iraqi government to send. As the 1990s progressed, it was revealed by British Petroleum that their estimate of how much oil was available in the Iraqi wells undersold the reality. Securing access to substantial oil reserves and ensuring they were safely in the hands of a friendly government grew ever more important, leading to occupation in 2003. This was undertaken by a coalition of forces from the United States and Britain alongside myriad other countries including Australia, Spain, Poland and New Zealand. Below we examine the swift way in which formal control over Iraq, at first embodied through a military governorship under a US general, gave way to informal control; indeed, this happened far more quickly than transitions to informal control had occurred in the British Empire. But first we turn to the use of informal imperialism as a tool to secure the economic frontiers of the metropolitan.

By informal means where possible

Given the dramatic and visible nature of formal imperialism, it has been of obvious attraction to scholars. Indeed, as we saw above, formal imperialism was the focus of many of the analyses of imperialism which abounded even whilst the age of empires was still ongoing. Both Lenin and Luxemburg saw the formal empire as being central to understanding capitalism's need for, and acquisition of, new markets and resources. But as we have also seen, Gallagher and Robinson, quite properly, brought this analysis into question. With the majority of capital and people not being exported to the empire, a working theory of imperialism needed to explain British capitalism's interactions with other parts of the world by reference to more than just the formal empire. This, then, brought Gallagher and Robinson to the idea of informal empire, the iceberg's mass below the waterline.

It was not the transfer of sovereignty that distinguished the informal empire; rather, for Gallagher and Robinson, informal imperialism was 'political action [which] aided the growth of commercial supremacy, and how this supremacy in turn strengthened political influence' (1953: 7). Informal imperialism offered the benefits of economic advantage without the costs or complications associated with formal control. Where local elites were open to British trade, the dominance of such trade made the interests of British capital paramount. Gallagher and Robinson gave the example of nineteenth-century Argentina. Argentina, an independent country which had overthrown formal Spanish control in the 1810s, was a destination for considerable investment by British companies, with virtually the entire rail network of the country being owned by British capital. America's Monroe Doctrine put a specific block upon European imperialism on the South American continent. But no such efforts were required. The dependence of the Argentine government upon British capital meant that it retained the free trade agreements upon which British capitalists depended and which disadvantaged a number of local industries. The effect was profitable and equally as forceful. Recent scholarship has demonstrated the massive loss of life caused by free trade policies in South America. Moreover, the costs of ameliorating the effects of such policies fell, of course, upon the people who suffered from them. The absence of formal control saved the British government and taxpayers from the costly business of governing an enormous territory but still afforded British capital preferential trading conditions.

For Gallagher and Robinson, a crucial factor in deciding the nature of imperial control in the British Empire was the existence of collaborators at the frontier. European settlers provided ideal collaborators given their desire to maintain close links to Britain and willingness to facilitate trade between their colonies (later dominions) and the metropolitan. Having learned the lessons of too strict a control over settler communities during the American Revolution, constitutional reform which slackened imperial control of what became known as the 'white dominions' characterised the relationship between Britain and the these dominions throughout the nineteenth and early twentieth centuries. As early as the mid-nineteenth century, separate to Britain, the Canadian government signed a trade agreement with the United States regarding fishing rights, and the white dominions generally took on more responsibility for international relations as the nineteenth century went on. Indeed, by 1931 the Statute of Westminster prohibited the British Parliament legislating for Canada, Australia, New Zealand, the Irish Free State, Newfoundland, and South Africa (though some of these dominions had to adopt the statute for its provisions to apply to them, a process that took a few years). The change is nicely demonstrated by the declarations of war in 1914 and 1939. In the Great War, all of the colonies and dominions entered the war automatically in 1914, but in 1939 they had to formally ratify entry into the war in their own parliaments. South Africa dithered, though did enter; the Irish Free State did not. By contrast, war was declared on behalf of India, to which the Statue of Westminster did not apply, causing considerable resentment and fuelling further the independence movement.

British interests even in its formal empire were thought to be best secured by reshaping local elites in the mould of the imperial agents that governed the colonies. This explains not only the extension of the principles of Westminster-style government and British laws to the empire, but also the encouragement given to elites in colonies to immerse themselves in British culture, not least of all through attendance at British public schools. In sum, whilst a map of the British Empire coloured much of the world red, the direction of travel was towards eliminating the need of the British Parliament to legislate for these territories and for informal control. Only where local conditions prohibited this was formal control considered a necessary long-term arrangement.

As the United States became the predominant economic power after the Second World War, its imperial methods incorporated not only the formal imperialism explored above but also forms of informal imperialism. We explore this informal control further here.

As we saw above, emblematic of the transfer of economic predominance from Britain to the United States was the Bretton Woods negotiations of 1944. The proposal for an international unit of account, the Bancor, designed to help put into operation a system for balancing out trade surpluses and deficits and which was proposed by the British Treasury delegation was rejected by the United States. Just as previously Britain had used its phenomenal potential for international trade to break open markets and to informally control political conditions at the periphery in order to ensure its interests, so too did the United States begin to turn to such methods.

The principles of the post-Second World War Marshall Aid programme stood in sharp contrast to the attitude taken by the central powers after the Great War. The United States realised that a strong European economy was beneficial in stopping the spread of Soviet satellite states not only to western Europe but also to the global economy, which the United States now surmounted. The significance of this was not lost on the Soviet Union, which refused Marshall Aid. Indeed, in 1948, the introduction of a new currency by the West German government, backed with money from the Marshall Aid programme, threatened to upset the Soviet Union's plan to destabilise the German economy by forcing it to use the devalued pre-war Reichsmark. Fearing a revived Germany, the Soviet Union blockaded Berlin, preventing supplies from reaching the Allied-controlled zones by land. It demanded that the new currency be withdrawn before supplies would be allowed to be transported overland from West Germany to Berlin. The Berlin blockade became a trial of strength between the Allied powers and the Soviet Union, with the United States leading an airlift that supplied Berlin up until the Soviet Union lifted the blockade, eleven months after it began. The response to the blockade demonstrated the desire of the United States to ensure the reshaping of the global economy in such a way as suited its interests.

American willingness to use the strength of its economy to shape the post-war economy was not confined to defending its position as the leading global economic power and as a bulwark against the Soviet Union. In addition, the United States sought to expand its influence globally through a process of informal empire that reconfigured the global economy and states at the periphery in a manner amenable to US capitalism. In part this was achieved through the United States's lead in new supranational organisations designed to help stabilise the global economy in the aftermath of the Second World War. Keynes had proposed that the International Monetary Fund and the World Bank be involved in the operation of the Bancor. Despite the rejection of the scheme, there was plenty of work for these two organisations to undertake. Both played a crucial role in pressuring countries to follow policies consistent with neoclassical economics which, in the decades following the end of the Second World War, underpinned neoliberal political economy.

Despite the World Bank's focus on the developing world, its first loan in the years immediately after the Second World War was to the French government. Part of the conditions for the loan's payment was that the French government had to produce balanced budgets (demonstrating a distinctly pre-war vision of macroeconomics) and it was required to drop Communist Party ministers from its coalition government. At the same time, Italy accepted an invitation to join the World Bank and the International Monetary Fund, which bolstered the governing Christian Democrats Party at the expense of the Italian Communist Party, the main opposition. During the Allied occupation of Italy between

1943 and 1945, the United States had already bolstered the Italian government's ability to resist the Communist Party at the polls. In the final year of the war, the United States had worked with the Italian Mafia to resist communist entry into power. Indeed, the notorious Mafiosi Vito Genovese acted as translator to the military governor of Sicily during the US occupation, and the handling of the distribution of supplies to the US Army was undertaken in conjunction with Mafia members. Thereafter, Mafia support against the Communist Party was forthcoming. Alexander Stille (1996) outlines how, in the ten years from 1945, 43 socialists or communists were killed in and around election times and an impressive showing from Sicilian communists in the April 1947 election was met with a massacre of 11 people attending a celebratory May Day event shortly thereafter. In the search for Cold War Italian collaborators who could secure US interests, the Mafia proved ideal.

Yet the interventions in French and Italian politics in the immediate aftermath of the Second World War were mere tinkering when compared to the United States's reconfiguration of other economies in the decades that followed. We have seen already the way in which the United States played a crucial role in the overthrow of social democratic governments in Guatemala and Chile. Chile became a policy testing ground for neoliberal political economy. Economists from the Chicago School of Economics (Milton Friedman's department at the university; Friedrich Hayek was part of the Committee on Social Thought at the same institution) were seconded to advise the Chilean government on 'sound' economic policy. In time, these policy interventions became received wisdom and formed the basis for access to IMF and World Bank assistance. Codified in the Washington Consensus, loans to governments in financial difficulties come attached with the need to commit to a series of neoliberal policy prescriptions (we see more about policy and informal imperialism in chapter 6). These include, the opening up of the national economy to foreign direct investment; the sale of nationalised industries; and a commitment to balanced budgets that prioritise the repayment of any loans. Reflecting the policies imposed upon developing economies in the 30 years after the Second World War, from the 1980s onwards the Washington Consensus was applied also to developed economies that found themselves in financial crisis.

An excellent recent example of the enforcement of Washington Consensus policies on countries is the provision of loans from the IMF, World Bank and European Union (known as the Troika) to Greece, which began in 2010 (an in-depth analysis of the Troika's work in Greece is given in chapter 7, whilst the European Union itself gets special treatment in chapter 11). Governments between 2010 and 2014 proved to be comprised of excellent collaborators, and bailouts were provided in 2010, 2011 and 2013 in a *quid pro quo* for policies that fitted well with Washington Consensus policies. Nationalised infrastructure such as ports were privatised, and labour laws were relaxed in order to make Greece attractive to foreign investors. The Greek government opened up its ministries to officials from the Troika, with advisors having access to ministers and the Greek prime minister, much as British residents had in parts of Britain's informal empire such as Egypt (the latter is examined in chapter 1). Yet, the social and economic consequences of these policies were dire. High unemployment of nearly 30% and especially high youth unemployment contributed to alarming increases in homelessness and suicide.

So dire did conditions in Greece become that in 2014 a mass popular movement was born in the form of Syriza. Elections in January 2015 saw Syriza become the largest political party in the Greek Parliament, and it took the lead in a coalition government. The incoming finance minister, Yannis Varoufakis, was portrayed as a radical whose policies threatened the economic 'sense' of the Troika. In reality, Varoufakis was, like many economists, a social democrat with an appreciation for Keynesian economics and an excellent knowledge of Marx, whom he nevertheless found reasons to dislike. His radical nature was not so much in his own brand of economics, but rather in his ideas for the reform of the Greek economy and sovereign debt (Varoufakis, 2017).

Varoufakis proceeded from the position that the Greek debt should not have been accrued in the first place. He argued that when the first loan was made in 2010, the Troika knew Greece was effectively bankrupt and that the debt could not be repaid. By keeping the Greek economy solvent, the Troika had not helped out the Greek economy but, rather, locked it into a debt loop which forced the reconfiguration of the economy in order to attempt to pay off a debt that could never be repaid. Varoufakis advocated that the debt be written off to levels that were sustainable and set about protecting industries that were not yet liberalised. Perhaps most egregious for the Troika, Varoufakis also set about expelling the Troika's technocrats from his ministry. Varoufakis was clearly not a collaborator with whom the Troika could work; his memoirs of that time recall a meeting in April 2015 where he stated the limits of his willingness to collaborate to friend Larry Summers, a former vice president of the World Bank. Happily for the Troika, the Greek prime minister, Tsipras, proved more pliable, eventually circumventing Varoufakis and engineering his resignation. The 'logic' of the Washington Consensus was maintained.

Just as formal imperialism developed in the decades following the end of the Second World War, so too did informal imperialism. As we have seen, broad coalitions of countries with mutual interests undertook formal action where necessary. And we have also seen this replicated with informal imperialism, with the case of Greece demonstrating a broad coalition of informal imperial agents. But it was not only in the operation of formal and informal imperialism that there were developments; there have been developments also in the way in which imperial powers could elide between the two. We saw above that the process of moving from formal to informal control in the British Empire was often a slow one. But in the case of the US-led invasion of Iraq, the goal was achieved extremely quickly. In the aftermath of the invasion, a US general was installed as governor in Iraq, at the head of a provisional government. This was followed by an interim government in 2005 and transitional government in 2006, both headed by elected Iraqis. Troop withdrawals were facilitated by the use of the private security industry to offer protection to Iraqi politicians and key figures while, at the same time, Iraqi forces were trained so that they could take over responsibility for security and defence. Not only did this allow for the training and recruitment of new collaborators within the Iraqi state, but it also had the effect of passing the cost for US informal control in Iraq onto the Iraqi people, who, effectively, pay US contractors for the continuation of US informal control (Godfrey et al., 2014).

Structure of the book

This volume is divided into four parts. Parts 1 and 2 develop analyses of events which Gallagher and Robinson would have recognised when they wrote their original essay in 1953. Part 1 covers informal interventions in the Sudan in the nineteenth century and in Spain in the nineteenth and twentieth centuries. It extends the analysis by offering these as fresh case studies of informal imperialism. We also see informal imperialism at work in US-Cuban relations, extending an analysis of attempts to informally control to the United States. Part 2 examines formal imperialism, in particular the methods by which states have attempted to secure control of imperial possessions. Parts 3 and 4 extend the analysis offered by Gallagher and Robinson by looking at developments in the global financial architecture and applying their concepts to these. Part 3 examines the role of supranational organisations in the pursuit of informal imperialism. We see the role that organisations such as the IMF, World Bank and European Union have played in pressing informal control over economies at the economic frontier. Part 4 examines the role of finance capital in securing advantages at the periphery in order to preserve the wealth acquired therein. We see here the role of the European Union and of tax havens in providing the agents of informal imperialism with opportunities to protect and increase their wealth and future investment opportunities. Throughout, we see how Gallagher and Robinson's ideas of a continuity of imperial purpose, of the use of informal and formal imperial means, and of collaboration at the frontier as being crucial to forms of control are extant not only in the era of British imperialism but up to the present.

Part I

The imperialism of free trade in historical context

Overview

In this first section we examine three historical examples of the imperialism of free trade at work. In chapters 1 and 2 James Fargher and Nick Sharman focus upon the British example, with Fargher examining formal interventions in Sudan designed to protect Britain's global trade, whilst Nick Sharman looks at the ways in which British investment and government policy towards Spain served to reconfigure the Spanish economy and political scene to the advantage of British capital. In both cases, British policy objectives were achieved. After a brief formal intervention, the Sudan remained part of the British informal empire and key to keeping open the short sea route to India. In Spain, access to mining concessions such as the Rio Tinto and the breaking down of Spanish monopolies on goods such as cotton manufactures proved lucrative for British capital. Adam Burns (in chapter 3) takes up the use of formal and informal means but, instead of examining Britain, looks to the relationship between the United States of America and Cuba since the latter was prised away from the Spanish Empire in 1898. Burns demonstrates neatly the ways in which, before the Cuban Revolution, the United States was able to exert its will over Cuba's elites, removing difficult political factions from power whenever trade with the United States was threatened and installing new collaborators through constitutional and occasionally military means. Access to constitutional methods of altering the Cuban government ended after the Cuban Revolution and the rise to power of Fidel Castro, and the full weight of US informal imperial power was brought to bear on Cuba – interestingly to no avail. Here we look at each chapter in greater detail.

Gladstone, Suakin and the imperialism of British liberalism

James Fargher explores the ways in which formal intervention in the Sudan was necessary to secure Britain's wider network of strategic bases and infrastructure which provided security to the British Royal and merchant navies – the life-blood of both formal and informal empire. In the latter half of the nineteenth century, various territories in the north and the east of the African continent became more important to British interests. The opening of the Suez Canal in 1869 provided a short sea route to India as well as to British colonies and trading partners in the Far East and Australasia. In Egypt and the Sudan (which was claimed as one of Egypt's territories), informal control was essential to maintaining the neutrality of the Suez Canal zone. Egypt remained an independent state but nevertheless was designated as a British protectorate, with British military and financial officials 'advising' the Egyptian government. A force of British troops was in place in the canal zone to ensure the area's neutrality. Thus, when a series of uprisings against the Egyptian government threatened the coast around the canal sea route, British firms lobbied the British government for formal intervention. Fargher examines how this was carried out in two interventions in 1884 and 1885.

Spain and Britain's informal empire

In nineteenth- and early twentieth-century Spain, Nick Sharman traces the exertion of informal imperialism over various successive Spanish governments by Britain. Much as with Gallagher and Robinson's example of Argentina, British ownership of key infrastructure in Spain gave it considerable leverage over the Spanish government. This leverage was used in two ways. First, strategic advantage. Spain guarded the western Mediterranean and could pose a threat to the naval base and fortress at Gibraltar, a particular concern after the opening of the Suez Canal made Mediterranean trade and access more significant in Britain's commercial interests. Keeping Spain neutral and preventing other European powers from exerting influence on Spain or its North African colonies was therefore vital. Second, Spain was a notably protectionist economy in the nineteenth century with a number of state monopolies protecting sizable industries such as the trade in tobacco and cotton manufactures. In Spain, therefore, we see a classic case of not so much the imperialism of free trade but imperialism *for* free trade. Substantial investments in Spanish industries such as mining increasingly forced the Spanish government to consider British interests in Spain. In addition, as Sharman analyses, the British government worked with economic and political liberals to press its vision of free trade at the expense of Spanish conservatives who realised that the opening up of Spain to British trade would be at the expense of the old order. With very little having been written about Britain's informal imperialism in Spain, Sharman's chapter provides an insight into British imperial tactics contiguous with examples cited by Gallagher and Robinson.

Economic imperialism in Cuba, 1898–2017: Hegemony and embargo

The Spanish formal empire in Cuba was deprived to them in 1898 as a result of the Spanish-American War, during which the United States annexed Cuba, Guam, Puerto Rico and the Philippines. Cuba was a significant loss to the Spanish economy because it had provided a ready outlet for Catalan textile manufactures. The weakening of the Catalan textile industry benefitted British textile exports, as Sharman demonstrates. Adam Burns picks up the story by examining the interactions of the United States with Cuba from the point of annexation. Having annexed Cuba, Burns examines the way in which the US government set about establishing a constitution for the island that suited US interests. Despite a reasonably brisk move to informal control, established by independence in 1920, the Cuban constitution contained a clause which allowed the United States the legal right to use military force to impose its will upon the Cuban government. Burns examines several of the occasions on which this was done, in every case the intention being to ensure US economic interests on the island. However, as Burns examines, the wantonly one-sided arrangement of the US-Cuban relationship bred such a degree of hostility against the United States that collaboration completely collapsed in Cuba. The Cuban Revolution, and Fidel Castro's accession to power in 1959, saw the expulsion or flight of economic and political elites who had collaborated with the United States and the installation of a government as hostile to the United States as the United States was to it. Informal attempts at control followed (with formal attempts having been hopelessly foiled by the Bay of Pigs incident). Yet, the cast-iron resolve of the Cuban government to resist the United States, combined with assistance from the Soviet Union, meant that the United States was unable to get any purchase in Cuba. As we will see throughout this volume, informal means often require a crack in a country's economic life into which a wedge can be driven. The example of Greek debt provides a good example of this in Part 3. Yet in Cuba, the refusal to be drawn into the US economic orbit, combined with a counterproductive blockade, gives us the opportunity to explore the failure of an economic superpower to successfully exert informal imperial control.

1 Gladstone, Suakin and the imperialism of British liberalism

James Fargher

Introduction

In 1884 and 1885, two British military expeditions were sent to Suakin, an ancient port city on the Red Sea in the eastern Sudan, to prevent it from falling to an Islamist insurgency. This chapter explores the significance of these expeditions, which were launched as part of a nascent strategy to uphold British global commercial and naval dominance in the face of rising challenges from imperial rivals. Lacking the natural resources, populations and industrial potential of the United States, imperial Germany and the Russian Empire, by the 1880s Britain began to face the prospect of permanent second-class status. To avoid this fate and to buttress Britain's position as a world power, strategists sought to integrate her scattered overseas possessions into a united, federal empire.

This sea-based imperium would be welded together along sea lines of communication acting as a nervous system along which would flow the vast British mercantile fleet as well as instant communications through the undersea telegraph cable network, the most important branch of which ran through the Suez Canal and the Red Sea. After its opening in 1869, the Suez Canal rapidly became vital for British trade and, more importantly, for telegraphic communication between London, Aden, South Africa, India and Australasia. In order to achieve the objective of fusing the British colonies into a true empire, Britain needed to ensure that the steamship and undersea telegraph routes connecting the principal territories could never be interrupted by a foreign power.

The Suakin expeditions were launched in order to protect the British Empire's most important sea line of communication at its most vulnerable point. Moreover, they were supported by influential commercial firms which were contracted by the British government to facilitate inter-imperial shipping and communication. Directors on the boards of firms such as the Eastern Telegraph Company were eager to protect their profits in the Red Sea and, as members of Britain's political elite, were also invested politically in the new imperial project.

Only by examining the Suakin expeditions from the context of oceanic imperial defence can these two military campaigns be fully understood. Though the British government and its corporate partners were ever eager to minimise costs by operating abroad indirectly through local actors, the military interventions at Suakin demonstrated that Britain was willing to resort to more formal means of control if her strategic and commercial interests were threatened.

Historical context

Egyptian colonial rule over Sudan began in 1820 with an invasion led by the Khedive Muhammed Ali, but until 1867 its rule remained limited to the central Nile Valley (Daly and Holt, 2000: 41). In 1865, Ali's successor, the Khedive Ismail, successfully persuaded his overlord, the Ottoman Sultan Abdülaziz, to devolve control over the two ancient Sudanese ports of Suakin and Massawa and the territory surrounding them to Egypt (Talhami, 1979: 236). Ismail had recognised that the Suez Canal, then under construction and due to open in 1869, would transform the backwater Red Sea into one of the world's great trade routes, and he was determined to lay claim to the small handful of ports between Suez and the Indian Ocean (Hill, 1959: 141).

Ismail's pursuit of an empire in central Africa combined with his lavish spending on domestic projects proved ruinously expensive. In addition to taking on huge debts from European creditors, Ismail financed his political development by imposing heavy taxes on his colonial territories (Theobald, 1951: 26). An ill-judged invasion of the ancient Christian empire of Ethiopia in 1874 increased Ismail's expenses still further and weakened his hold over Sudan when his troops were repeatedly routed by the Ethiopians. In Sudan, the combination of high taxes, Ismail's decision to outlaw slavery in 1877 and his ostentatious use of Christian European officers as provincial governors caused widespread resentment against Egyptian rule, which was supported only by a dwindling number of isolated garrisons (Theobald, 1951: 26).

By 1879, Ismail was so heavily in debt that his European creditors, principally British and French, effectively controlled the country's finances, and they used their influence to impose unpopular political reforms. An army revolt broke out, led by Colonel Ahmed Arabi. Despite pressure from London and Paris, Ismail was either unwilling or unable to quell the insurrection. The exasperated British and French governments subsequently deposed Ismail and replaced him with his young son Tewfik. This did nothing to quash the nationalist rebellion led by Arabi, who remained Egypt's *de facto* ruler until a British 'army of occupation' led by Sir Garnet Wolseley crushed the rebellious Egyptian forces at the Battle of Tel-el-Kebir in 1882 and occupied Cairo. Not only did Wolseley's victory signal an end to Egyptian independence, but it also placed Egypt within Britain's sphere of influence – at the expense of France.

Revolt in Sudan

Political paralysis in Egypt caused by the failed Arabi revolt combined with long-standing popular resentment towards Egyptian rule created an explosive atmosphere in colonial Sudan (Daly and Holt, 2000: 76). In 1881, a young Sufi sheikh, Muhammed Ahmed, declared to his followers that he was the Mahdi (the Expected Guide) who, according to Islamic scripture, would return at the end of time to establish an earthly kingdom in preparation for the Day of Judgement (Theobald, 1951: 32). Respected for his reputation for piety,[1] by 1881 Ahmed had gathered a small band of disciples and felt confident enough to call on his supporters to rise up in revolt against Egyptian rule, promising to replace the tottering colonial administration with a militant theocracy.[2]

The colonial government unsuccessfully attempted to arrest the Mahdi and his followers. Evading capture, he established a camp in the Nuba Mountains and began rallying the Sudanese to his cause.[3] By 1882, he had acquired an army sufficient to lay siege to the city of El Obeid in Kordofan province, severing the line of communication between Khartoum and the remote garrisons in Darfur (Theobald, 1951: 43). By the time the city had fallen to the Mahdi in early 1883, he had succeeded in establishing his own proto-state capable of seriously challenging Egyptian rule over Sudan (Ohrwalder, 1892: 52).

Amongst those who were persuaded by his victories to join the Mahdi's cause was a former slave-dealer from Suakin, Osman Digna. Appointed Emir of the East by the Mahdi, his orders were to cut the Egyptian government's main supply route, which ran between the port of Suakin and through the Red Sea hills to the Nile (Serels, 2013: 54). Digna duly returned to his native Red Sea Hills, and by the autumn of 1883 he had raised an insurgent army in the mountains, which he used to attack and besiege key towns along the Suakin-Nile road. Columns of government troops sent from Suakin to relieve these isolated posts were relentlessly ambushed and destroyed.[4] In December 1883, Digna's troops had reached the outskirts of Suakin itself (Talhami, 1979: 192). Cut off from Darfur and from its regular line of communication to the sea, Khartoum appeared increasingly isolated.

Reaction in Britain

Prime Minister William Gladstone already opposed Egyptian rule over Sudan on both economic and ideological grounds,[5] but Suakin proved to be a different matter. The advance of Osman Digna's forces on the port through the autumn of 1883 had already caused concern in London, and military officers warned that if the Egyptian ports – Suakin, Massawa and the Somali towns of Berbera and Zeyla – fell, the French or the Italians could easily capture them and turn them into naval bases.[6] In response, gunboats from the Royal Navy were deployed to Suakin to boost the town's defences, but the situation continued to deteriorate.[7] Secretary of State for War Lord Hartington announced to the cabinet that if held by a hostile power, Suakin would pose a direct threat to the security of communications with India (Robinson and Gallagher, 1981: 133).

Nevertheless, in 1883 the Liberal government remained reluctant to send troops to the eastern Sudan.[8] The presence of warships alone, it was hoped, would act as a sufficient deterrent to shore up Egypt's eroding control over the Red Sea coast.[9] Gladstone aimed to induce the Sublime Porte to send troops to prevent the area from falling under Mahdist control even as the Egyptians continued to evacuate their own troops from Sudan (Gladstone, 1990: 94). Despite its insistence on the Egyptian evacuation, the government confirmed that it would continue 'to protect the ports of the Red Sea'.[10]

This cautious policy was upended in February 1884 when Valentine Baker, a disgraced former cavalry officer who was now serving in the khedive's army, led 4,000 Egyptian troops into a disastrous defeat at the hands of the Mahdists outside Suakin. The blow crushed all hopes of extinguishing the rebellion in eastern Sudan (Burleigh, 1884: 15) and raised a storm of protest in Britain, with both the press and Parliament calling on the government to avenge this defeat (Glasgow Herald, 1884).

The Cabinet came under renewed pressure to send troops. Although Gladstone was extremely reluctant to do so, the War Office, the Admiralty and the India Office formed a powerful faction pushing for action. Hartington requested a special meeting of the Cabinet on 8 February 1884 to discuss the possibility of deploying troops to Suakin,[11] during which the War Office (Buckle, 1928: 477) and the Admiralty presented arguments in favour of establishing British military garrisons in the Red Sea ports.[12] Hartington and the Earl of Northbrook, First Lord of the Admiralty, also persuaded Gladstone to telegraph General Charles Gordon for his expert opinion on the matter.[13] Gordon had famously been sent to Khartoum in January 1884 as Governor-General to oversee the evacuation of Sudan (Davenport-Hines, 2004). However, there is some evidence to suggest that Gordon never intended to evacuate Khartoum at all (Vetch, 1901: 257), and he telegraphed back his support for the intervention.[14]

Buried under the weight of these arguments and faced with further news of Mahdist advances towards Suakin (Colvile, 1996[1889]: 21), Gladstone conceded. Four thousand troops embarked for Suakin, with instructions to 'tak[e] any measures necessary for defence of ports'.[15] Less than a month after Baker's defeat, on 22 February 1884, this force under the command of General Sir Gerald Graham appeared off the eastern Sudanese coastline (ibid.: 22).

The expeditions

At first glance, it would appear that the Suakin expeditions were tactical victories but strategic failures. Neither accomplished their publicly announced intention of destroying the Mahdist insurgency in the eastern Sudan, and both were withdrawn after several months in the field. More importantly though, the expeditions did succeed in preventing the port of Suakin from falling into Mahdist hands.

1884

The first Suakin expedition lasted from February to April 1884. Shortly after landing in the port, General Graham and his 4,000 Regulars marched on El Teb, where the infantry squares drove Osman Digna's fighters from dug-in positions with artillery and machine-gun fire (Burleigh, 1884: 49). Further battles between the British and the Sudanese over the next few months went much the same way, with superior British firepower overcoming the 'human wave' assaults launched by Digna's spearmen. Alarmed at the scale of the conflict, Gladstone soon decided to recall the expedition in early April. As he argued to the Cabinet, Britain was positioning itself to occupy eastern Sudan permanently, despite having no legal claim to the territory.[16]

This had become true of Suakin, which quickly became a *de facto* British possession. A British officer, Herbert Chermside, was appointed by the Egyptian khedive to the post of governor-general, and Egyptian military and civil officers in Suakin were quickly replaced with British counterparts (Serels, 2013: 56). By July 1884, the Royal Engineers had begun constructing piers and coal depots in the harbour, capable of accommodating troop transports and large cruisers,[17] as well as fixed defences (Anon, 1885: 24). Parliament soon began demanding that the government clarify its position on retaining the port. Responding in the House of Commons, Secretary of State for War Lord Hartington remarked,

> I consider it a matter of importance to British interests that the ports of the Red Sea should not be in a position which would tempt any other European Power to occupy them. ... It appears to me that the importance of the Red Sea, as being on our line of communication with our Indian Possessions, makes it of great importance that no other European Power should be established in any of these ports.[18]

The Foreign Office put it more succinctly: 'the Red Sea and Gulf of Aden are British interests ... because they are the road to British interest'.[19]

Gladstone hoped that Suakin and the other Red Sea ports could be returned to either Egypt or the Ottoman sultan once the situation stabilised,[20] but it was quickly becoming apparent that neither government would be able to resume effective occupation of the African coast. In Cairo, the khedive decided to recall his garrisons from the two Somali ports of Zeyla and Berbera and to abandon Somaliland, prompting the Foreign Office to declare that Britain would assume responsibility for it.[21] When the Sublime Porte objected to this development, the Foreign Secretary replied that as the Ottomans had taken no steps to secure the territory, Britain had no choice but to do so itself.[22]

1885

Deliberations over Suakin's status continued until early 1885, when events once again forced the Liberals to revisit the eastern Sudanese question. Since being sent to Sudan to evacuate the Egyptian garrisons in 1884, General Gordon had come under siege in Khartoum. Although the government sent a column under Sir Garnet Wolseley to rescue him, it arrived too late, and in February 1885, the Cabinet learned that the city had fallen and Gordon was dead.[23]

Gordon's death was a serious blow, and the national press screamed for a response to the humiliation. Hartington and the War Office had already been calling for a second expedition to Suakin for some time,[24] and Gladstone seized this opportunity to mitigate the disaster. On 7 February, he announced that 10,000 troops under Graham would be sent back to Suakin in a show of force to the Mahdi (Vetch, 1901: 286).

Despite bellicose rhetoric, the second Suakin expedition proved a greater disappointment than the first. Although Graham achieved two victories in the field, in May 1885, before he had a chance to achieve any meaningful gains, his troops had to be recalled in response to an emergency on the northern Indian frontier (Wolseley, 1967: xlii). Though brief, the second expedition did result in the effective addition of Suakin to Britain's growing imperial defence network, and Britain would retain control over Suakin until Sudanese independence in 1955.

Imperial defence

In order to make sense of the Suakin expeditions, they must be examined within the context of imperial defence, a new school of strategic thought pioneered in the 1870s and 1880s which caused a profound shift in attitudes towards the empire. The Royal Navy's victory at the Battle of Trafalgar in 1805 had initially placed Britain as the world's pre-eminent naval power. As early as the 1830s, however, tensions between Britain and France were again beginning to rise (Caquet, 2013: 702) as the French began rebuilding a battle fleet, fortifying the Channel harbours and investing in steam propulsion technology (Partridge, 1989: 23). When France launched *La Gloire*, the world's first modern ironclad in 1859, she even appeared to be on the verge of surpassing the Royal Navy technologically (Sandler, 2004: 22).

The initial reaction in Britain was to devote increasingly large sums of money to line the southern coast with fortresses (Fergusson, 1849: 134). However, even before some of these fortresses were completed, some astute observers by the 1860s began to question this approach to strategy and defence. The cruise of the Confederate raider CSS *Alabama* in 1862 demonstrated the destruction a single ironclad could wreak on commercial shipping.[25] The advent of mass industrial warfare in the US Civil War also implied the future belonged to great continental powers. By contrast, Britain was a small island nation reliant upon undefended shipping lanes for her prosperity and on food imports to feed her population.[26]

One of the first people of the period to recognise this fact was John Colomb, a retired naval artilleryman who in 1867 published a short but far-sighted book on Britain's strategic future (Beeler, 2004). Colomb recognised that the key to preserving British global power was mastery of the world's oceans (Colomb, 1867: 2). Britain depended upon the sea for commerce and for information which flowed along exposed and vulnerable undersea telegraph cables. In order to protect these vital lines of communication, the Royal Navy needed fortified overseas bases and coaling stocks to allow new steam-powered warships to maintain a constant presence along the world's principal sea lanes. These bases, constructed at natural choke points such as Aden, would allow Britain to act as gatekeeper to the global trading commons (ibid.: 3). Colomb pushed his new concept of imperial defence through a series of later publications and speeches, and his ideas were taken up by a small but influential circle of statesmen (Harcourt, 1873: 585). The Carnarvon Commission of 1879 was largely a product of Colomb's writing.[27]

At the same time, the influential historians James Anthony Froude and Sir John Seeley introduced a new perspective on empire. Whilst most mid-Victorians had previously regarded the settler colonies as burdens on the British taxpayer, Froude and Seeley re-envisioned them as integral components of a 'Greater Britain' united by the world's oceans (Seeley, 1883: 172). Like other small states throughout history, Britain alone would be swallowed up by the continental powers, unable to compete with larger rivals if she could not match their territorial size (ibid.: 301). Unlike contiguous powers, however, Greater Britain would depend on control over the world's oceans in order to protect the sea lanes which bound the empire to the British Isles like veins in an imperial body politic. Only through instant communications and steam shipping could Greater Britain achieve a degree of unity comparable to rival continental empires, and this depended on the Royal Navy's ability to maintain cruiser squadrons and overseas coaling stations to protect global shipping and cable routes (Froude, 1871: 173).

Froude's and Seeley's ideas were not confined to the academy. Froude was personally connected with at least five Cabinet ministers, four of whom were in office at the time of the Suakin expeditions. The Earl of Carnarvon was 'one of his greatest political friends' (Paul, 1905: 435), turning to Froude's historical work for guidance on plans to federate the colonies in southern Africa (Gordon, 2009: 219). Froude was also able to influence the Earl of Northbrook, who in February 1884 argued in Cabinet in favour of the proposed military intervention at Suakin.[28] Lord Hartington owned several of Froude's books in his personal collection at Chatsworth House (Anon, 1879: 157).

Whilst Froude enjoyed access to the political elite, Seeley's influence was felt more widely amongst the British public. His 1883 book, *The Expansion of England*, helped to transform Victorian attitudes towards the empire by presenting the idea of imperial union in terms of national survival, galvanising support for the Imperial Federation League, which Seeley joined in 1884 (D'Egville, 1913: 99). Later, when the Liberal Unionists broke away from the Liberal Party in 1886 over the issue of Irish Home Rule, Seeley played a leading role in establishing a local branch in Cambridge,[29] and he invited the navalist and imperialist Thomas Brassey to deliver a speech at the university.[30]

Strategy and economy

The imperial fantasy provided by Colomb, Froude, Seeley and their supporters in Cabinet was backed by influential inter-imperial commercial interests. As agents of the imperial government, the private communications and shipping companies necessary for building a pan-imperial market and defence capability grasped the opportunity to fulfil their duty as patriotic British firms whilst also pleasing their shareholders.

The fantasy of a Greater Britain came at a critical juncture in British economic history. In 1870, the British economy reached its zenith before entering into decline relative to Britain's closest industrial rivals, the United States and Germany. Britain remained an industrial powerhouse but was reliant on the export of manufactured goods abroad (Kitson and Michie, 2014). Moreover, one of the effects of the US Civil War in the 1860s was to interrupt the flow of raw cotton to the textile mills in Lancashire, leading to a boom in cotton production in British India (Harnetty, 1971).

Critical to sustaining this economic arrangement was rapid transit provided by steamships from sources of raw materials to export markets, as well as access to the global communications network. In 1869, the opening of the Suez Canal revolutionised world transportation by redrawing the trade routes between Europe and the East. As already noted, this had originally been anticipated by the Khedive Ismail, who had overseen the project and had in the 1870s attempted to seize control over every African port between Suez and Somalia in an attempt to place the new great highway of world trade under his control.[31] Although the number of ships passing through the canal was initially small, it increased rapidly over the next decade. Between 1870 and 1873, the annual amount of cargo passing through Suez rose from 436,618 tons to over 2 million, three-quarters of which were British (The New York Times, 1875). By the end of the nineteenth century, Britain had become so dependent on the canal for shipping that foreign observers noted, 'it is ... necessary that she should retain the control not only of the canal itself, but of its approaches' (The New York Times, 1893). Should the Royal Navy ever lose control over this new route in wartime and shipping be rerouted around the Cape of Good Hope, 'the whole trading interest of the British Empire would revolt' (ibid.).

Indeed, some of the largest shipping firms and telegraph operators had played a critical role in the development of the Suez route. Although the canal was dug by a Frenchman, Ferdinand de Lesseps, the Peninsular & Oriental shipping line had long advocated for a direct link between Britain and India via the Red Sea and had established itself as an agent of the imperial government through its position as the government's subsidised mail carrier (Harcourt, 2010: 19). Similarly, the operators of the major undersea telegraph lines which bound the empire together were eager to see the British government intervene to protect their vulnerable cables. Sir George Elliot (1884), chairman of the first transatlantic cable company, for example, argued in favour of the Suakin expeditions before the House of Commons. John Pender, chairman of the Eastern Telegraph Company, enjoyed close connections with leading members of the government as he controlled two-thirds of all British undersea cables, including the only links with India, Aden and South Africa (Headrick, 1988: 105). These figures included the Prince of Wales as well as the Earl of Northbrook, First Lord of the Admiralty, who appointed Pender's brother, Lord John Hay, commander-in-chief of the Royal Navy's Mediterranean Fleet (Lambert, 2004). Pender added Suakin to the Electric Telegraph Company's (ETC's) telegraph network just prior to the 1884 intervention and likely supported the intervention in his elite social circle.[32]

Given that the ETC's main line was laid between Malta and Bombay, this was perhaps unsurprising, as Pender had a financial interest in maintaining British naval dominance over the Red Sea. That is not to say that influential commercial firms were motivated solely by profit. As the ETC acted on behalf of the government in maintaining inter-imperial communications, Pender would have been well aware of his pivotal role in imperial defence. He was not alone in this regard. His friend, the Indian Ocean shipping magnate Sir William Mackinnon, led the annexation of Kenya with his Imperial British East Africa Company in pursuit of a combination of private profit, spiritual salvation and maintainance of British naval dominance of the waters between Aden and Zanzibar (Galbraith, 1972: 385).

The close working relationship between shipping and communication firms and the imperial government was a symbiotic one. Britain wielded her indirect influence through these companies, London repeatedly intervened in regional affairs to secure their privileged positions when local actors could not. For example, the India Office successfully lobbied the government to annex the island of Socotra, which lay on the route between Aden and Bombay, in order to prevent other European powers from building rival coaling stations or telegraph cables.[33] The prime beneficiaries of the Royal Navy's surveying work in the Red Sea were the shipping firms and undersea cable operators subsidised by the government to form an imperial nervous system with the Suez Canal acting as its spinal cord (Hull, 1875: 58).

Conclusion

Fears about Britain's relative industrial decline and the emergence of new powers combined with the new possibilities offered by steamships and the telegraph laid the foundation for a sense of imperial unionism. The evidence suggests that by 1884 senior members of the Cabinet had embraced the idea of closer union between Britain and the empire bound together by the undersea telegraph cable and chains of naval coaling stations. It was within this context that the Suakin expeditions of 1884 and 1885 must be understood in order to make sense of the seemingly contradictory policies pursued by the Liberal government. The Red Sea was a crucial link in a much wider nervous system which linked the imperial body politic, without which, Britain would be unable to maintain her position as one of the world's predominant powers.

Notes

1 British Library, London, IOR/MSS Eur/D604/5–11, India Office Records, Confidential Memorandum on the Insurrection of the False Prophet, 23 November 1883.
2 Ibid.
3 Ibid.

4 British Library, London, IOR/MSS Eur/D604/5–11, India Office Records, Confidential Memorandum on the Insurrection of the False Prophet, 23 November 1883.
5 Earl of Granville, December 1883, quoted in Sanderson (1965: 17).
6 British Library, London, IOR/L/PS/20/MEMO39–43, India Office Records Foreign Office Prints: Correspondence Respecting the Red Sea and Somali Coast, Admiral Sir William Hewett to the Secretary to the Admiralty, report, 7 January 1884.
7 British Library, London, IOR/MSS Eur/D604/5–11, India Office Records, Confidential Memorandum on the Insurrection of the False Prophet, 23 November 1883.
8 British Library, London, IOR/MSS Eur/D604/5–11, India Office Records, Confidential Memorandum on the Insurrection of the False Prophet, February 1884.
9 British Library, London, IOR/R/20/E, India Office Records, Sir Julian Pauncefote to the Secretary of the Admiralty, letter, 3 January 1884.
10 British Library, London, IOR/MSS Eur/D604/5–11, India Office Records, Confidential Memorandum on the Insurrection of the False Prophet, February 1884.
11 National Archives, Kew, PRO/30/29/144, Correspondence and Memoranda: Cabinet Opinions, Marquess of Hartington to Lord Granville, letter, 7 February 1884.
12 National Archives, Kew, CAB 37, Cabinet Minutes and Papers, Photographic Copies of Cabinet Letters in the Royal Archives, Lord Northbrook to the Cabinet, Confidential Memorandum, 8 February 1884.
13 British Library, London, Add.MS 44645, 2nd Earl Granville: Minutes and memoranda by: 1853–1886, William Gladstone, Personal minutes of Cabinet meeting, 8 February 1884.
14 National Archives, Kew, PRO/30/29/144, Correspondence and Memoranda: Cabinet Opinions, Marquess of Hartington to Lord Northbrook, letter, 14 February 1884.
15 National Archives, Kew, Ad. WO 33/42, War Office Records, Adjutant-General to the General Officer Commanding in Egypt, telegram, 12 February 1884.
16 William Gladstone to Lord Northbrook, letter, quoted in Gladstone (1990: 152).
17 Surrey History Centre, Woking, LM/COR, Major W. Emerson Peck to the Inspector-General of Fortifications, Report, 13 July 1884.
18 Marquess of Hartington, Speech to the House of Commons, 15 March 1884, *Hansard Parliamentary Debates*, Commons, vol. 285 (1884), 1149.
19 Lord Edmond Fitzmaurice, Speech to the House of Commons, 10 March 1884, *Hansard Parliamentary Debates*, Commons, vol. 285 (1884).
20 British Library, London, IOR/MSS Eur/D604/5–11, India Office Records, Earl Granville to the Earl of Dufferin, letter, 14 May 1884.
21 Ibid.
22 British Library, London, IOR/R/20/E, India Office Records, Earl Granville to Musurus Pasha, letter, 22 August 1884.
23 Diary entry, 6 February 1885, in Gladstone (1990: 275).
24 British Library, CM/IOR/026, India Office Records, Lord Hartington to Sir Garnet Wolseley, telegram, 7 January 1885.
25 Captain Bedford Pim, Speech to the House of Commons, 19 March 1877, *Hansard Parliamentary Debates*, Commons, vol. 233 (1877), 136.
26 National Archives, Kew, CAB 7/3, Cabinet Office Records, Royal Commission appointed to inquire into the Defence of British Possessions and Commerce Abroad, Second Report, 1882.
27 National Archives, Kew, CAB 7/3, Cabinet Office Records, Royal Commission appointed to inquire into the Defence of British Possessions and Commerce Abroad, Second Report, 1882.

28 National Library of Scotland, Edinburgh, Acc.11388/60, Lord Northbrook to Lady Louisa Ashburton, letter, 18 May n.d.
29 Senate House Library, Papers of John Seeley, MS903/1B/17, Lord Hartington to Sir John Seeley, letter, 27 October 1887.
30 Senate House Library, Papers of John Seeley, MS903/1B/17, Lord Brassey to Sir John Seeley, letter, 11 February 1888.
31 National Archives, Kew, Foreign Office Confidential Records: Correspondence Respecting the Red Sea and Somali Coast, Sir Bartle Frere, Memorandum on the Treaties with the Somalis and other Tribes on the African Coast of the Red Sea and Gulf of Aden.
32 National Maritime Museum, Caird Library & Archives, Goodsall Papers, GDL/6, Logbook of SS *Chiltern* cable laying in the Red Sea, December 1883–February 1884.
33 British Library, India Office Records, IOR/R/20/E/88, W. Wedderburn, Acting Political Secretary, Memorandum on the Red Sea Route, 5 July 1870.

2 Spain and Britain's informal empire

Nick Sharman

Spain's failure to use its abundant natural and human resources to achieve industrial 'take-off' in the nineteenth century has long fascinated economic historians. From being one of the wealthier European countries in 1800, its per capita GDP had fallen to barely a half of the advanced countries by 1910 (Berend and Rankí, 1982: 154). Explanations have pointed to a wide range of domestic institutional and historical factors. Most have highlighted the largely unmodernised, often quasi-feudal, agricultural sector operating alongside a small and unstable industrial sector, creating a dualistic economic structure, 'respectively growth-generating and growth-resisting' (Trebilcock, 1981: 312). Others have pointed to the failure to achieve the balance of factors necessary for successful industrialisation, highlighting an inadequate financial sector oriented to financing public debt, an undeveloped entrepreneurial class and a weak state, all factors leading to consistently poor policymaking (Nadal, 1975: 226; Tortella, 1977: 12). Some early explanations (including in Spain itself)[1] rejected such structural causes in favour of psychological factors: an 'inherent racial vice', a lack of practical sense and an instinct for conspicuous consumption over efficient production (Carr, 1980: 27). Nearly all these approaches have had a common link; namely, that 'Spain's backwardness is its own doing' (Tortella, 1977: 4). However, these analyses of Spain's halting progress to industrialisation have typically underplayed the impact of the new international political and economic environment created by the emergence of Britain's extraordinary industrial and trade dominance in the early nineteenth century.

A complete explanation of Spain's intensely uneven process of development needs to take full account of the strong external factors operating on Spain from the first decades of the nineteenth century. Gallagher and Robinson's work suggests that Britain's leadership of the industrial revolution, supported by its command of the sea, allowed it to dominate weaker economies, such as that of Spain. Britain was able to shape the economic and political development of these 'informal colonies' around its own imperial interests; notably, its insatiable need for raw materials and markets for its industrial products. Less developed economies were incorporated within its 'informal' empire. They were exploited economically and dominated politically, though never acquired as formal colonies. The advantage of this strategy was that it largely avoided the costs and risks of direct military and political oversight. Britain intervened directly only when domestic political circumstances threatened its economic aims of trade and investment (Gallagher and Robinson, 1953: 6). It was the needs of the rapidly growing British economy that led Spain in the nineteenth and early twentieth centuries to become, in effect, such an informal British colony. For over a century, between the 1830s and 1940s, Britain had a dominant economic and political role in the country. Although France (and later in the period, Germany) also exerted a strong cultural and economic influence over Spain, the imperialist character of British dominance was apparent in its readiness to deploy military force to support its interests. It intervened militarily in Spain, both by threat and directly, from the Napoleonic Wars right up to the end of the Second World War. Initially, Spain had been drawn into Britain's expanding economic sphere through the consumer markets it offered for British textiles and, later, machine tools. Toward the end of the century, when Spain's mineral resources became crucial to the second wave of Europe's industrial revolution, Britain established a near monopoly in the extraction of the country's copper, sulphur and iron ore resources. Combined with French dominance of Spain's financial credit market and its railway network, the result was the country's highly fragmented economy, which ranged from feudal agricultural areas to modern, urbanised industrial centres. Such extraordinarily uneven development created fiercely opposed factional and regional interests, which radically distorted Spain's politics throughout the nineteenth and early twentieth centuries.

The turning point for the Anglo-Spanish relationship was the Napoleonic Wars. In 1800, Spain, with its substantial worldwide empire and a slowly developing domestic industrial base, was still one of Europe's great powers. By the 1830s, it was mired in a bitter civil war of succession following Ferdinand VII's death in 1833, having lost its naval fleet at Trafalgar and its Latin American empire to Bolivar's and San Martín's campaigns in the 1820s. Nonetheless, Spain was still a significant country in 1830: it had a growing population of some 14 million, the same size as the population of England and Wales at the time. Together with the remnants of empire in Cuba and the Philippines, this population provided good markets for its expanding domestic textile and metal-based industries.

For Britain's rapidly growing international oceanic trade, the Iberian Peninsula (and Spain in particular), commanding both Mediterranean and Atlantic sea routes, was strategically vital. There was intense British concern that another European power might exploit Spain's military weakness and threaten Britain's near monopoly of the world's shipping routes. Meanwhile, Spain was a highly attractive market for its fast-growing manufacturing economy, particularly the Manchester-based textile industry. This combination of strategic and commercial factors led Britain to actively intervene in Spain's domestic political turmoil of the 1830s. As Foreign Secretary, Lord Palmerston set three objectives for British policy towards Spain. First, he worked to ensure that a liberal monarchy and government, supporting British interests, won the civil war against the Carlist rebels, monarchist absolutists who were hostile to British trade and allies of the Holy Alliance of Prussia, Austria and Russia. Second, Palmerston wanted to install the British-supporting liberal parliamentary faction in power. His objective was to exclude both the French-supporting 'moderate' faction and the 'ultra-progressives', committed to a radical extension of suffrage and economic independence. Third, Palmerston wanted to secure an exclusive trade agreement to reduce Spain's high tariff barriers and open its markets, especially to the Manchester textile merchants. By the end of the decade and despite opposition from the French monarch, Louis Philippe, the first two objectives were secured with the help of a 10,000 strong British government-financed private army and the active political interference of the British ambassador, George Villiers (Webster, 1951: 427). However, the liberal monarchy's victory in the civil war in 1839 did not definitively end the internal conflict between traditional landed interests and the emerging middle classes. Over the next four decades, chronically unstable governments in Madrid periodically drew in the military to re-establish order. Nonetheless, for the rest of the century there was no 'great power' threat to Britain's strategic dominance of the Iberian Peninsula.

Economic domination proved more difficult. The 1830s saw the launch of Britain's international free trade campaign, designed to break down high European tariff barriers to allow the more technologically advanced British cotton, wool and machine tool industries access to foreign markets. With its combination of trade protection, weak governments and a substantial and accessible population, Spain was a highly attractive target for British manufacturers. Moreover, Palmerston was under pressure from his own parliamentary colleagues to show a return for Britain's military investment in the civil war. He therefore worked with the increasingly powerful industrial lobbies in Manchester, Liverpool and Glasgow to open up the Spanish market, with a very deliberate policy of eliminating the Catalonian textile industry (Rodríguez Alonso, 1991: 200). A combination of military, diplomatic and ideological pressure was applied in a coordinated attempt to undermine Spain's economic independence. This was one of the first examples in the new, industrialising world of a systematic campaign to take forward the 'imperialism of free trade' by breaking into protected markets and destroying potential industrial rivals.

However, two groups in Spain resisted British pressure for radical tariff reductions. Conservative landed interests, notably some of the wheat producers of Castile and landowners of Andalusia, saw the policies of the Madrid-based liberals, especially their support for a national domestic market and for free trade, as threatening established political and economic institutions. From an opposite, modernising perspective, the Catalan cotton manufacturers fought an existential struggle to protect their growing, but still relatively backward, industry from the invasion of low-cost British manufactured goods. This was an often uncomfortable and contradictory protectionist alliance based on diametrically opposed interests. On the one hand the Catalan manufacturers wanted low food prices, while on the other the conservative agriculturalists were interested in maintaining high land rents. The alliance was nonetheless to last for the rest of the century, an outcome of the manufacturers' institutional and political weakness. Crucially, they failed to win over the Madrid bourgeoisie, which remained firmly wedded to individualist English liberalism and its associated ideology of free trade as the foundation of its modernising project for the country. Unlike their British equivalents, the Manchester manufacturers, the Catalan industrialists were never able to build a Spanish counterpart to the great liberal political alliances of mid-nineteenth-century Britain, which had united landowners, manufacturers and financial interests to develop industry and trade. Instead, Spanish liberal and business supporters of British free trade ideology joined with conservative aristocratic landed interests to reject an active state role in the economy and to vilify the Catalan protectionists.

For the Catalans, intellectual inspiration came from the collectivist ideas of German and French political economists. They were particularly attracted to Friedrich List, the German-American economist who argued that a strong state had an essential role in defending and developing infant industries so they could compete on equal terms with more advanced economies (Pugés, 1931: 22). List's arguments were widely used to justify the high tariffs that protected the successful industrialisation of the agriculture-based economies of the United States and Germany. The Catalans too supported List's proposals for broad-based state interventionist policies. Led by an indefatigable representative, the cotton industrialist Juan Güell y Ferrer, their campaign saw protection of the domestic cotton industry as part a broader economic policy for Spain. Through an institute of national industry, the Instituto Industrial de España, established in 1841, Güell championed a country-wide movement which aimed to persuade the Spanish government to adopt an active interventionist policy. They had little success in undermining the already deep-seated and enthusiastic support of the Madrid liberals for radical economic individualism. Indeed, the enthusiasm for free trade broadened following the end of the Carlist War. When Richard Cobden toured Spain in 1845 on a campaign in support of free trade, financed by British industry and supported by the British government, he was rapturously received in all the major cities as 'the Christopher Columbus of the modern world' (ibid.: 74). His argument, that free trade was the key to world economic development and peace as well as to economic prosperity, appealed to a wide constituency anxious to see Spain once again a significant European power. Güell and his supporters were characterised as narrowly self-interested, 'voracious birds of prey, hungry wolves who devour the substance of the Spanish, monopolists, barbarians, Bedouins, detestable tyrants, executioners of the workers' (ibid.: 91).

Despite the overwhelming support for a British-inspired ultra-liberal economic policy among much of the political elite, the Catalan protectionist alliance was strong enough, with French support, to stop Palmerston from forging an exclusive Anglo-Spanish trade agreement in the 1840s. Moreover, tenacious rearguard political campaigning by the Catalan cotton manufacturers, supported by the periodic mobilisation of their workers, managed to protect much (though not all) of the textile industry for the rest of the century. This, in turn, enabled the industry's very rapid growth so that by the 1860s it was Europe's third-largest textile manufacturing centre. Despite this partial success, the protectionists could not resist the overwhelming British-led pressure to reduce general trade protection. From the 1840s over the next 30 years, both tariff levels and the number of prohibited imports were steadily cut. At its free trade high point in 1869, Spain's Tariff Law committed the country to becoming one of Europe's most open economies. As a result, outside the Catalonia-based textile industry, Spain became a 'semi-peripheral' economy, its foreign trade, balance of payments and production increasingly tied to and subordinated to northern Europe's industrial core (Berend and Rankí, 1982: 9). Spanish exports were dominated by raw materials and food – the classic primary products of a peripheral economy. Between 1849 and 1913, minerals and metals made up 25% of all exports (Nadal, 1975: 94), with wine and fruit contributing a further 20%. The paradox was that Spain had the 'right' kind of exports, especially in its minerals and metals, for broad-based industrialisation. This wasn't enough by itself: as the Catalan protectionists and others at the time recognised, such new industries needed to be widely and deeply embedded in the national economy if they were to be successful drivers of transformation.

Buttressed by the wealth of the old Spanish Empire, the landowning aristocracy retained the political initiative after the failure of the progressive Liberal-led First Republic and the restoration of the monarchy in 1874. Many of the substantial bourgeois entrepreneurs took on the traditional values and role of the great landowners, while at the same time vigorously supporting free trade policies. These free trade policies benefitted the growing bourgeois classes, both by giving a direct impetus to domestic consumption and by integrating Spain in the European market system. However, the outcome of attempting to modernise without substantial change to the old institutional and political framework was a fatal struggle between the forces of reaction and change, leading to economic stagnation.[2] Moreover, as many countries have subsequently discovered, adoption of a free trade policy by a less developed economy simultaneously undermines its economic independence. In Spain, as in similar 'informal' dependencies, the 'imperialism of free trade' became closely linked to a parallel process of 'imperialism of capital' as the demands of economic transformation drew in foreign investment (Berend and Rankí, 1982: 77). With much of the income from Spain's raw material exports wasted on luxury imports and nonproductive spending (especially a succession of military adventures), external finance was essential for the country's substantial infrastructure needs. There was an added factor: landowners systematically evaded tax and blocked any substantive public finance reform to the feudal tax system. The result of this mix of persistent overspending and underfunding were chronic budget deficits, largely financed by British and French loans.

For the rest of the century, the country was caught in a spiral of financial indebtedness for which it paid dearly in terms of lost economic independence. The conditions attached to foreign debt quickly became an instrument of informal imperialism: by giving investors the contractual right to intervene to secure debt, foreign bond owners are able to take control of key economic sectors. In the Spanish case, the sovereign debt crisis of the 1850s forced the government to sell off the country's prime mining and rail concessions to French and British investors. The Spanish rail network was largely developed by French interests and became heavily oriented to the transport of minerals and food out of the country. Built around Madrid-based radial routes and connections from coast to frontier, the network was 'an instrument of extraction and international traffic, and not of production and circulation … from the beginning, most of the investment in railways was considered as an instrument of colonisation and exploitation rather than an authentic instrument of development' (Nadal, 1975: 50). The French dominated the sector: by 1914 French companies controlled some 85% of the network, 9,722 km of the total 11,378 km. Meanwhile, the Rothschilds secured control over the world's largest lead and mercury mines as security for loans to cover the deficit arising from the successive government funding crises of the 1840s and 1850s. British investors were quick to follow: in 1874 a British consortium bought, at a cut price of £3 million and in perpetuity, the Royal Mines of Rio Tinto, the world's largest deposit of pyrites and the main mineral source of its copper and sulphur for the next 40 years. For Spain, the most damaging effect of the disposal of these critical mineral assets was the lost opportunity to use its natural resources to develop a domestic metal-based industry to supply the equipment for its new rail network. As a result, almost all the benefits of rail investment went abroad. This was a crucial failure, as Güell pointed out at the time (Güell y Ferrer, 1880: 770), and was to haunt Spain for the next hundred years.[3] Instead of helping to create a modern industrial base, over 90% of the country's irreplaceable copper, sulphur and iron ore wealth became the feedstock for industrial development of the northern European core. As late as 1910, iron ore smelted in Spain was only 8.8% of the total produced (Trebilcock, 1981: 305).

The 1870s proved to be a turning point for the Anglo-Spanish relationship, a decade of upheaval and change for Britain as much as Spain. Both countries were hit by the agricultural depression that followed the opening up of wheat supplies from the American prairies and Russian steppes. The crisis in the Spanish economy brought an abrupt halt to the progressive abolition of trade tariffs and a turn to protectionism as conservative landowner interests came under increasing pressure from the dramatic reductions in world wheat prices. The realisation that 'like Latin American nations Spain had become an export economy supplying raw materials to the developed West' fed a growing economic nationalism, especially among conservatives (Carr, 1980: 27). Cánovas, one of the leading statesmen of the time, wrote that 'political economy must accept the concept of the *patria* and subordinate itself to it' (ibid.: 28). Spain in the twentieth century was to see two dictatorships which attempted to build on this conservative patriotism to break out of the country's economic dependency on international investors.

The economic crisis of the 1870s also saw Britain's industrial dominance under serious challenge for the first time, especially by the new chemical and electrical industry technologies emerging from the United States and Germany. Despite the growing threat to its competitiveness, Britain fought hard to maintain its free trade economic primacy by resisting the growing international movement towards protectionism. It managed to mitigate the effects of the gradual and inexorable erosion of its free trade competitive advantages by acquiring foreign assets on an enormous scale. Some 5% of Britain's gross national product was invested abroad in the final decades of the nineteenth century. Spain was a particularly important target for this 'imperialism of capital': from the 1870s, some 13% of all British investment in Europe went to Spain, initially concentrated in the mining sector. This proved to be an astonishingly profitable investment. For the next half-century, Spanish copper, sulphur and iron ore were essential to the world's industrial expansion, especially to the new industries being built around chemicals and electricity. Some 66% of the world's pyrites output between 1875 and 1915, for example, came from Spanish mines, and Britain secured a strong grip on these raw material lifelines. Rio Tinto alone was responsible for two-thirds of Spain's output, some 58 million tons over the period, supplying an extraordinary 44% of the world's needs (Nadal, 1975: 108). With a parallel investment in the second-largest mine, Tharsis, British firms achieved a domination of the world pyrites market that lasted into the 1920s.

British firms also invested heavily in the mining and smelting of the rich iron ore deposits of the Basque Country. These low-phosphorous minerals were ideally suited to steel production and became a staple source for the British industrial economy. Between 1881 and 1913, over 80% of the iron ore imported into Britain, some 136 million tons, came from Spain (ibid.: 120). This amounted to some 60% of Spain's total output of 231 million tons, clear evidence of the growing interdependence of the British and Spanish economies. In the same period, Spain itself managed to smelt just 19 million tons, some 8.4% of the total. Even this concealed a further symptom of the country's dependence on Britain: Welsh coal, shipped back to Bilbao in the iron ore ships, was used for smelting the Spanish ore. The concerted use of the returning ore vessels meant that British coal cost less than the lower-quality coal from the Asturias province just down the coast. As a result, coal imports from Britain rose by 47% between 1865 and 1881 as the Basque iron industry developed a strong dependence on Britain imports. Meanwhile the lack of internal transport connections led many other areas of Spain, especially in Andalusia, to become highly dependent on British coal supply and distribution (ibid.: 141). By 1900, Britain's economic influence was pervasive. As well as a near monopoly in pyrites and a dominant role in iron ore mining and coal supply, British companies invested in a range of urban services, including water, gas, electricity and transport. For example, British finance (and, later, ownership) was behind one of Spain's largest enterprises, Barcelona Traction, responsible for the Catalonia region's electricity generation and transport system. Even as late as 1936, Britain's total share of foreign investment in Spain was some 40% (Edwards, 1979: 65).

Britain's economic imperialism – both its 'free trade' and its investment capital form – had a strong political dimension. During the last half of the nineteenth century, as rivalry sharpened between the 'great power' empires, Spanish foreign policy became increasingly constrained by British strategic interests. In 1859, Spain, encouraged by a measure of economic prosperity and political stability, had mounted a colonial adventure in Morocco aimed at recovering its imperial and European status. Britain made it quickly evident that it would not allow a European power to exert influence over the North African coast or to interfere with its favourable trade relations with the Moroccan sultanate. Spain was forced into a humiliating withdrawal by Britain's total naval dominance. Later, during Spain's disastrous war against the United States in 1898 when it lost its last colonies of Cuba and the Philippines, Britain underlined Spain's subaltern role. In a famous Albert Hall speech, British Prime Minister Lord Salisbury implicitly referred to Spain as a 'dying nation', suggesting the country needed direct 'oversight' by an imperial great power. Less than a decade later, Britain showed what this meant in practice when it settled the terms of the agreement between the great powers, including the United States, over the carving up of the Moroccan sultanate. Although the 1906 Algeciras agreement gave Spain residual colonial role over the northern coast of Morocco, this was explicitly designed by Britain to frustrate France's aspiration to colonise the whole of Morocco. French acquisition of the coastal ports would have enabled it to challenge Britain's command of the Mediterranean sea routes through the Strait of Gibraltar. Britain felt sufficiently confident of its influence over Spain to allow it a measure of control as a buffer state. Both subsequent world wars were to confirm just how limited, even in highly adverse circumstances for Britain, was Spain's foreign policy freedom of manoeuvre.

While Britain's ability to project its imperial political power in the Iberian Peninsula remained strong, its dominant economic role had reached its apogee by the first decade of the twentieth century. Its mining assets were passing peak production, while other European powers, notably the French and the Germans, were investing heavily in Spain. In Spain itself, the long 70-year campaign for trade protection finally succeeded with the passing of the 1906 tariff law. This imposed significant barriers to foreign dominance and stimulated foreign and domestic industrial investment, partly designed to evade the new trade barriers. However, the tariffs, primarily aimed at protecting existing economic interests, failed to provide the basis for a Spanish industrial take-off. The critical failure was the lack of a parallel national programme of comprehensive state intervention to support industry, so long demanded by the Catalans and the Basques.

The failure of conservative and landowner-dominated Madrid governments to respond to the needs of the industrialising areas, centred on Barcelona and Bilbao, had dramatic political consequences. From the 1890s, industrialists in both regions began to ally with the populist regional nationalist movements, enabling them to win significant political and electoral support. By 1906, the Catalonian Lliga led by Cambó was able to win a majority of the region's parliamentary seats while in the Basque Country Arana's conservative nationalist movement, the PNV (Basque Nationalist Party), gradually established itself as a major political force once industrial interests began to join the demand for devolution. Over the next two decades, this regional political fragmentation was reinforced by the continuing failure of the Madrid-based liberals to break with their orthodox economic beliefs and develop interventionist policies to support domestic industry. Many were to remain ardent adherents of Britain's nineteenth-century *laissez-faire* economic ideology into the 1930s, even as Spain fell further behind the advanced economies with the quickening pace of international economic competition. Awareness of the need for a more interventionist economic policy grew in the decade before the First World War, but the political stalemate among the established parties and the marginalisation of the emerging workers' organisations meant there was no consensus about the shape of an alternative approach.

Paradoxically, it was an increasingly powerful populist section of political conservatives that took the lead in pressing for more state-sponsored intervention in the name of nation-building. Although heavily contested, both by liberals and landowners, a developing nationalist movement argued for the state to take a more active role, especially in the development of new infrastructure and the reform of agriculture. In parallel, this nationalist-inspired movement demanded that Spain should develop its 'buffer' colony in northern Morocco as the foundation for a new Spanish imperium. Neither strategy succeeded. Fierce Moroccan resistance and a chronic failure to invest undermined Spain's colonial campaign, which eventually collapsed. Meanwhile, at home, proposals for an ambitious programme of investment, led by progressive conservative Finance Minister Santiago Alba, came to nothing, defeated in Parliament by an alliance of regional, liberal and landowner interests in 1916. The failure of both conservative and liberal economic models to provide the basis for modernising the country undermined the uneasy coalition of landowner and bourgeois interests supporting the regime. At the same time, the slowly growing development of working-class organisation created further deep fractures in the regime: trade-union-led strikes in the mining and urban industrial areas were increasingly frequent from the 1890s and added to the regime's growing economic and political crisis.

Spain's deep political contradictions were brought into the open by the shattering impact of the First World War. Although formally neutral, the country was inexorably drawn into the war. Its textile industry became a major supplier of military clothing while the mineral and metal industries were crucial for the munitions industries of both sides, enabling some sections of Spanish industry to make fabulous profits. On the other hand, the inadequacies of the country's social and physical infrastructure meant that many rural areas faced severe food shortages and even starvation. In towns and cities, workers were hit hard by largely uncontrolled price inflation. The resulting social misery led to rising industrial and political militancy, including a brutally repressed general strike in 1917, initiated by the anarchist trade union, the CNT, and supported by the usually highly moderate socialist trade union, the UGT.

Behind this deep internal social and political wartime crisis lay the influence of Britain, which set – and, importantly, enforced militarily – the boundaries of Spain's economic and political independence. The First World War made brutally evident the underlying neocolonial nature of the Anglo-Spanish political and economic relationship. The Iberian Peninsula, at the hinge of Atlantic and Mediterranean shipping routes, took on crucial military significance, especially when, in April 1917, Spain became a focus for the submarine war. Meanwhile, for all the belligerents, Spanish minerals were increasingly essential for munitions production. Britain was especially dependent on Spanish iron ore and sulphur for its munitions, arms and shipbuilding industries, crucially so once the war intensified from 1916. Despite this, in a clear indication of Britain's overwhelming power, Spain was unable to take advantage of this vulnerability. Instead, Britain used its naval blockade to ration supplies, especially coal, to Spain, allowing it to impose – and directly police inside Spain itself – a licensing system for both Spanish and foreign-owned firms (Garcia Sanz, 2011: 56). This was a clear demonstration that when its core interests were threatened, Britain was able and prepared to use military force to discipline its informal colonies, a strategy neatly summarised by Gallagher and Robinson as 'trade with informal control where possible, trade with rule where necessary' (Gallagher and Robinson, 1953: 13).

The First World War marked a decisive turning point for Britain's economic hegemony in Spain, as elsewhere in the world. From the 1920s onwards, Britain's share of Spanish imports, investment and finance declined as US and German consumer-based industries in particular took pole position in Spain's developing mass markets. Meanwhile Spain's politics took an increasingly nationalist turn as the country tried to modernise its economy and escape its peripheral economic role as food and raw material supplier to the European core. This was reinforced by the growing influence of popular and working-class organisation seeking to improve industrial prospects and conditions at work. Strikes against British-owned enterprises took on an explicitly nationalist and populist character. The six-month-long strike at Rio Tinto's mines in 1920 became a national movement: towns and cities throughout Spain supported the strikers with demonstrations, funding and accommodation for strikers' children. There were widespread demands by politicians of both left and right for Rio Tinto's nationalisation. Another strike, the 1919 shutdown at the British-owned Barcelona Traction Company, which resulted in legislation guaranteeing an eight-hour day, also aroused bitter resentment of foreign domination.

These strikes were part of an extraordinary upsurge of country-wide industrial action in the years following the First World War. Combined with the disastrous failures of the Moroccan military campaign and deep domestic political divisions, these industrial struggles showed that the narrow political base of the liberal-conservative regime was totally unable to cope with the intense post-war economic and social changes. In 1923, it collapsed when General Primo de Rivera mounted a successful *coup d'état* and established an authoritarian dictatorship. Over the next eight years, the Primo regime, loosely modelled on Mussolini's, introduced a range of measures to support investment in infrastructure, industry and agriculture. Its economic agenda took on elements of populist nationalism: chosen workers organisations were given a voice in management, and there were promises to take back control of the country's natural resources from foreign owners. In the boom years of the mid-1920s, Primo's economic policy mix of pragmatism and mild nationalism appeared to restore stability and achieve a measure of industrial and urban expansion. There were some threats to foreign-owned enterprises – Rio Tinto, for example, was forced to make significant tax payments for the first time, and a state enterprise took over petrol and oil distribution. On the other hand, the regime actively encouraged foreign investment in new industries; for example, contracting the development of the country's phone network to the US multinational, ITT.

At root though, the Spanish economy was still highly dependent on its raw material exports and a largely unchanged agricultural base: the world trade crisis at the end of the decade revealed how little the structure of the economy had changed. In 1930 Primo fell, driven out by the same old landowner interests which had looked to him to reimpose social order but which were now threatened by the world trade slump. Shortly afterwards, the monarchy itself was swept away amid widespread accusations of corruption. In April 1931, in the middle of the world's worst financial crisis, a progressive alliance of republicans and socialists established the Second Spanish Republic. Although signal for an enormously ambitious programme of democratisation, the new republic adopted an economic policy that was rigorously orthodox. In an attempt to preserve the international value of the peseta and under direct pressure from the Bank of England, it agreed to balance its public sector budgets while meeting all the Primo dictatorship debts. As a result, the new republic was unable to meet the intense social aspirations of its supporters or to make the infrastructure investment the country desperately needed.

Five years later in 1936, these unfulfilled economic expectations contributed to the military uprising and the Republic's defeat in the devastating civil war that followed. The Franco regime's answer to Spain's economic needs was to adopt a highly nationalistic and autarkic form of economic planning (Quiroga and Ángel del Arco, 2012: 161). This had two essential elements. One was a programme to repress the social and political aspirations awakened by the Republic, which was carried through with savage and murderous intensity. All independent institutions including trade unions were abolished and political opponents systematically exterminated. Alongside this programme, the regime initiated a largely unsuccessful policy to eliminate Spain's dependence on foreign finance and investment by building a self-sufficient economy. Foreign investors were bought out and large sectors nationalised, with British companies representing a particular target.[4]

Remarkably, the profound changes of the interwar years – notably Spain's growing national assertiveness and the weakening of Britain's imperial influence – left the underlying 'informal colonial' relationship between the two countries fundamentally unchanged. The outbreak of the Second World War showed the economic and geostrategic interdependencies were as strong as they had been during the First World War. Once again, Britain used its naval dominance to impose a tight naval blockade on the Iberian Peninsula and to ration Spain's imports and exports. Meanwhile, Britain's war industries proved to be as dependent on the supply of Spanish minerals as they had been 20 years before. Despite Franco's Nazi sympathies and deep hostility to Britain, Spain was again forced to recognise its dependence on British trade and finance, and it remained neutral throughout the war. For his part, Churchill saw Spain's geostrategic position and its economic role as crucially important in the maintenance of the British Empire. Although finding Franco personally distasteful, he tenaciously argued, against Roosevelt and his own foreign secretary, Anthony Eden, that the survival of his military regime was a bulwark against the social disorder which might follow its replacement. More surprisingly, these arguments were to find enthusiastic Cabinet support in the Labour government of 1945.

By the end of the war, Britain's grip on its informal, as well as its formal, colonies throughout the world was weakening. Nonetheless, the new 1945 Labour government ensured that the Allies, and later the United Nations, took no effective action against the Franco regime despite widespread international calls to do so. The Attlee government maintained, just as Churchill's War Cabinet had, that any social disorder in Spain would threaten its investment interests as well as essential mineral and food supplies. Ernest Bevin, Attlee's foreign secretary, argued that any social breakdown in Spain would threaten the imperial supply lines through the Mediterranean to Suez and India. At a crucial Cabinet meeting in January 1946, Bevin used Britain's economic vulnerability as his central argument against taking any action against Franco. The rest of the Cabinet meekly accepted his suggestion that toppling Franco would fatally undermine Britain's desperately vulnerable industrial economy.[5] The rationalisation for giving priority to British economic self-interest over democratic principles was still – as much for a radical Labour government as it had been for British governments in the previous century – that the Spanish were not ready for democracy. In 1947, the British *chargé d'affaires* in Madrid registered his 'sickening doubt about the whole thing [democracy] as regards Spain', and he had 'come to the conclusion that a strong hand – police or army or what have you – is probably the only thing for these wild and extravagant people' (Balfour and Preston, 1999: 221).

Spain's experience as a notionally independent state operating within the influence of 'informal' empires of Britain and France provides one of the first examples of such a colony in a world economy driven by industrialised great powers and finance capital. There are clear parallels with the experience of ex-colonies and other peripheral nations in the aftermath of the Second World War.[6] Spain was to have many post-war successors, informal colonies forced to operate within the US-dominated free trade regime (Panitch and Gindin, 2012: 67–87). Indeed, Gallagher and Robinson's hypothesis has proved just as applicable to the new US imperium, as it sought to bring new states within its expansionist economy, as it had to the British Empire and its relationship with less developed countries, such as Spain, in the previous century.

Notes

1 A strong sense of self-doubt suffused intellectual Spain, especially in the wake of the 1898 'Disaster' when the country lost its last colonies in the Spanish-American War. A leading thinker of the time, Ortega y Gasset, for example, titled one of his major polemical works *Invertebrate Spain*.
2 As Berend and Rankí put it, 'the bourgeoisie in its long and ultimately successful struggle against the old feudal ruling class, took England for its example, concentrating primarily on doing so with the old restrictions and barriers' (1982: 66).
3 As Güell put it, integrated development of 'our foundries and coal sources' would have avoided 'an open wound in the body of the nation from which flows without interruption the blood of Spanish jobs and capital which fertilise foreign capital and jobs' (Güell y Ferrer, 1880: xlviii).
4 The impact of Franco's autarkic industrialisation was limited: through the 1940s and 1950s, Spain remained very largely dependent on its raw material exports. Not until the opening up of the economy in the late 1950s was there a degree of industrial 'take-off' (Tortella, 2000: 232).
5 National Archives, Kew. CAB 129/16/2, Cabinet Papers: Paper from Foreign Secretary, 6 January 1947.
6 As Trebilcock points out, Spain's experience, as 'a nineteenth century LDC (less developed country), anticipates the ambitions of twentieth century LDCs from a similar background of deprivation and colonisation' (Trebilcock, 1981: 378).

3 Economic imperialism in Cuba, 1898–2017

Hegemony and embargo

Adam Burns

This chapter traces US imperialism in Cuba through two distinct phases: US economic hegemony (1898–1959) and the US embargo (1960–present). Throughout these seemingly very different periods, Gallagher and Robinson's (1953) theory of economic imperialism provides a, perhaps unlikely, link. Despite taking different forms across the years, the thrust of US policy has been largely based on economic dominance. Though Gallagher and Robinson term their theory the 'imperialism *of* free trade', Grocott and Grady (2014: 543) suggest it might be more accurately called 'imperialism *for* free trade', and across the last century US policy has been consistent in interfering to ensure the option *for* free trade. The United States has, however, rarely submitted to entirely unfettered and bilateral access to their markets. For example, despite very close trading links through both nations' membership of the North American Free Trade Agreement (NAFTA), the United States has continually opposed tariff-free access for Canadian softwood lumber exporters (Devadoss et al., 2005). This is not so dissimilar to the situation in the British Empire in the 1880s when, as Peter Cain (1999: 1) notes, though the British were broadly in favour of 'free trade', duties were still charged on goods such as tobacco, tea, spirits and wine. Indeed, though the United States has often spoken of free trade as an economic cornerstone of its foreign policy – as the British Empire did in its heyday – its contradictory actions towards nations such as Cuba have shown many US rivals that free trade is often 'a self-serving policy to be used only when it serves US political interests' (Petras and Morley, 1996: 282). So, when it comes to the so-called 'imperialism of free trade', this chapter explores, more precisely, the informal imperialist course the United States took to create market conditions in Cuba that were more favourable to itself and then passed off under the guise of 'free trade'.

Few have had a stronger view of the United States as a *bona fide* imperial power than Fidel Castro. In March 2016, the father of the Cuban Revolution, rebuffed President Barack Obama's attempts at rapprochement with the words, 'we don't need the empire to give us anything' (Gomez, 2016). Indeed, from the late nineteenth century onwards, US imperial intrigue regarding Cuba has dominated the island's destiny. After belatedly helping Cuba to oust its Spanish rulers in 1898, the United States occupied the island, only to grant it a humiliating form of conditional independence in 1902 that presaged half a century of total US domination. The Platt Amendment, which was forced into an independent Cuba's constitution, provided the United States with *carte blanche* to intervene in the island's affairs, and troops were sent in on numerous occasions prior to the abrogation of the amendment in the 1930s. Between 1898 and 1959 – the period of hegemony – the United States virtually controlled the island's economy, and Cuba became the jewel in the informal empire of the United States.

Understandably, not all in Cuba were happy with this often one-sided imperial deal. When Fidel Castro finally gained power in 1959, the disastrous Bay of Pigs invasion of 1961 served only to confirm the new Cuban leader's claims of 'Yankee imperialism' to most remaining sceptics in Cuba. Following the failure of this violent incursion, the United States attempted instead to assert its economic sway to oust Castro and install a leader with an economic outlook of which it approved. This policy caused Cuba, ultimately, to fully embrace the Soviet Union until the latter's demise in the early 1990s. The period of the US-Cuban embargo – known in Cuba as El Bloqueo – has lasted until the present day, and its primary purpose remains, as LeoGrande (2015: 939) puts it, 'forcing Cuba's revolutionary regime out of power or bending it to Washington's will'. At the time of writing, the United States has failed to achieve either, but has continued to assert its economic power to the detriment of Cuba for more than half a century.

Before going on to explore these two phases of US hegemony and sanctions, it is useful to briefly contextualise the US-Cuban situation within some of the more canonical historiography on informal imperialism. The historiography of US and British imperialism has, until more recent decades, tended to develop along parallel, rather than directly comparative, lines. While Gallagher and Robinson's 1953 essay introduced a new dimension of economic continuity to the British occupations and annexations of the late nineteenth century, the historiography of US imperialism tended to look instead to the work of William Appleman Williams and Walter LaFeber (of the so-called 'Wisconsin School'). The Wisconsin School took a broadly analogous line when re-evaluating US imperialism, though not without due recognition of the work of Gallagher and Robinson (Kunz, 2000; Palen, 2015). Not unlike Gallagher and Robinson's re-evaluation of British imperialism, the Wisconsin School rejected the idea that American overseas annexations at the end of the nineteenth century were a change of direction – or aberration – in the course of US history and, instead, posited that they were part of a continuous line of economically led imperial expansion (Palen, 2015: 157–159). When revisiting his 1959 landmark work, *The Tragedy of American Diplomacy*, first published in the year of Castro's revolution, Williams singled out US-Cuban relations from 1898–1961 as 'symbolising' his titular tragedy. This period, Williams argue, saw the United States exercise 'continuous, extensive influence in and over all aspects of Cuban affairs' but fail to allow Cuba to run its own affairs, to modernise and to become the nation US propaganda had always suggested it should (Williams,

1972: 1–4). Inevitably, Williams's thesis, like that of Robinson and Gallagher, came under attack from a variety of critics, and it would be difficult for any historian to claim that either thesis is unimpeachable (Louis, 1976; Wolfe, 1999; Kampmark, 2010; Kramer, 2011). At the same time, their parallel arguments about British and US imperialism have continued to provoke and intrigue for more than half a century.

Just as Gallagher and Robinson argue that British imperialism in the nineteenth century was relatively constant, rather than seeing a sharp move to formal imperialism with the Scramble for Africa, such is true of the United States and Cuba across the twentieth century – despite outward appearances. The United States took on a more formal type of imperialist rule (via an open-ended occupation) in Cuba in 1898 but did not shed their imperialist intent in 1902 when they left Cuba; they simply moved to assert informal control instead. Indeed, for an empire to prosper, it need not control other nations directly in order to assert its commercial power, but only intervene when a state fails to 'provide satisfactory conditions for commercial or strategic integration' (Gallagher and Robinson, 1953: 6). From 1902 to 1959 Cuba broadly fulfilled, with some short exceptions, the criteria that the United States required of it to remain free from direct US intervention. Yet these exceptions do help to prove the rule, as explored below.

Duménil and Lévy (2004: 660) argue that imperialism is not a stage of capitalism, as Lenin famously posited, but a constant feature of capitalism: 'The crucial factor is to impose, within the dominated countries, a government prone to the development of economic relations favorable to the interest of dominating countries'. This has been consistently true of the United States in Cuba across the last century. As Grocott and Grady (2014: 559) note, one primary difference between British and American imperialism is that supranational organisations have allowed the United States to exert its informal imperial might all the more effectively in the twentieth century and beyond. As they put it, 'the speed with which finance capitalists can withdraw from a region allows elites not only to take advantage of a crisis, but also to create the crisis in the first place'. In Cuba, this is exactly what the United States has attempted to do since 1960 (and most successfully in the 1960s): create a crisis using its economic sway that would lead to the overthrow of the Castro government and, with it, the installation of a neoliberal, capitalist-friendly government more amenable to the will of the United States. The rest of this chapter will explore the two phases of US imperialism in Cuba – hegemony and embargo – as two very different but nevertheless continuous forms of the attempt to bring the Cuban economy under the informal control of the United States.

Hegemony

In 1898, the United States vanquished Spain, and the victors occupied the majority of the remnants of the once-great Spanish Empire: Cuba, the Philippines, Puerto Rico and Guam. There is little doubt that – economically speaking – Cuba was the prize, and one which had been coveted by the United States since the time of the Founding Fathers. Cuba offered a nearby market for US goods, a strategic position for further economic projection into Latin America and control of vital Caribbean trade routes (Lane, 1972). For numerous reasons, ranging from slavery and race to the fears of US sugar beet growers and the reluctance of the Spanish to sell the island, the United States had never taken control of Cuba prior to 1898 (Burns, 2017: 59–66). From the end of the war until Cuba's 'pseudo-independence' in 1902, the island was controlled by US administrators who set the groundwork for the informal imperialism that was to follow. This was necessary because the United States had promised to grant the island independence. The Teller Amendment of 1898 placed a condition on the United States that once a *stable* government could be established, the United States would leave the island under Cuban control. Indeed, given the emphasis the US media had given to freeing the Cuban people from Spanish imperial oppression, formal political annexation was almost impossible, though it was never too far from the minds of the US occupiers. However, as Lane (1972: 327–329) illustrates, many in the United States – and key US administrators on the island – felt that Cuban *stability* was contingent upon its economic well-being, which in itself rested upon selling vast quantities of sugar (and to a lesser extent other agricultural products) to the United States, and by 1902 the island was 'well on its way to becoming an appendage of America's new commercial empire' (Lane, 1972: 330). Between 1900 and 1903, Cuban exports to the United States tripled at the expense of the US sugar trade with the Dutch East Indies and Europe (Lebergott, 1980: 236). In the decade or so that followed the initial US occupation of the island, an array of commercial networks developed between the United States and Cuba (Santamarina, 2000). As notions of reneging on the promise not to annex the island ebbed, the period of formal occupation became focused firmly upon establishing a stable economic base for the United States to exploit; and if this happened in conjunction with democracy, then all the better.

Cuban independence, however, was not really to be – at least not in 1902 when, in theory, it was formally granted. The Platt Amendment of 1901 provided for future – if temporary – US intervention in Cuba, as required to *stabilise* the country, if anything were to disturb the calm economic base the United States had established during the occupation. A reluctant Cuba was forced to accept this significant caveat to secure their titular independence, and in the following years, the United States was not afraid to assert its right to intervene. When Cuba faced political crises in 1906, 1912 and 1917 and during an economic crisis in 1920, the United States stepped in to assert control over the island (militarily and/or politically) and restore stability. The final phase of direct military intervention, often referred to as the 'Sugar Intervention' (1917–1922), began after a contested election in 1916. The United States issued diplomatic instructions that only a 'legally established' government would be permitted, and it deployed US military forces in 1917. Though the rebellion died down in the subsequent months, US forces remained on the island, and at the end of 1920, when another contested election coincided with an economic downturn, President Woodrow Wilson sent General Enoch Crowder to

Havana to reassert control once more (Aguilar, 1998: 46–47; Schoultz, 2010: 12). This entire final phase of formal occupation was overtly commercial, reflecting the US administration's eagerness to protect US-owned sugar interests on the island. The United States intervened and then retreated only as necessary to assure uninterrupted commercial domination.

When the United States left Cuba in 1902, they might have departed militarily (with the exception of Guantanamo Bay and the aforementioned periods of intervention), but they had certainly not retreated economically. Indeed, as Speck (2005: 451) observes, when considering the US grip over Cuba after 1902, one must consider not only the interventionist blank cheque that was the Platt Amendment, but also the Reciprocity Treaty of 1903. Speck notes that many historians see the two measures combined as part of 'a general strategy of hemispheric domination, launched to further U.S. economic interests' (ibid.). Cuba's economy became the virtual possession of US business interests. Within only three years of Cuban independence, 60% of its rural property was in US hands, as well as substantial sectors of its economy from tobacco and mining to railroads and electricity (Pérez, 2015: 157–158; Chomsky, 2011: 27). However, this relationship has often been depicted with too broad a brush. More recently, historians such as Speck (2005) and Palen (2015: 162–163) have challenged the idea of the US being a champion of free trade, an image which they convincingly argue contains a number of contradictions. The true story of this period is not one of unbridled US free trade with Cuba, but rather a mismatched policy of US economic domination of Cuba coupled with US domestic protectionism, or as Palen (2015: 163) puts it, 'an expansive closed door'. Palen (2015: 182–183) argues that despite the preferential nature of the initial 1903 Reciprocity Treaty, by 1909 this had been replaced with a more 'stringent retaliatory tariff' that failed to encourage Cuban economic independence – not true 'free trade' but trade slanted heavily in the US national interest. The United States was in a bind: to attempt to show some good faith in terms of economic policy (given the far-reaching powers they claimed under the Platt Amendment to interfere in Cuban politics) while at the same time trying to appease US sugar and tobacco producers fearful of cheap and plentiful Cuban competition. The result was not so much the imperialism of free trade as the coercion of Cuba to trade along preferential lines, generally more beneficial to the United States than to Cuba. Though the trade between the United States and Cuba was significant – particularly from a Cuban point of view – it was not a simple tale of continuing growth. Indeed, though the United States supplied 71% of Cuba's imports between 1915 and 1924, this fell to 61% between 1925 and 1929 (Speck, 2005: 462–463). However, this decline was not the sign of things to come, and though trade and investment fluctuated before 1959, commercial links continued to grow.

Despite the important nuance added by recent scholarship to the often one-dimensional image of US-Cuban economic relations, the overall picture between 1898 and 1959 was one of increasing trade and continuous US investment and control of key Cuban industries by the mid-century. In the

1930s, a Reciprocal Trade Agreement (1934) and Sugar Act (1937) were passed enabling Cuba to trade with and, most importantly, sell sugar to the United States at preferential rates, providing a far more attractive market for Cuba's primary agricultural staple. By the early 1950s, the United States remained closely bound to the Cuban economy through private investment and preferential trade, to the extent that US firms owned most of the telecommunications facilities on the island and around half of the railroads and sugar production capacity as well as having substantial investment in a number of other smaller concerns (Helwege, 1989: 214–215).

US presidents and officials have often pointed beyond US economic interest in Cuba to their supposed desire to nurture democracy and improve human rights, but such matters have always been preferable side effects rather than *raisons d'être* for US informal imperialism (Schoultz, 2010). Indeed, as Grocott and Grady (2014: 559) argue, the United States has shown itself to be more than happy on several occasions to 'find collaborators … even at the expense of democratically elected governments' to help impose neoliberal policies to serve the interests of 'capitalist elites'. For the United States between 1934 and 1958, Fulgencio Batista, whose second term as president came on the back of a military coup, was one of the primary collaborators who would help secure its interests. Only when Batista's repression of the Cuban populace and rigging of elections made him a liability to the United States's international reputation (for example, when Batista's US-supplied air force killed innocent civilians) did the United States stop supplying his regime with arms in March 1958 (Rabe, 1988: 121). Batista fled Cuba at the end of December that year, and the United States began considering the unpalatable prospect of working with a socialist, Castro-led Cuba. This unlikely transition proved to be the end of the first phase of US economic imperialism in Cuba: the successful phase.

Interim

When Fidel Castro's revolution proved successful, the possibilities of Castro replacing Batista as the new stooge of the United States deteriorated rapidly. President Eisenhower snubbed Fidel Castro's visit to Washington in April 1959, leaving him to meet instead with Vice-President Nixon. However, Nixon did little to assuage the concerns of intelligence chiefs that Castro, if not a communist himself, was dangerously close to the communists in Cuba. Instead, they reverted to their initial conviction that the removal of Castro (and his replacement with a more economically amenable leader) should be the first-choice policy of the United States (Gott, 2005: 178–179). For Chomsky (2011: 69), 'U.S. policy makers greeted the Cuban Revolution with a single-minded focus on the interests of U.S. investments in Cuba'. Suspicions of Castro's threat to the economy, whether he was a fully fledged communist or not, turned into more distinct fears when, in May 1959, a land reform measure was brought forward that would restrict farm sizes in Cuba to 3,333 acres, with any excess being expropriated (with compensation) (ibid.: 71). Castro's co-revolutionary, Che

Guevara, was keen to move the Cuban economy as far as possible from what Gott (2005: 186) calls the 'economic embrace of imperialism', which would require the abolition of US-owned economic enterprises and their transferal to state ownership. By 1960, US plans were underway to stage a covert operation to oust Castro, akin to the CIA operation which had successfully removed a left-wing government in Guatemala in 1954. The resulting Bay of Pigs invasion in April 1961 (Operation Zapata), planned under Eisenhower but executed under Kennedy, was an outright failure – mainly due to poor US intelligence gathering – and served only to bolster Castro's popularity (Burns and Gallimore, 2017).

The Bay of Pigs fiasco was firm evidence that sending in troops, albeit in this case US-backed Cuban exiles, to secure good economic conditions was not a policy confined to the first two decades of the twentieth century. Indeed, it illustrated that perhaps the United States was more willing to pursue an aggressive foreign policy in the interests of economy hegemony in Cuba than Robinson and Gallagher suggest the British had been during the nineteenth century, at least in some cases (Platt, 1968: 306). The failure of US force played a final, decisive role in solidifying Castro's embrace of the Soviet Union and communism and left the United States with few options on the table. Aside from ongoing covert operations (such as the infamous Operation Mongoose), the tactic most likely to succeed was hurting the island economically in order to force Castro out and allow US businesses to retake control of the informal empire. This tactic was underway even before the Bay of Pigs invasion, with a tit-for-tat economic battle between the United States and Cuba steadily ramping up throughout 1960. As the United States gradually attacked the Cuban sugar industry, Cuba responded with further nationalisation and increased trade with the USSR. In November 1960, the United States took the step of imposing an embargo upon all US exports to Cuba (except medicine and food), a policy that came to last more than half a century.

Embargo

Historians and commentators of US-Cuban policy after 1959 have tended to fall into roughly three broad groups: the first seeing it as guided by pre-existing economic imperialist tendencies, the second by Cold War concerns, and the third as a bit of both (Bernell, 1994: 70–71). However, the end of the Cold War has, in many respects, taken one of the most substantive variables out of the equation; and with little sign of the embargo coming to an end, even more than 25 years since the collapse of the Soviet Union, this chapter argues that the first approach has proven the most resilient interpretation. The Cold War certainly changed the nature of the discussion, but it did not fundamentally alter the core economic focus that both predated and succeeded it.

The US policy of using a trade embargo against Cuba was not a rejection of economic imperialism, but instead an aggressive measure to attain the same freedom to trade with, and invest in, Cuba that it had prior to 1960. The US embargo imposed in November 1960 had two significant impacts: first, it put enormous pressure on the Cuban economy; and, second, it forced the Soviet bloc to continually increase its support for the island to stop its economy from collapsing. In this sense, the Cold War context played a far bigger role in changing Soviet relations with Cuba than did shifting US policy. After the Bay of Pigs invasion failed, Kennedy made the embargo all-encompassing so that, by 1962, it included all US imports from Cuba, and his successor, Lyndon Johnson, attempted to get Latin American and Western European allies to follow suit (Schreiber, 1973: 389; LeoGrande, 2015: 942). 'As a result of such pressure, between 1964 and 1966, Cuba's trade with the United States' western allies almost halved, though it never stopped entirely' (Morley, 1984: 46). This diplomatic pressure, when combined with a lack of sufficient expertise to handle the Cuban economy, exacerbated the turmoil caused by the embargo. This lasted, by degrees, until rising world sugar prices, alongside the increasing support of Soviet subsidies, helped remedy Cuba's finances in the early 1970s. Soviet support was essential: between 1960 and 1974 Soviet subsidies of bilateral trade deficits with Cuba came to around $3.8 billion, and where commerce with the USSR accounted for 45% of Cuban trade up to 1975, it exceeded 60% in the early 1980s (Dominguez, 1998: 112–114, 142). Also, by this time, the willingness of other Western powers to follow the US line on the embargo began to wane, and this allowed Havana to regain access to much-needed international capital (Morley, 1984: 46–47). The embargo might have achieved its aim had it not been for Soviet economic intervention to its own political ends. By forestalling a collapse of the Cuban economy, Soviet aid compelled the United States to maintain the embargo for such an extended time that it inevitably began to draw criticism from other nations across the globe.

In the late 1970s Cuba appeared to be reconsolidating itself in the Americas. Though not permitted entry to the Organization of American States (OAS), it played an active role in a number of other regional groups and established diplomatic relations with several countries in Latin America and the Caribbean (Pérez-Stable, 1993: 148). In 1975 the Ford administration, in recognition of the problems that would inevitably arise due to the increasing normalisation of Cuban trade relations with the United States's neighbours and allies, revoked some of the provisions of the US embargo regarding shipping and trade via overseas subsidiaries with Cuba and voted to relax OAS sanctions (Petras and Morley, 1996: 269; LeoGrande, 2015: 944). However, when Ronald Reagan entered the White House in 1981, the small efforts to ease the extremes of the blockade – under Presidents Gerald Ford and Jimmy Carter – came to an abrupt end. Reagan, in line with a hardening of approach to the Soviet Union, worked to reduce Cuban access to hard currency even further and attempted to expand the reach of the embargo by banning the import of products containing Cuban nickel (LeoGrande, 2015: 945).

However, though the 1980s saw a reversion to a harsher form of the existing embargo, it was the collapse of the Soviet Union at the beginning of the 1990s that finally seemed to offer a chance for the policy's full impact to be brought to bear. For opponents of Castro in the United States, the time was ripe to deliver a decisive economic blow against Castro's government, now without its seemingly vital Soviet support. Backed by the right-wing Cuban-American National Foundation (CANF), legislators forced President George H. W. Bush to revisit the embargo (Castro Mariño, 2002: 47). In the election year of 1992, Bush's Democratic opponent, Bill Clinton, added his support to the administration-backed Cuban Democracy Act (also known as the Torricelli Act), that sought to resurrect the extraterritorial provisions of the embargo that were repealed under President Ford. When elected, Clinton went on to ratchet up the pressure on Western allies to stop trading with Cuba as well as limiting the Cuban government's access to hard currency. By 1993 trade between Cuba and US overseas subsidiaries had fallen to almost nil (Petras and Morley, 1996: 270–271). In 1996 the passage of the Cuban Liberty and Democratic Solidarity Act (also known as the Helms-Burton Act) further tightened and extended the reach of the blockade as well as more formally codifying it into law. However, by this point international condemnation for US policy was so widespread that no other countries were willing to respect the terms that the United States unilaterally imposed; the European Union even challenged the act at the World Trade Organization (Castro Mariño, 2002: 62–63; LeoGrande, 2015: 948). In 1998, Pope John Paul II capped off a decade of increasing international distancing from the United States on its Cuba policy when he visited Havana and called for an end to the embargo.

In the decade that followed the end of the Cold War, lobbying by US-based businesses for a reopening of Cuba also began to emerge, led especially by agribusiness. In 2000, these voices finally managed to secure a law permitting the sale of food to Cuba, and by 2008, US farmers had become the largest suppliers of food and agricultural products to the island (Schoultz, 2010: 3–4; LeoGrande, 2015: 949). However, in spite of this seeming progress on a single economic front, the overall approach of the United States had changed little since the end of the Cold War, and as most commentators agree, this is due in part to the role of older, anti-Castro Cuban Americans in Florida – a swing state that has proved essential to presidential candidates' success in the twenty-first century (Schoultz, 2010: 4; Landau, 2009: 343). In response to the lobbying of Cuban Americans, President George W. Bush created two Commissions for Assistance to a Free Cuba (CAFC), in 2004 and 2006, to outline plans for transition to a neoliberal economy in Cuba with the aim, at least in the eyes of its critics, of a post-Castro return to its traditional economic hegemonic relationship with the island (Núñez Sarmiento, 2014: 148–149). Yet, despite foundations for a post-Castro US-Cuban relationship being set, the rule of the Castros did not end. In 2006, Fidel's brother Raúl took charge, a move formally confirmed in 2008; and despite Fidel's death in 2016, a Castro is still (at time of writing) the President of Cuba. The pressures of agribusiness and the Cuban-American lobby led to fluctuations in the severity of the embargo during the first decade of the twenty-first century, not dissimilar from those of the 1970s; but fundamentally El Bloqueo, and US-Cuban policy in general, remained intact.

When Barack Obama was elected in 2008 on the back of wider promises for an overhaul of US foreign relations, there were signs that Cuban-American opinion in Florida also favoured a toning down of US intransigence towards Cuba, and a series of reports in 2008 and 2009 by the Brookings Institution recommended a constructive re-engagement with the island (ibid.: 150). Between 2009 and 2011 the administration lifted certain travel and remittance restrictions, and in 2014 Obama appealed for the embargo to end. In 2015, the United Nations voted 191 to 2 to condemn the US embargo of Cuba, and Obama pointed out that perhaps, after 50 years of implementing the same policy, it was time to 'try something new' (LeoGrande, 2015: 939, 951). The following year, Obama became the first US president since the Cuban Revolution to visit Havana, with polling suggesting that Cuban Americans no longer showed such strong support for the embargo, especially among the younger generations (Roberts, 2016). Nevertheless, in spite of Obama's overtures, the embargo did not come to an end.

As Joy Gordon (2015: 863) remarks, in an age of so-called 'smart sanctions', the US embargo against Cuba remains 'deliberately overbroad in every aspect. … These sanctions are as thoroughgoing and indiscriminate as it is possible to be, and that has not changed significantly with the reopening of diplomatic relations'. Yet, in spite of the small vacillations in the severity of the embargo, after more than half a century it remains and is a sign that – even after the fall of the Soviet Empire – the aim of US policy towards Cuba, requiring submission to US economic hegemony, has remained generally consistent since 1898. The counterproductive nature of the embargo has not gone unnoted, bringing international sympathy to a government that might have otherwise faced greater external pressure to reform (Giuliano, 1998; Bernell, 1994: 67). However, for the United States to back down on a half-century-long embargo, particularly before the end of the Castro government, is still too difficult for many politicians in the United States to countenance. The election of Donald Trump in 2016 has promised, in areas well beyond the Cuban sphere, to provide a stark contrast to the more open diplomacy advocated by Obama, even if Obama's rhetoric was not always matched by concrete achievement in foreign affairs. In June 2017, Trump announced new restrictions on trade and travel with Cuba, but left off rescinding all of the changes made by his predecessor (Kunović 2017). Though prognostication is not within the remit of this short chapter, it is safe to say that the US embargo looks secure at least until the end of Castro rule in Cuba. However, even when the embargo ends, it is more than likely that the unbroken policy of US informal imperialism will simply revert to its previous approach and see the United States reassert its economic hold over the island through lop-sided trade and investment policies. The continuity of US economic imperial purpose in regard to Cuba – informal where possible, formal when necessary – looks to be far from over.

Part II

Periphery-metropolitan relationships

Overview

In this part we explore two examples of the operation of formal imperialism. In the first instance, we examine the ways in which empires have co-opted a particular element of colonial societies, peasants, into the imperial war machine. In chapter 4 Gibson Burrell ranges across a variety of empires to show how peasants have been incorporated into imperial armies. Formal imperialism has always been costly, and where it has had to be undertaken to secure and advance the economic frontiers of an imperial power, there has been a concerted effort to defray the cost of imperial defence to imperial possessions themselves. Recruiting troops from imperial possessions helps to minimise the need for a large standing army recruited from the metropolitan. Paul Stewart and Tommy McKearney look at the British experience in the island of Ireland and, in particular, Northern Ireland since the 1970s. They examine the use of hard and soft power in Northern Ireland, with soft power forming part of an extended policy of retaining influence and control even should formal control end. Both chapters in this section draw our attention to the way in which conditions at the periphery dictate imperial actions.

Imperialism and the military-peasantry complex

In the introduction of this book, we saw how the United States used neoliberal principles to aid its informal imperialism in Iraq. By using the private security industry, the United States was able to allow for a swift change in imperial control from formal, in 2003, to informal, as quickly as in 2006. In this way, the cost of formal control was quickly transferred from the metropolitan to the periphery. Gibson Burrell prefaces this by an examination of the recruitment of peasants into the imperial forces of colonising powers. Ranging from ancient Rome to post-war Vietnam, Burrell demonstrates the ways in which colonial forces were, where possible, comprised of local troops. In part, this then helps to explain, for example, how Britain was able to control its vast empire with a standing army of around 100,000 troops. Even in India, substantial forces were recruited locally, as Burrell investigates. But it is not just that local forces are raised by imperial governments, but also that such forces were often recruited from the peasantry, creating a military-peasantry complex. Burrell explores this phenomenon, in particular giving thought to the reasons why this collaboration with imperial forces occurs amongst the peasantry, for whom collaboration and resistance are contingent upon the local conditions in which they find themselves. And indeed – and this was one of Gallagher and Robinson's crucial points – this results in conditions at the frontier affecting policy in the metropolitan.

The Good Friday Agreement and Britain's 'deep state': Britain's long goodbye and speedy return

Paul Stewart and Tommy McKearney examine the contemporary history of the relationship between Britain and the island of Ireland. Drawing upon concepts of soft and hard power and the deep state, they examine the ways in which the British state in Northern Ireland used differing tactics to ensure formal control of a territory which was, and remains, highly contested. Parallels with British policies elsewhere in the empire are clearly extant, such as the use of 'special' judiciary proceedings and of the military to put down insurrections against the state. Likewise, the use of democratic proceedings and structures in an attempt to bring opposition within the machinery of the state was a common tactic throughout the empire.

4 Imperialism and the military-peasantry complex

Gibson Burrell

Introduction

Kwame Nkrumah (1965: 1) argues that the methods and form of colonial exploitation differ. He says, 'For example, in an extreme case the troops of the imperial power may garrison the territory' but the exploitative range covers systems as diverse as those found in South Vietnam and within the Congo. Whilst colonial exploitation allowed social conflicts within the metropolitan core to be reduced by distributing some of the spoils of empire amongst domestic industrial and agricultural workers, the only sort of 'aid' sent in return to the colonies tends to be military aid because the cost of maintaining 'peace' within the empire is designed to be borne by the periphery. Lattimore (1970) maintains that formerly big territories were conquered in Asia with small forces. Income, first of all from plunder, then from direct taxes and lastly from trade, capital investments and long-term exploitation, covered with incredible speed the expenditure for military operations. This arithmetic represented a great temptation to strong countries. It is this range of military operations within the empire and how it was managed in different places and at different times, with or without indigenous peasantry, that is the focus of this chapter.

Colonial experiences have been remarkably different across time and space. They include differential systems of coercion and retaliation, varieties within 'the consent of the colonized to colonialism' and the varying role of non-players (Gandhi, 1998: 172). All of this problematizes 'colonialism' (and imperialism) as generalisable theoretical object. Another question, of course, is how one could speak for subaltern peoples, how one could understand their worldview and their political desires and fears. And, relatedly, how does the subaltern voice relate to the colonial archive, which records only certain voices and totally ignores others? A further complication is what types of colonialism exist with which to understand 'post'colonialism. It has been argued that, on the one hand, there is the physical conquest of territories, a violent bandit mode of building a colony based on rapaciousness, greed and capitalist self-interest. For example, it is estimated that from 1545 until 1825 8 million people of Bolivian and African origin died in the Potosí silver mines after the discovery of the pre-existing Inca mine by the Spanish conquistadors. Imperial rapaciousness and greed indeed. On the other hand, says Nandy (1983), there was a colonial commitment to 'soft power' and control of ideological and cultural forces by those who thought they would be bringing 'civilization' to 'their' colonies via rationality, liberal values and modernity. Happily, one is reminded that when asked about 'Western civilization', Gandhi replied that it would be a good idea. This sort of reaction is exactly one form of resistance which postcolonial theory would welcome because of its denaturing of many usual assumptions held within the imperium.

This raises the question, of course, of whether a piece such as this chapter approaches anywhere close to understanding the 'military-peasantry' complex when the terms we are to use are so European in 'orientation' (sic). My concern is to look to the history of some anti-colonial movements – and imperial gambits too – which involve, in one way or another, that category known here as 'the peasant'. This is not to engage substantively with the discourse of the imperial power such as that undertaken by Said where one finds 'a subject race, dominated by a race that knows them and what is good for them better than they could possibly know themselves' (1991[1978]: 35). It would be well for every European author writing about colonialism to bear this in mind.

Moreover, Spivak (1993: 55) has written that 'If there is a buzzword in cultural critique now, it is "marginality"'. In an inversion of the core-periphery trope, my point here would be that we should make the assumption that, today, perhaps the majority of humanity upon the planet are peasants (Van de Ploeg, 2010). This term requires definition, of course, to which we will return in a moment. Suffice it to say here that the global core is the peasantry, in numerical terms at least, and the rest of us are peripheral in some major senses to them.

> In 1970 the world's agricultural population stood at 2.0 billion, while by 2010 it will have grown to 2.6 billion. Phrasing it differently, agriculture directly supports the livelihoods of more than three billion people (data derived from Borras, 2009: 15).
>
> (Van de Ploeg, 2010: 29)

The military-peasantry complex

As befits a 'complex' of any sociological and political kind, the military-peasantry complex is extraordinarily difficult to unpack. When President Eisenhower was about to leave office in 1960, he spoke of the problematic nature of the 'military-industrial complex' in which the close ties between the military forces of the United States and industrial companies in the munitions trade were perceived to be out of the control of the ruling party in government. What is meant here by the military-peasantry complex is not dissimilar to this. It is the full range of ties between imperial forces and the peasantry within the colonies – some close, some not. At one extreme, the peasantry may be engaged in armed conflict against the colonial forces. At the other, members of the peasantry are enrolled not necessarily to maintain order within their own society but to occasionally help 'police' activities within other colonies of the imperial state. This 'complex' of social forces and relationships appears to give the imperial entity greater control over the subjected peoples by creating within the oppressed groups those who are willing to become oppressors themselves. Of course, another intermediate possibility is that the peasantry are not first in line for this selection, for often the groups chosen for recruitment are already somehow socially superior and may be drawn from pre-existing militarised groups (such as the Sikhs and the Gurhkas) in order to take them into the tent of empire. In the imperial regimes of Europe, it was often the so-called 'martial races' that were sought out for entry into colonial forces. But sometimes and in some circumstances, it is the landed peasantry who provide the bulk of lower ranks within militarised forces. This was true in Ireland for many decades and also perhaps was relevant in India in some measure, especially in those times of global conflict in the twentieth century when the British Empire was particularly threatened.

Who are the peasantry?

The peasantry here are defined as rural cultivators who produce for subsistence and the market, using family labour with little capital and for whom non-market considerations are crucial. Thus, a peasant is a member of a traditional class of farmers, either labourers or owners of small farms, especially in the European Middle Ages under feudalism or, more generally, in any pre-industrial society. The word 'peasant' is also commonly used in an 'othering' sense as a collective noun for the rural populations in the poor and underdeveloped countries of the world. Their rural lifestyle, location in the primary sector of the 'feudal' economy, commitment to traditional patterns of belief and authority, especially witchcraft, particular conceptions of time and space, illiteracy, oral histories, a focus often upon bare survival, and so on all mark them as different from industrial workers. Thus, the use of many derogatory terms for 'the peasant' across many nations reflects their low status in urban, metropolitan, science-based cultures. They are, quite literally, soiled.

There are many commentators, of course, who see the term 'peasant' as unsuitable for states and social systems outside of Europe. Cohen (1984) for example, asks why the rural population in China were called 'peasants' rather than 'farmers', a distinction he called political rather than scientific. Modern Western writers often continue to use the term 'peasant' for Chinese farmers, typically without ever defining what the term means. This Western usage suggests that China is stagnant, 'medieval', underdeveloped and held back by its rural population. Cohen (ibid.: 6) maintains that the 'imposition of the historically burdened Western contrasts of town and country, shopkeeper and peasant, or merchant and landlord, serves only to distort the realities of the Chinese economic tradition'. So in considering China or India or Ireland and their military-peasantry complexes, we should be very careful in our usage of the term 'peasant'.

What is meant here is much more akin to 'semi-proletarian' peasants who eke out an existence through subsistence farming and seasonal work for large landowners or, more importantly, to the agricultural proletariat (so called 'ag labs') with no possession of land. Of course, each of these status positions leads to very different conditions of possibility. We must also be very careful in addressing the sorts of colonial organisation that imperial states often adopted, for these differ considerably. Fieldhouse (1999) drew up a fivefold categorisation of colonial territories that has proved influential. He distinguishes 'pure settlement colonies' – for example, the United States, Canada and Australia, where indigenous peoples were to all intents and purposes excluded from the sociopolitical system – from 'mixed colonies' – such as Algeria, which included the original inhabitants and the colonial settlers in large numbers. Different from these two was the classic 'plantation colony', such as Jamaica, where immigrant workers were 'imported' to work on the land under the control of a small group of Europeans. Fieldhouse differentiates this system from colonies of occupation, like the Philippines, and from 'trading enclaves', such as Shanghai (ibid.). Perhaps there is also an additional category – 'the internal colony', which was suggested by Hechter (1975) and is a territory possessed of a separate identity and culture, such as in the case of Ireland.

Whatever the system, the perennial imperial themes are how to manage these very large systems without overstretch or underperformance. How to police a frontier, how to train local forces and how to create 'security producers' rather than 'security consumers', all at the lowest cost possible, are the pragmatic concerns of imperial systems. Thus, the colonial system both around and within the military affected almost all levels of society. Killingray and Omissi (1999: vii) claim that almost all colonial armies were a mixture of expatriate troops and officers and local recruits of one sort or another. The recruitment, maintenance, interaction and deployment of both these categories has to be interpreted … in the context of the distinctive social, cultural, intellectual … formations of both metropolitan powers and colonial territories. And this complexity of cultural differentiation must be recognised; but almost everywhere it was widely accepted that 'The military was the only obvious way to a more comfortable life' for 'the army offered paid employment, regular food, welfare services for the man and his family, clothing, status, new opportunities and for some anonymity' (Killingray, 1999: 14). This set of inducements was crucial to understanding how landless peasants might join up and enter into imperial military forces. Or not.

Conceptually, it is important to distinguish between the different sorts of relationship that the colonial military forces might 'enjoy' with the peasantry of the colony. First, one can imagine total hostility between colonial troops and the local agricultural labour force. For example, one thinks here of China under the Japanese occupation at the time of the Nanking Massacre or of Bolivian Indians around Potosí.

Second, one can imagine total identity of the peasantry with their own military force, as in war against another power (North Vietnam against the French and then the United States). Here, the military *are* the peasantry through recruitment of the dominant demographic grouping. Third, one could imagine 'partial hostility', as in an ongoing colonial occupation which has become established, though troops and peasants often remain mutually suspicious. Certain parts of Ireland around 1915 showed this sort of relationship.

The military are seen primarily in these circumstances as external occupiers, often utilising punishments though also offering rewards for quiescence. Fourth, there might be 'partial identity' in which peasants are encouraged to enter the military, travel abroad as agents of colonialism, are fed regularly and are routinely offered material advantages. This was the case also in parts of Ireland in the late nineteenth century. Fifth, one can imagine 'hostile identity' where peasants are encouraged by political agents to enter the military in order to subvert it and learn military methods for use in liberation against the imperial power. This entryism is unusual but is known across colonial circumstances. Finally, there will be movement between all five of these positions as political and economic conditions change.

What does this simple categorisation allow us to do? Well, first it shows that it cannot be taken for granted that the closely knit overlapping military-peasantry complex is likely to be present in all imperial circumstances. Far from it. We must remember that peasant revolution has been widely seen as a response to capitalism and imperialism and that far from being passive and undemanding concerning what their life chances are, elements of the peasantry have from time to time risen up against their oppressors and have certainly not always joined the armies of the imperial power in enthusiastic ways. Rather, they have militarised themselves, as has been the case across parts of Latin America. Second, this categorisation suggests that there is no single military-peasantry complex but several, and these can change with ongoing social and economic perturbations. Third, we must expect the peasantry not to be in the forefront of colonial forces in many instances. Pye (1962) maintains that many colonial forces did not utilise landless agricultural workers. So the question must be: why are the peasantry overlooked by colonial forces seeking to recruit into their ranks? Well, first is the perceived unimportance of the landless peasantry. We are told by Akram-Lodhi and Kay that they are virtually invisible to the imperial regime because 'contemporary peasants are "petty commodity producers", operating as both petty capitalists of little consequence and as workers with little power over the terms and conditions of their employment' (2010: 178).

Similarly, Van de Ploeg (2010: 20) claims that powerlessness is the issue in point. Indeed, 'the first editorial of the *Journal of Peasant Studies* referred to peasants as "the most underprivileged", although it also referred to their long "history of struggle against such conditions"' (Byres et al., 1973: 1). In the same issue Hobsbawn discussed the 'general subalternity of the peasant world', claiming that 'peasantness' was defined by 'subalternity, poverty, exploitation and oppression' (1973: 7).

Third, is the besmirchment of the peasant across time and space. Jim Handy in the *Journal of Peasant Studies* (2009), referring to 'a long history of blaming peasants', specifically cites *The Economist* of 1841 as the source of much of the vilification of the peasantry by business and for the construction of an anti-peasant rhetoric. Fourth, Max Weber in his writings advocated 'de-peasantization', just as *The Economist* did, because the peasantry were a deep pool of non-rationality. The peasantry are 'most lacking in culture' (Gerth and Mills, 1959: 368). They engage in 'primal, naturalist and unsublimated sexuality' (ibid.: 349). They 'have been inclined towards magic' since 'they are bound to nature and depend upon elemental forces' (ibid.: 283). And, worst of all perhaps, they have not been trained 'to produce in order to gain profit' (ibid.: 365). Fifth, it might be possible to see some transnational features of peasant impoverishment which lead to questions of a lack of moral propriety as seen through the eyes of the imperial recruiters into the colonial military. Impoverishment comes about through enforced property sale if the peasant has any property whatsoever to sell. This leads to unemployment and after a considerable period of time maybe to abandonment by the wider extended family. Once familial ties are cut, it is but a short step to beggary and starvation. Some expropriated peasants are forced into slavery, especially into prostitution (Gerber, 2014), or even suicide.

For these reasons, then, the peasant is widely seen as unlikely to 'make a go of it' in military forces being recruited by the imperium. They are seen as a drag on 'modernisation', whereas the armed forces are often portrayed as one of the most 'modern' sections of the socio-economic life of the colony (Rettig and Hack, 2006). What the colonial recruiters thus undertake is the identification of 'martial races', not drawn from the peasantry but often from those groups peripheral to mainstream agriculture, such as 'hill tribes' who were seen to reflect positive virtues by being adventurous, bellicose and apolitical. After the Indian Rebellion of 1857, the British authorities classified each caste and tribal people into one of two categories, 'martial' and 'non-martial'. The reason cited in many works was that a 'martial race' was typically brave and well built for fighting, having been assigned this set of characteristics as one of four 'varna' in the Vedic system of Hinduism, while the 'non-martial races' were those whom the British believed to be unfit for battle because of their sedentary lifestyles. In other words, the majority of agricultural labourers were deemed unfit for martial activity. By using a racially inspired system, the colonial forces succeeded in creating internal divides within the Indian polity in order to avoid a repeat of the so-called Indian Mutiny of 1857. It became an accepted part of all imperial recruitment manuals that only 'the martial races' should be recruited into the military (Peers, 2013). Greenhut (1984) argues that 'The Martial Race theory had an elegant symmetry. Indians who were intelligent and educated were defined as cowards, while those defined as brave were uneducated and backward'. What this ignores, of course, is the millions who were not educated at all – the peasantry.

Once identified as a martial race, particular sections of the Indian population contributed 1 million men to the British Imperial forces in the Great War and double this in the Second World War. It is estimated that 40% of the Indian government's budget went on peacetime 'defence', making it to all intents and purposes 'a garrison state' in which the cost of its defence (and imperial aggression elsewhere) was carried by the people of India. Local troops were perceived to be cheaper and healthier than their European counterparts but less reliable. The Indian soldier cost one-quarter of his British counterpart, and since the cost to the empire of colonial forces was of central concern to those in London, this calculation was seen as paramount.

In 1928 Nehru said, 'our army is a mercenary army employed by foreigners to put down their own countrymen and to keep them under foreign heels' (1928: 5). Economic policies emanating from London had led to the ruin of traditional handicrafts, particularly in textile manufacture. So as dispossession of the peasantry increased, landownership became concentrated and overcrowding of the remaining land was increasingly found. This led to massive debt and impoverishment of the peasantry across large parts of India. The result of this project of immiseration was peasant uprisings during the colonial period and the subsequent development of peasant movements after formal independence. Other solutions to imperial control of territory were attempted elsewhere on the planet where capitalism was not fully developed and other socio-economic arrangements pertained.

The problem of recruitment into imperial armies

In the long history of Rome, the army moved from a citizen militia drawn from property-owning small farmers and came to depend increasingly on recruitment among both the rural peasantry and low-status city dwellers. The maintenance of a property qualification for legionary service had led to a manpower crisis in the second century BC as more and more citizens fell below the qualifying level. There was also concern about whether the peasantry were bearing and rearing enough children to fulfill their civic duties (Rich, 1983). By the time of Augustus a decision had been made to set up a regular standing army with fixed terms of service and guaranteed retirement bonuses (Raaflaub, 1980), which ended the chronic insecurity experienced by soldiers under the republic. Formal annual levies of property owners no longer took place in the traditional way (Cornell and Matthews, 1991: 157). It had not been until the dictatorship of Caesar that a large-scale programme of overseas settlement was undertaken, allowing for the gradual transformation of the Roman army from a citizen militia to a professional force. As Roman armies became more involved in many theatres of war lasting for years on end, campaigning no longer followed a seasonal annual pattern and ceased to have the natural rhythm that had been known for centuries. Rich (1983) argues that the economic and social status of the legionaries was very low even during the second century BC, when the levee existed. With permanent armies drawing their manpower from peasant groups inside both Rome and Italy, the social status of the troops fell even further. The Romans had successfully exploited their Italian conquests by demanding troops rather than by taxing them, but if they were to continue to profit from the alliance, they had to keep finding ways of employing Italian soldiers outside Italy. Wars of conquest were soon to follow.

During the first century AD, 'the legions were increasingly, and in the end almost exclusively, recruited in the provinces' (Forni, 1953). This policy of recruitment had the paradoxical effect of enlarging the army's recruitment base but widening the gap that separated it from Imperial and civilian society in Rome itself. The patricians regarded the army with increasing fear and loathing. Indiscipline and low-class impudence were to become the problems perceived by all Roman aristocrats. During the empire, the rapid spread of Roman citizenship had allowed for this development of integrating the provinces, and whilst the centurions were likely to be drawn from the local provincial aristocracy, the troops were much more likely to be rural workers whose owners had allowed or encouraged them to join the army. Yet, there is evidence of resistance by landowners, even in periods of military crisis, to the call-up of 'their' peasants. Many high-status landowners were able to sabotage the wholesale recruiting of their agricultural labour force simply by refusing permission or utilising other evasionary tactics.

By the fifth century AD, as the empire crumbled, the Roman forces seem to have consisted not of Romans or even Italians, but entirely of 'federates': tribes and peoples enjoined with Rome by way of a federal structure rather than as Imperial citizens. There is no mention of Roman soldiers at all. In the twilight of the empire, provincials were heavily subjected to conscription, billeting and other requisitions by the army. But as Roman control disappeared from the forests and mountains and concentrated increasingly upon the fertile river valleys, many provincials sought some protection in commanding their own weapons, 'even if they were no match for trained soldiery' (Brunt, 1975). The empire was soon to collapse, as empires do (Rich and Shipley, 1993).

Two millennia later, in Russia, there was eastward expansion of the Tsarist Empire wherein large numbers of previously independent regions were coming under the control of St Petersburg. Such an expansion raised the problem of how to fight on two fronts with divided forces. The solution lay in the mix of soldiering and agriculture. Military settlements represented a special organisation of the Russian Imperial army in 1810–1857, allowing the combination of military service and agricultural production. These were designed by Alexander in 1812 to produce an inexpensive military reserve. The settlements were made up of married men who had at least six years' military service and their families, and men aged between 18 and 45 who were selected from amongst the local peasantry. The peasants had to undergo military training, which often caused a certain unseasonableness in the annual round of agricultural activities. The peasants rioted against this issue of timing when it affected their own areas. Alexander said that any peasant resistance would be suppressed even if it meant lining the 100 km road out of St Petersburg with the dead bodies of settlers.

When military settlements were instituted near St Petersburg, every settler was ordered to grow wheat, but this led to malnourishment because the land around the capital was marshy and labourers had eked a living by hunting and fishing rather than by grain production. Due to such changed circumstances surrounding subsistence, the military performance of settlers was exceedingly low. These settlements could be productive primarily of marshland diseases, and many 'cholera riots' took place in the years before 1850. So far from being a device to suppress resistance to Tsarist control, military settlements became centres of resistance. Eventually, however, a quarter of the Russian Army was stationed in, and produced by, such military settlements. But by 1857 the military settlement programme had been abandoned and the 'communities of ploughing soldiers', as they had come to be known, were no more.

In Ireland, of course, the picture is very complex. Karsten (1983) maintains that 300,000 Irishmen served in the First World War for the British Army and 49,000 lost their lives. However, in peacetime before the world wars, Irish soldiers were more represented in the British Army than they would come to be. By 1915, 'the general disinclination of the farming class to join the colours' had been noted by Bishop O'Dwyer of Limerick, saying of the local agricultural labour force that 'they preferred to till their own potato gardens' rather than enlist (1915: 455). In Victorian times, Irish soldiers had noted that they would fight for Queen Victoria so long as she did not ask them to fight in Ireland against their own kith and kin. They were paid the equivalent of £40 per annum, whereas the Irish farm labourer could expect £25 per annum if he was to remain on the land. It was therefore an attractive option for many to leave the land and take up a musket. By 1830, 42.2% of the British Army was from Ireland. Having been described previously in War Office Reports on recruitment in both 1795 and 1801 as the 'peasantry', in 1889 they were described as being 'adventurous, bellicose and apolitical'. Just what the empire needed everywhere. What the empires of the world do not want are peasant armies rising up against them.

Peasant armies against imperial forces

Che Guevara (2000: 221) wrote about his time in the Congo thus:

> The peasants pose for us the most difficult and absorbing problems of a people's war. In all wars of liberation of this type, a basic element is the hunger for land, involving the great poverty exploited by latifundistas, feudal lords and, in some cases, capitalist-type companies. In the Congo, however, this was not the case, at least not in our region, and probably not in most of the country.

So in the massive continent of 'Africa', these sociological categories of feudalism and capitalism were ill formed or non-existent, and relationships were typically much more tribal in nature. The essence of this tribal/state relationship is perhaps encapsulated in what Hyden (1980) describes as an 'uncaptured peasantry'. Guevara (2000: 223) argues that where he was in the Congo, the peasantry were completely independent, capitalism was barely to be seen and 'imperialism [gave] only sporadic signs of life in the region'. Mkandawire broadens out the analysis to all of sub-Saharan Africa when he claims that

> There are two striking features of the African countryside that have shaped the prospects and conditions for rebellion. The first is that peasants still have direct access to the main means of production – labour and land … with the exception of countries of settler agriculture and concessions,

> production of export crops in much of colonial Africa has remained in the hands of peasants. Capitalist relations of production entailing mass land alienation are thus rare.(2002: 193)

Guevara believed that there was little with which to revolutionise the African peasantry because there was no land shortage and the land was already divided, no desire to produce for more than subsistence needs and no need for credit facilities amongst the peasantry (Mkandawire, 2002: 181).

These writers emphasise that it is unusual within Africa for the peasantry to engage in military action. The character of peasant revolt is highly localised and highly episodic whenever and wherever it does occur. Armed rebel militia engaging in violence against the state are rarely drawn from within the ranks of the peasantry. Instead, peasants have generally resorted to a whole range of 'everyday forms of resistance', such as 'tax evasion, withdrawal from official markets, deception, pilfering, dissimulation, feigning loyalty, theft, and exit from the national territorial or officially assigned spaces' (Mkandawire, 2002). Scott (1976) points to the constant struggle between those seeking to extract labour, produce, taxes and interest from the peasantry, whilst Hobsbawm (1973) describes these peasant behaviours as 'working the system to their minimum disadvantage'. African exceptionalism of this kind should be contrasted to other 'national liberation movements, which fared better with respect to the responsiveness of the peasantry' (Mkandawire, 2002). In other words, across large parts of Africa the military-peasantry complex did not take shape as might have been expected.

Of course, this variability is true elsewhere. What we mean by 'imperial forces' differs over time, but here it is as well to note that whilst the French occupation of Indo-China was as an imperial power, there have debates about whether the United States can be seen in the same light. By the time the Americans became the dominant power broker in the south, the term 'imperialism' may be seen by some as inaccurate. However, Jasanoff argues that as the United States grew in stature, its 'material interests' superseded its 'liberal' attitude to ending empire and would 'make imperialism continue to thrive whether or not it had the word "empire" attached to it' (2017: 267). The theory of globalised capitalism looked remarkably like empire. In Vietnam, the people had fought the French, the Japanese, then the French again, all in the name of opposing someone else's empire. For the majority of the Vietnamese people, the Americans were next in this line of imperial exploiters. Macak (1989) informs us that the rural population were central to the contestation we know as the Vietnam War.

> This Viet Cong infrastructure (VCI) recruited peasants for its army, collected taxes, and undermined GVN influence by intimidating local officials. The GVN's initial attempts to counter this Communist influence in the countryside were the agroville and strategic hamlet programs. The agroville program failed because it removed the peasants from their ancestral lands

> arousing bitter resentment against the GVN. Likewise, the strategic hamlet program, while not requiring any population shift, neglected to isolate the population from the Viet Cong, and it also failed.
>
> (Macak, 1989: 8)

It was widely accepted that 'reaching down into the rural heartland' was crucial for all sides in the conflict, but 'reaching down' is a hierarchical giveaway and is clearly an American conceptualisation. In South Vietnam, we find the following from a report undertaken by the RAND Corporation on behalf of the US military as early as 1967:

> The pattern of VC [Viet Cong] recruitment has changed over time. It has varied, moreover, from one locality to another, the most striking difference being that between GVN- and VC-controlled areas. In recent years, strict criteria of proven political reliability, limits on the age and sex of recruits, the exclusion of youths supporting families, and attempts to station men near their homes have been subordinated to the demands of intensified warfare.
>
> (RAND, 1967: 15)

The class basis of recruits from urban areas was of central concern so that despite these changes, this army remained throughout the 1960s as a peasant army in that many of its rank-and-file members were agricultural labourers. The young men in the rural areas of South Vietnam faced chronic land shortage, and since the Viet Minh in the north had succeeded in effecting much more egalitarian land distribution, the promise of the 'Viet Cong' to engage in land reform was a key inducement to join up. However, Jonker and Meehan (2008) suggest that the government of South Vietnam also offered such reforms, redistributing land to poor tenant farmers and paying reasonable compensation to landlords with financial help from the United States.

As the war intensified, dislocation from home and farm increased. And since male farm labour was seen as crucially important by those remaining in villages, it became more important for the military authorities to seek conscription rather than voluntary enlistment. We must also remember that these rural areas were the districts in which the ARVN (Army of the Republic of Vietnam) were simultaneously recruiting. Rather than assume they could stay in the fields and villages untouched by war raging around them, the choice was open, in some senses, to young peasants as to which way they wished to pursue their military 'careers': Viet Cong or ARVN. Naturally, both sides attempted to disrupt the recruitment efforts of the other.

After the Tet Offensive ended in 1968 with Vietnamese casualties amounting to perhaps 35,000, we are told that '[c]learly, the resistance movement needed soldiers. Viet Cong officials fully realized that without the participation of the masses of women in the revolutionary struggle, the revolution (would) never succeed' (Pothier, 2003: 9). The achievement of women soldiers in the Tet Offensive had been very significant, and this received considerable publicity in both North and South Vietnam. The vast majority of the young people keeping open the so-called Ho Chi Minh trail in Cambodia between 1965 and 1975 were women from agricultural backgrounds. They engaged in fighting, construction, repair work and supply of troops in the South. As Pothier reveals, the experiences of all women involved in the resistance movement showed that 'these were no Rosie the Riveter who stayed home, hoped for peace and gained new skills doing men's work while the men went off to take care of the dirty business of war' (2003: 15). Thus, when we speak of peasant movements against imperial powers, we must see the peasantry in a much more gender-neutral way as they engage in their version of the military-peasantry complex.

But the importance of land, working it, holding it, pacifying it, making a livelihood from it can be overdone in wartime. The main elements of the Viet Cong army within South Vietnam were becoming much more technically sophisticated. The assumption was that the level of literacy, technological understanding and ability to follow complex orders that is required by modern main battle armies was 'beyond' the peasantry's capabilities. Recruitment became much more urban based.

> [B]y the end of 1971 (the Viet Cong army) had an overall strength of 433,000 men – up from about 390,000 in 1968. Forty-six percent of these troops were 'technical speciality branch troops' (such as communications, sapper, artillery, and armour), up from 30% in 1965. This was a much more sophisticated and well-trained fighting organization than that faced by General Westmoreland.

The peasant and modern warfare were apparently becoming separated.

Conclusions

It is clear from this brief excursion across the planet that there is a certain grossness to the terms 'colonial', 'postcolonial' and 'imperialism'. Yet their very scope offers us some hope of providing generalised understandings of the plight and possibilities facing fellow human beings, seen not as individuals or families but as peoples. In all of these cases, the role of military forces and military action cannot be denied. Nor can it be denied that in many societies across the globe, even in 2018, the peasantry exist in a numerically strong position within politico-economic systems. Putting the military issues together with demographic features within nation states and continents, one is forced to conceptualise how these social categories interact and in some ways collide. Yet, empires often ignore the agricultural labourers upon whom food production often depends. For the peasantry are believed to be powerless, besmirched, irrational and historically irrelevant to the march of empire and capitalism (and, it should be said, socialism). Half of the world's population is seen as technologically backward, unwilling to embrace literacy, embued with non-scientific ideologies and far too self-contained. This makes them unfit for military service for or against empires.

The peasantry, in some circumstances at some points in time, however, are more than capable of picking up agricultural tools and forming them into weaponry and then marching out to seek to disrupt the citadels of the imperium. They are more than capable of joining the colonial forces in times of deep agricultural malaise. They are also most likely to seek to remain where they and their families have lived for centuries, within a mile or so of the ancestoral land. Thus, there are at least several ways in which a military-peasantry complex might be understood. What this chapter has attempted to do is to show this variety whilst emphasising as much as is possible the real potency of the peasantry within imperial and colonial circumstances – and to note finally that this potency has by no means run its course.

5 The Good Friday Agreement and Britain's 'deep state'

Britain's long goodbye and speedy return

Paul Stewart and Tommy McKearney

Introduction: the continuity state repressive apparatuses of imperialism's deep state

> If you remove the English army tomorrow and hoist the green flag over Dublin Castle, unless you set about the organization of the Socialist Republic … England would still rule you … through … the whole array of commercial and individualist institutions she has planted in this country.
>
> (James Connolly, 1897: 124)

This is the story behind the story of Britain's long goodbye from the island of Ireland.[1] It reveals the United Kingdom's broader political concerns, the concerns of the new imperialism. In the island of Ireland, these are often deeply hidden to ensure that withdrawal will take place in such a manner as to ensure that the chance of an ultimate departure will be minimised. In fact, it is a departure to end departure. The chapter considers how this story can be told by exploring the continuities in the exercise of state power during the long insurgency from 1969 to 1998. A mixture of hard and soft power (force plus consent) has been mobilised to manage the anticipated unification of Northern Ireland and the Republic of Ireland sometime in the coming decades.

While the theme of the use of soft power is considered, the majority of the chapter is concerned with the development of apparatuses and institutions of hard power into what we term the continuity state repressive apparatuses (CSRAs). While these apparatuses are not unusual in aspects of their development as understood by imperial powers elsewhere, the chapter describes their evolution during the period of the long insurgency in the north. The argument is that these apparatuses were constituted by, and represented, the practices of the deep state. The deep state is present in all capitalist societies and, in the case described here, has an essential role in shaping, or preparing, political and civil society for outcomes which are congruent with the interests of the 'departing' imperial state.

The chapter delineates three periods in the development of the CSRAs: 1969–1981 (from the start of the insurgency until the Hunger Strikes); 1981–1998 (from the Hunger Strikes until the Good Friday Agreement, GFA); 1998 to the present.

When Britain eventually leaves the north, it will not do so in any commonly understood sense – just as in 1922 when Britain conceded independence to southern Ireland, it did so while retaining overall influence. What can be said, though, about the kind of political, social and economic changes attendant on a perceived British withdrawal? Clearly, Britain will not simply let the north go if by this is meant 'let go' without the protection of the political, economic and other strategic interests central to British imperialism. In this respect, and notwithstanding its current relationship with the Democratic Unionist Party (DUP), given the febrile nature of Northern Irish politics, the British government will be happier dealing primarily with the Republic of Ireland. How to remain while appearing to leave – that is the question. Attending this question is the issue of the way Britain seeks to exit the North and the kinds of state apparatuses – repressive and consensus building – that it is endeavoring to fashion.

We concentrate on key features of state practice couched within Gramsci's concept of hegemony; that is, state rule premised upon force plus consent. The concept allows us to account for the changing balance between the use of force – the police, army and other repressive institutions in liberal democracy – and consent – including consensus-forming bodies and notably the liberal democratic institutions of parliamentary democracy, education and the media. The latter are sometimes described as soft power institutions operating within soft power networks, while the former can be labelled as hard power operating within hard power networks.

Within this framework it is argued that Britain has been preparing for a range of so-called soft power and hard power institutions that in a number of aspects meld with *re*-formed state repressive, or hard power, apparatuses, which include the Northern Ireland police service and Britain's deep state repressive apparatus, MI5, in the period up to and including the signing of the GFA in 1998. This CSRA network included an assemblage of deep and extra-state forces organised within, or in proximity to, loyalist paramilitary groups. One of the deep state forces included the Force Research Unit created in 1982. CSRAs have been developing since the beginning of the long insurgency.

The latent, sometimes manifest, objective of the deep state's CSRA is to ensure that Britain can both guide the final break from Ireland and remain hegemonic. Institutions are designed to allow for departure and re-entry: this is the work of the deep state. Its activities mingle, at intervals, with the practices of regular state repressive apparatuses such as the Royal Ulster Constabulary (RUC, now Police Service Northern Ireland, or PSNI) and the British Army. Worth noting is that while hard and soft power are ever-present, the status of the institutions making up the network of the deep state are contextually specific. While the state seeks to retain its *agents influents* within extra-state institutions, over time their import ebbs and flows. We know this because prominent state actors have highlighted it, as evidenced many years ago in the secret memo of the discussion between British Prime Minister Harold Wilson and Irish Taoiseach Garret Fitzgerald (see appendix).

Thus, the activities of the deep state can be detected principally in various network apparatuses, some of which continued the intersection of soft and hard networks developed during the period of the anti-Orange state and anti-imperialist insurgency from 1969 to 1998. While quite distinctive in their chief practices, the boundary between the activities of the two aspects of state rule (i.e. force plus consent) are often more difficult to untangle, as we shall see especially in the context of the use of deep state *agents influents* since 1998.

The evolution of the network of deep state institutions and actors, as a means to demonstrate Britain's desire to play the critical role in the gradual evolution of the island of Ireland into a separate entity, is highly significant. Whether a new country will take the form of an all-Ireland state or a semi-federal state (e.g. one state, two systems – the Hong Kong solution) is not of pressing concern to London. The practices of hard power institutions, the state repressive apparatuses, link to the outworking of a range of soft power institutions that include not so much the Northern Ireland Assembly as the activities, and more specifically the management of the activities, of the Orange and Green political class (Stewart *et al.*, 2018).

Ready to go, while preparing to stay

Britain is as comfortable with the unification of Ireland as it is with its continued division, because its principal concern is the strategic relationship with the island as a whole. One needs to add an important caveat: Britain, as the major player, has conditioned the political class in the Republic as all the while it dominates the political class, and its significant ways of thinking, in the north (Stewart *et al.*, 2018). This is because of the wider political economy context, which now allows the United Kingdom to govern in the absence of territorial domination. This is not to say that Britain would not prefer territorial integrity, merely to make the point that in the era of neoliberal financialisation, the driver of contemporary imperialism ('neoliberal imperialism'; Wilder, 2015), Britain can rule just as comfortably without territorial subordination.

Specifically, as the GFA became embedded after 1998 with the formation of the new cross-sectarian political class, the older, repressive forms of forceful subordination gave way to a new domestication of the state's repressive apparatuses. Whereas during the period of the long insurgency, the state's coercive agencies (the RUC, RUC Special Branch, MI5, the British military) together with its extra-state apparatuses within loyalism worked to repress the nationalist population as a way to undermine the insurgency, since 1998 the role of these state repressive apparatuses has inevitably evolved as circumstances and the balance of forces have changed.

With respect to the period since 1998, we consider the way in which the state sought, by means of soft power, to compromise, at intervals *pour encourager les autres*, a number of key political figures and movements and parties to keep them on track with Britain's wider prospectus of all-island political synchrony according to its reading of the GFA. One feature of our argument is that in contrast to the period of civil conflict, the institutions of hard power have now been domesticated, hidden as they are behind the face of democratic participation in the new North. No longer hidden faces behind armoured cars, tanks and guns, the new face of hard power is as likely to wear the uniform of a civil servant. Hard and soft have combined, but now the fist that is raised is carefully hidden in a velvet glove.

Hard and soft networks of power: force plus consent in the new financialised world of Northern Ireland

Neoliberal financialisation has redefined the context of contemporary imperialism, preferring the proliferation of soft power networks of subordination in Western Europe and North America and parts of Australasia to its various national sociopolitical settlements. The latter are increasingly characterised by patterns of conflicted consensual governance, which has seen growing disaffection with the political class to an unprecedented degree as witnessed in the presidential elections in 2016 in the United States and France in 2017 and in the Brexit vote in the United Kingdom in 2016.

The political and historical character of the reconstitution of UK state hegemony in Northern Ireland in the period both before and after the signing of the GFA in 1998 provides a unique example of this process of reformation of British state power. Recent accounts of the character of imperialism from the point of view of imperial state power have, for good reason, focused on state repressive apparatuses, including the use of torture (see, especially, Gott, 2012; Cobain, 2012; Cadwallader, 2013; Urwin, 2016; Campbell, 2017). Recently, Cobain (2016) assessed the significance of institutions and practices of the bureaucracy of state secrecy in the maintenance of empire. This is a highly significant account of a number of ways in which civil power colludes in the constitution of forms of coercive (hard) power and shines a light on a level of imperial state activity that requires attention in our context. Arguably, less focus has been brought to bear on the way in which the British state has interacted, sometimes in partnership, with a range of social and political forces in order to retain a hegemonic role in the remaking of its relationship with Ireland after the end of the long period of civil conflict.

Our interest is not with the role of the United Kingdom in prosecuting the GFA, but rather with the unscripted, hidden role played by Westminster together with its much wider association of social familiars (social and political class allies) and colonial satraps. 'Westminster' includes the formal liberal democratic state but also what is often referred to as the 'deep state'. More than simply describing the state's repressive apparatuses, the deep state denotes the state's alter ego. Thus, we are referring not only to the level at which decisions are put into effect beyond legislative, democratic oversight. This is not about the play of the executive, the government. 'Deep state' characterises the evolving network of political and social affiliation beyond democratic control. The deep state established the apparatus of collusion discussed here.

These networks of collusion were developed in the period between 1969 and 1998 and operated initially to undermine the insurgency in such a way as to steer it in a direction favourable to the British state. This operation of hard power by the state's repressive and consensual apparatuses was crucial to the institutionalisation of the activities of the deep state in seeking to shepherd those leading the insurgency. The consensual apparatuses included the shift towards legislation as a mode of incorporation that ran hand in hand with collusion networks involving the police service (the RUC, which became the PSNI in November 2001), the Ulster Defence Regiment (UDR), the RUC Special Branch, MI5 and loyalist paramilitary organisations, principally the UVF, UDA and UFF.[2] Internal subversion of the republican movement necessitated finding and then running *agents influents*.

In this instance, the state used individuals in key internal institutions, such as the Provisional IRA's[3] internal security apparatus, to garner information about individual volunteers, anticipate combat operations and search for internal divisions. Loyalist *agents influents* were used for two purposes: to act as proxy state assassins of republicans, especially those opposed to leadership's parliamentary-road-to-a-settlement; and to intimidate nationalist communities through killing civilians, especially those with family ties to IRA volunteers.

Though fixing precise dates is problematical, we can delineate three overlapping phases in the development of Britain's deep state agenda. This comprised a set of CSRAs whose advance depended on particular conjunctures. We will concentrate on the evolution of the CSRAs over the period from 1969 beginning with the recent insurgency proper. The first phase, 1969–1981 goes from the rising insurgency to internment without trial in 1971 through to the Hunger Strikes ending in 1981; the second phase is the end of Hunger Strikes in 1981 until the GFA in 1998; the third phase is from the GFA to the present.

1969–1981 – Phase One: gathering as much information as possible about the insurgents. We know from an inquiry by the RUC's Detective Superintendent George Caskey that the deep state was finessing its techniques with a still underdeveloped CSRA network and was prepared to risk the lives of its operatives. This was highlighted by the case of SAS officer Robert Nairac killed in 1977 (Campbell, 1984).

From the beginning of the insurgency until internment without trial in 1971, Britain's intelligence agencies found themselves having to rely on outdated pre-insurgency information. The character of the insurgency, initially one of mass community involvement (McKearney, 2011), had found Britain sleeping at the helm. Britain's response reflected a fact it would characteristically seek to hide from public view, which was that this was indeed a new form of uprising in the Irish context. It was not one dependent solely upon an armed movement but one involving whole communities. It was a mass uprising to which Britain responded with tactics of widespread repression of entire communities including the use of curfews and flagrant disregard for civilian lives, as exemplified by the Ballymurphy killings by Paratroopers in 1971.[4]

To that extent, the state's attack on the early mass movement, culminating in the murder of 14 unarmed civilians on Bloody Sunday, 31 January 1972, was important to the development of a strategy that sought to separate, through physical repression and fear, the mass movement from the armed struggle. ('Mass movement' is used both in its typically understood sense of campaigns, such as the rent and rates strikes in Belfast and elsewhere in the 1970s, but also as way of recognising that support for republicanism in its variant forms was inherent within nationalist communities.) One outcome of the atrocity was that it accelerated the development of an armed movement that had only weakly existed before the bloody assault. This hastened the evolution of the war into one that the British state was more comfortable with. It mattered little to Britain that it might not win this war in the short term.

What mattered was that the outcome would be favourable to British interests. Britain, like any imperial state, develops apparatuses of repression precisely so it can seek to manage opposition though fragmentation, isolation and, eventually, dissolution. It would now have a security apparatus, built up since internment in 1971, with its assemblage of *agents influents* in the republican movement, within loyalist organisations and within parliamentary parties and civil society as well. In its favour of course it also had the state ideological apparatuses, including the media, very much on-message (Mclaughlin and Baker, 2015).

If Bloody Sunday was important in the development of the state's repressive apparatuses during Phase One, now it became essential to embark on a ruthless campaign of repression of nationalist communities. Renewed vigour was put into defeating the republican movement, and it was here that the prisons became a focal point of contestation from the mid 1970s up until 1981.

If the war was also a war of definitions, it was imperative that the conflict not be seen as a war. To be seen as a normal society subjected to terrorism, Britain would have to convince the world that those fighting the war were not revolutionaries. This would necessitate a soft power-hard power agenda, which became known as Ulsterisation. Ulsterisation, a creation of the British military, MI5 and the RUC, began under the Labour government and was outlined in an unpublished British strategy paper in 1975, *The Way Ahead*. The idea, similar to the Vietnamisation strategy adopted by the United States in Indonesia, was to make the locally recruited RUC the main state agent. This required 'normalisation', the key feature of which was to remove British troops from the front line to demonstrate that the war was not a war at all but rather an issue requiring conventional policing. The other prong to the strategy of Ulsterisation was 'criminalisation'. If it wasn't a war against insurgents, still less revolutionaries, it must be a campaign against criminals. This was the political basis of the refusal of Republicans to accept criminal status, leading to the Hunger Strikes.

1981–1998 – Phase Two in the development of the CSRA marks the response to the political impact of the Hunger Strikes. Force before consent in the dog days of the 'dirty war' might be the best way to sum up this period. The wider social and political response was unexpected by the British and others, including some within the Republican movement, because of the effect it had in terms of creating forms of mass civil disobedience not seen since the early civil rights movement. This time, however, the state was better prepared. In contrast to 1969, as a result of its intelligence assets and networks of collusion, the British were clearer about divisions amongst those opposed to its rule. The changed context of the mass popular fight against Ulsterisation forced the deep state to re-energise its prospectus. Now we would see, with greater urgency, the use of loyalist terror gangs, the SAS and other proxy deep state agents. It became essential to undermine the new mass movement by intimidating the communities from which it emerged.

If Bloody Sunday had been the catalyst to try to break the civil rights movement, loyalist terror gangs, *agents influents* within the republican movement and the SAS, would be necessary to push back the newly energised mass movement that was coalescing around a campaign that demonstrated the limited legitimacy of Ulsterisation. Why were the British adopting a strategy of greater (largely covert) repression when it might seem that the republican movement was embracing a 'republican parliamentary road to a united Ireland – eventually'. How was state terror going to win hearts and minds? The reason was that because of its *agents influents*, the deep stare could now identify with reasonable certainty who was opposed to *this* political process. Terror is often, and especially in the context of insurgency, a precondition of incorporation: defeated, demoralised communities eventually can be forced by attrition to sue for peace.

The British were aware that absence of mass participation on the streets is not the same as absence of mass support in the communities, and it would come as no surprise that the communities providing sustenance to IRA volunteers had to be disciplined. The reign of terror in nationalist communities, the 'dirty war', lasted until the GFA in 1998.

Had it recognised the mass civil campaign beginning in 1968 for what it was, it could have sought an early political solution. Britain's imperialist perspective privileged mass repression as a means of responding to mass civil disobedience. The Ulsterisation agenda that had sought to individualise the conflict as a means of normalising repression, depended on the use of a criminal justice system that functioned, seemingly ironically, to jeopardise the necessary social consensus which is everywhere a condition for the rule of law. Yet, it was indifferent to the inherent contradictions of its strategy.

Pushing the fiction that society was becoming normal ironically could only work where juries were abolished via no-jury Diplock courts. This perversion of one of the institutions of soft power was organically tied to the deep state's hard power CSRA network. The fantasy of normality required that state repression be hidden, and in practice, hiding required that it be outsourced.

Westminster's propaganda attempts to depoliticise the conflict were taking place against a backdrop of increasing state repression. The policy of Ulsterisation, seen as a means to solve the government's media image while absolving it of responsibility, wrought great suffering for many communities. This second stage of Ulsterisation would witness the increasing dependency on extra-state forces. Whereas Ulsterisation Phase One was characterised as being led by the RUC and the UDR – the role of *agents influents*, if still relatively underdeveloped, was naturally ever-present – the next phase witnessed a deepening of Ulsterisation.

Now, not only could the main visual presence of the state be seen in the shape of the RUC and the UDR, but the actual conflict would be fought increasingly by the state's proxies under the coordination of Britain's deep state. Ironically, while Ulsterisation continued to be pedalled for public consumption, behind the face of the RUC, the British military – notably, the SAS and other military state agents – were given considerable autonomy to run the war as they thought fit.

Agents influents and the role of the Force Research Unit[5]

For the imperial state, the mobilisation of intelligence has to focus on intervention for orchestration. It has to be concerned with more than finding out what the enemy is doing. The enemy, after all, contains the population of the country needed in the context of a new imperial dispensation. The purpose is not to eliminate the enemy *per se*, but rather to change it. This is the background and purpose of the use, in Phase Two, of proxies, *agents influents* and terror gangs. The state necessitated an array of institutions bringing together expertise from across its armed forces, including the RUC. Their *modus vivendi* was necessarily that of semi-autonomous operations. (See Moloney and Mitchell, 2013. For an extended account of collusion between the British state and loyalist paramilitaries, see Urwin, 2016).

Research by the latter allows us to shine light on several institutions set up to orchestrate the repression. It is commonly acknowledged that these were essential in attacks upon both civilians and IRA volunteers. State-directed IRA actions included the manipulation of volunteers by *agents influents* in the republican movement. In addition, loyalists gangs, either directly or under the direction of the deep state's CSRA (the Force Research Unit, the SAS, MI5, the RUC/ Special Branch), were used to intimidate and/or assassinate republicans and members of their families whether or not they were themselves sympathetic to republicanism and anti-imperialist politics. The killings of Pat Finucane and Rosemary Nelson are the most well-known in which the Force Research Unit (FRU) was embroiled. Brian Nelson, a former British soldier and senior intelligence gatherer with the UDA, was a central figure in the killing of Pat Finucane.

Interdiction and assassination were widespread state-sponsored, and state-led, tactics of repression as revealed most recently in the case of the infamous Glenanne

Figure 5.1 'Collusion = state murder'

Gang, arguably the most 'successful' of the deep state's CSRAs. Moloney and Mitchell (2013) unearthed important documents from 1974 on government commitment to the development of the CSRA:

> a Northern Ireland Office briefing paper … April 1974 [for] British Prime Minister Harold Wilson and his Irish counterpart, Garret Fitzgerald … explains in some detail the origins of the Military Reaction Force [MRF] and its replacement by a much larger, better trained outfit called the Special Reconnaissance Unit Simply [SRU] … (NIO 1974).

According to the paper,

The SRU had the task of putting terrorist suspects under covert surveillance as well as recruiting and running informers. Former SAS soldiers served with the SRU which liaised closely with the RUC Special Branch (NIO 1974). Moloney and Mitchell (2013) make the point that the MRF, set up in 1970/1971, which preceded the FRU, was the brainchild of Frank Kitson, a British commander at the start of the insurgency and British hero in the war against the Mau Mau in Kenya:

> The MRF consisted partly of regular soldiers drawn from a variety of regiments and partly members of the Official and Provisional IRA's who had been turned. … Known as 'Freds', these double agents both provided intelligence on their organisations and were available for undercover operations.

The conflict saw the continuation of a set of bureaucratic links that began to be instituted during Kitson's regime. He was supported by a police and state bureaucratic apparatus connecting key figures and offices of state (De Silva, 2012).[6] The MRF was professional and lethal.

> The MRF became publicly known about when its members were involved in a number of drive by shootings in Belfast. … [O]n September 26th 1972 … 18 year old Daniel Rooney was shot dead and 18 year old Brendan Brennan wounded when they were fired upon by … an MRF unit.
>
> (Moloney and Mitchell, 2013)

In 1982, the Force Research Unit[7] was set up by Brigadier Gordon Kerr, formerly in the Gordon Highlanders. Kerr's role was to run loyalist assets, extending the CSRA.

> many of the functions performed by the SRU were ultimately undertaken by the Force Research Unit … [and] it is by no means certain that a straight line connects them. Various other intelligence units … followed the SRU's wake.
>
> (Ibid.)

The FRU would operate as the decisive part of the CSRA that included MI5 and the RUC. The All-Source Intelligence Cell was set up in 1988 to coordinate intelligence between RUC Special Branch, MI5 and the FRU.

In 2007, as a result of the Stevens Inquiry into state and loyalist paramilitary collusion in murder, the FRU's name was changed to the Joint Support Group (JSG) (Rayment, 2007; Sharp ,2014). Special attention is paid to the FRU, not because it was the worst or most terrifying of the CSRAs but because, as a result of the Stevens Inquiry, we now have greater knowledge of its activities. The Stevens Inquiry demonstrated that from its inception, the FRU and loyalist paramilitaries colluded. Neil Mackay (2000) of the *Sunday Herald* quotes a former British intelligence officer:

> My unit conspired in the murder of civilians in Ireland. … There's no doubt about this. My unit was guilty of conspiring in the murder of civilians in Northern Ireland, on about 14 occasions.

1998–present – Phase Three: The CSRA shift from hard to soft power. With the signing of the GFA, we now begin to see a shift in the character of the operations of the deep state. While never disappearing completely, egregious acts of state and extra-state terror are increasingly substituted by the velvet glove. Now, rather than deny state repression, concessions are made, excuses crafted, apologies given. The most prominent was the apology by David Cameron for the Bloody Sunday massacre. Now that the guns are mostly silent, policing assumes the appearance of normality. Proper politics has resumed; the GFA allows everyone to vote for parties which are paying heed only to the will of the people, as opposed to the heel of the British. If the SAS has returned to Hereford and the heirs to the FRU fortune are quiet, MI5, nevertheless, 'hasn't gone away you know'. Its role has been to maintain constant vigil over its endowment in the northern part of Ireland.

Two facts about the role of MI5 in Northern Ireland should give rise to serious questioning. The first is that MI5's budget is paid from the British government's Single Intelligence Account (Morris, 2017) and is currently £1.8 billion a year, increasing to £2.3 billion by 2020. Of that, almost a fifth is spent directly in Northern Ireland. The second fact relates to the observation that around 1,000 MI5 operatives are employed at Loughside inside the Palace Barracks complex in Hollywood, County Down, making it by far the largest MI5 base outside London (McDonald, 2015).

Think about that. One-fifth of the UK intelligence budget spent on the largest MI5 base outside of London, and all for Northern Ireland. To the casual observer this may not seem strange. After all, did not the IRA carry out a violent 25-year insurgency, and do not the Chief Constable of the PSNI and senior officials of British Intelligence frequently remind us of the 'terrorist threat in Ulster'?

Yet by any reasonable standard, the level of politically motivated violence in Northern Ireland has dropped dramatically. Over the past 15 years, 60 deaths can be attributed to politically motivated violence, and of those only 6 have been fatal attacks on members of the state security services. Of course, there have been many failed attempts, but whether this has been due to the work of MI5 or to routine police intelligence is difficult to ascertain. What can be said is that the PSNI undoubtedly has inherited a very substantial and effective intelligence network from its predecessor, the RUC, and it is difficult to see why this has to be supplemented by such a substantial input from MI5.

That is, unless MI5 has additional responsibilities that go beyond merely monitoring the activities of armed anti-state activists. What if the County Down spooks spend much more of their resources on a form of political/social engineering? What if their principal task is to steer Northern Ireland politically in the direction desired by London and not just to monitor, intercept and frustrate the weak, divided, faction-ridden, police-infiltrated and unsupported armed republican sects? While it is almost always impossible to prove a direct link between political events and incidents and the hidden hand of an intelligence agency, it is reasonable to speculate.

To what extent was IRA authority undermined within the wider republican movement when it emerged that one of its more spectacular operations, the break-in at the Castlereagh police station, was perhaps not all it was deemed to be? Questions were raised when the police investigation into the Castlereagh break-in led to a raid on Sinn Fein offices in Stormont in October 2002 with damaging consequences for the party's intention's vis-à-vis participating in the Northern Ireland Executive. Worse was to follow when it emerged that Sinn Fein special advisor and long-time undercover British agent Denis Donaldson was a close acquaintance of the man believed to have facilitated the operation for the IRA (McDonald, 2005). Moreover, it had been Donaldson's idea to bring the man to Northern Ireland, set him up with a house in East Belfast and burrow his way into Special Branch headquarters in Castlereagh.

What, on the other hand, of the political demise of the House of Robinson – Peter Robinson, former First Minister of the Northern Ireland Assembly and leader of the DUP, and his wife, Iris Robinson? Some have said that they resembled a Northern Irish version of Frank and Claire Underwood from *House of Cards*. They were powerful, shrewd, hard-line, apparently invulnerable and seemingly embedded in office for decades. Yet how the mighty tumbled when a minor indiscretion was revealed to the BBC *Spotlight* programme by Mrs Robinson's pastor and political adviser, former RAF officer Selwyn Black (*Irish Times*, 2010). There is absolutely no evidence, and never has it been suggested, that Mr Black worked for the intelligence agencies, yet some have suggested a possible connection resulting from his background in the armed services. Whatever the possible conspiracy theories, the Robinson scandal damaged the DUP and undermined confidence in that particular leadership. While the party has certainly recovered since then, the lesson has not been overlooked by others aspiring to the leadership.

The question remains unanswered, why do we need such a large and costly MI5 presence? During the reign of the first Elizabeth, it was taken for granted that every diplomat was a spy. Now perhaps we have the situation where every spy has a diplomat's role of advancing central government's policies.

Conclusion: They haven't gone away you know

For much of its early history, the British ruled their empire through terror. '"Special" courts and courts martial were set up to deal with dissidents, and handed out rough and speedy injustice. Normal judicial procedures were replaced by rule through terror; resistance was crushed, rebellion suffocated' (Gott, 2012: 5–6).

The period after the Hunger Strikes in 1981 marked the renewal of the CSRA, which would consolidate essential features of the deep state. Britain saw its chance to push the major current in the republican movement, centred on the leadership, in a favoured direction. With an emphasis on hard power, this era, which lasted until 1998, perhaps more than any other could claim the soubriquet 'the dirty war'. It was characterised by state-sponsored and, in certain instances, direct state murder of both republicans and civilians from nationalist communities (Urwin, 2016). Informants, the so-called 'Freds', and loyalist terror gangs were important parts of the jigsaw.

Creating an informant network was both strategy and outcome of the operation of the deep state. If it seems something of a paradox that the use of both republican informants and loyalist terror gangs became more important as Sinn Fein acquiesced to the strategic aims of London, it is only seemingly so. Anyone objecting to the political direction of the leadership of the republican movement had to be challenged. This is not about the leadership consciously answering to the needs of the British state. The point was that the state was able to identify, at an early stage, particular ideological currents and utilise or disable them.

A significant objective for the UK state, wherein a critical role is played by its deep state, is how to remain in Ireland when it 'leaves'. This is contrary to much commentary and received wisdom which has interpreted the GFA as a fix, ensuring that Britain would be able at long last to leave Ireland without having to return. This is the story of Britain as civiliser, Britain as neutral – beyond Pax Britannica. The view taken here has been that on the contrary, Britain does not 'want to leave Ireland' in any straightforward fashion. This is evident from the role played by, and import of, the deep state that gives the lie to the anodyne view that it is seeking disengagement.

Our alternative interpretation sought to explain the significance of the deep state as the central driver for Britain and a range of institutions – legal, semi-legal and 'illegal' – that have been fundamental to ensuring its successful departure-return.

Notes

1 An unabridged version, complete with footnotes, is available at www.tommymckearney.com/blog-/the-good-friday-agreement.html.
2 The UVF is the Ulster Volunteer Force; the UDA is the Ulster Defence Association; the UFF is the Ulster Freedom Fighters.
3 The IRA is the Irish Republican Army.

4 The killing of ten civilians by the 1st Battalion, Parachute Regiment, in Ballymurphy, Belfast, occurred between 9 and 11 August 1971 during Operation Demetrius.
5 We now have a range of excellent sources on the activities of the CSRAs *inter alia*: Security Service (2002), Rayment (2007), Sharp (2014). The Force Research Unit was found to have colluded with British loyalist paramilitaries in the murder of civilians (BBC News, 2003). This has been confirmed by some former members of the unit.. From 1987 to 1991, it was commanded by Gordon Kerr (Mackay, 2000).
6 "The complex intelligence machinery in Northern Ireland was grown out of the history of security emergencies and the different, complementary and supportive roles played in them over the years by the intelligence agencies and security forces" Security Service (2002). Throughout the period of direct rule after 1972, the Secretary of State for Northern Ireland had constitutional responsibility for the administration of law and order in Northern Ireland. The Northern Ireland Office (NIO) advised government ministers on security policy issues, including legal and resourcing issues and information strategy. The Secretary of State was supported in his responsibilities by the NIO's Permanent Secretary and by three primary security advisers; namely, the Chief Constable of the RUC the General Officer Commanding Northern Ireland, who provided military support to meet the requests of the RUC, and the Director and Coordinator of Intelligence, a senior officer of the Security Service who was the Secretary of State's principal intelligence adviser (De Silva, 2010: Volume 1 Chapter 3, Intelligence structures Report of the Patrick Finucane Review).
7 See De Silva (2010) Volume 1 Chapter 3, Intelligence structures Report of the Patrick Finucane Review.

Appendix

Top secret Defensive Brief D

Meeting between the Prime Minister and the Taoiseach
Friday 5 April 1974
[Army plainclothes patrols in Northern Ireland]

Plain clothes teams, initially joint RUC/Army patrols, have operated in Northern Ireland since the IRA bombing campaign in Easter 1971. Later in 1971 the teams are reformed and expanded as Military Reaction Forces (MRF) this without RUC participation. In 1972 the operations of the MRF were brought under more centralised control and a higher standard of training achieved by establishing a Special Reconnaissance Unit (SRU) of 130 all ranks under direct command of HQNI.

2. The term 'Special Reconnaissance Unit' and the details of its organisation and the mode of operations have been kept secret. The SRU operates in Northern Ireland at present under the cover name 'Northern Ireland Training and Advisory Teams' (Northern Ireland) – NITAT (NI) – ostensibly the equivalent of genuine NITAT teams in UKLF and BAOR.

3. The prime task of the SRU is to conduct covert surveillance of terrorists as a preliminary to an arrest carried out by security forces in uniform. The SRU may also be used to contact and handle agents or informers and for

the surveillance and protection of persons or property under terrorist threat. The SRU works to a great extent on Special Branch information and the Special Branch have a high regard for it.

4. Men who have served with the SAS are serving in the SRU but no SAS units are operating in Northern Ireland. One officer and 30 soldiers serving with the SRU since early January are due to resume service with 22 SAS by 7 April. Their presence with the SRU went undetected until the Robert Fisk.

Source: Moloney and Mitchell (2013)

Part III

Supranational agents of imperialism

Overview

Many of the forms of formal and informal imperialism investigated so far in this volume would have looked familiar to Gallagher and Robinson. In this section, we advance on their ideas by turning our attention to supranational organisations. Many of these organisations did not exist when Gallagher and Robinson wrote their original thesis, and those that did (such as the International Monetary Fund and the World Bank) were in their infancy. In this section we investigate the ways in which metropolitan powers can operate collectively through supranational organisations to reconfigure parts of the periphery to the grouping's preference. Martin Quinn, in chapter 6, lays a solid foundation for this by examining from a policy studies perspective the way in which supranational organisations have continued the work of pressing informal imperial methods on the periphery. And whilst Quinn finds one example where this informal imperialism has failed to have the desired effect, we see in other chapters in the section the ways in which peripheral economies have been disciplined by supranational organisations. The Greek crisis is the focus of chapter 7 by Costas Eleftheriou and Orestis Papadopoulos. Here, of course, three supranational organisations converged to ensure the implementation of neoliberal political economy. Elsewhere, in South Africa and in Chile, Jasper Finkeldey and José Miguel Ahumada, in chapters 8 and 9 respectively, analyse the ways in which supranational organisations have locked in peripheral economies to that of the metropolitan.

Policy as a tool of economic imperialism?

Martin Quinn looks at the role of the World Bank, the International Monetary Fund and the European Union in spreading informal imperialism through policy transfers. We saw in the introduction to this volume the ways in which deregulation and the opening up of countries to foreign investment have been crucial to the reconfiguring of peripheral economies to suit metropolitan ends. Quinn examines the mechanisms by which this occurs, exploring the ways in which supranational bodies have imposed neoliberal economic policies on countries. In particular, the imposition of the Washington Consensus upon countries requiring economic assistance is shown to be designed to open up those countries to outside influence and control (we see this yet more clearly in Costas Eleftheriou and Orestis Papadopoulos's chapter on Greece, of which more soon). Interestingly, Quinn also detects that the extent to which the informal imperialism of policy transfer can be enforced may have limits. Whilst the hold of the European Union on Greece has been cast-iron, informal means have been less successful elsewhere. Quinn examines the case of Brazil and the use of conditional cash transfers by the World Bank. Whereas elsewhere these transfers had indeed been conditional, in the Brazilian case stipulations were not put on how the government could spend the money dispersed to it from the World Bank. And so, the Brazilian government allowed local communities to use the money as they saw fit without the need to restructure local economies along neoliberal lines, much to the chagrin of the World Bank. Whereas in the past the British empire might well have undertaken a swift dose of gunboat diplomacy in response, clearly the World Bank is unable to enforce its will formally. True enough, Brazil may not receive future payments from the World Bank as an outcome of this episode; nevertheless, the cash has now been spent. Quinn therefore shows that supranational agencies are not omnipotent when it comes to the imposition of informal imperialism. Perhaps more so than when a nation state undertakes informal imperial means, there is scope to push back against supranational organisations when circumstances allow.

The role of the Troika in the Greek economic crisis and its social and political consequences

Picking up the threads of Quinn's argument, Costas Eleftheriou and Orestis Papadopoulos investigate in depth the Greek economic crisis and the role of the Troika of the European Union, World Bank, and International Monetary Fund in providing loans to Greece. Unlike the misstep in Brazil, the bailout loans offered to Greece did indeed come with conditions, and stringent ones at that. These conditions were accepted by Greek capital, which, Eleftheriou and Papadopoulos argue, has suffered only slightly during what has been for Greek society as a whole a prolonged and devastating crisis. This analysis ties together ideas about collaboration and the operation of informal imperialism. We see the way in which the Greek economy has been reconfigured along neoliberal lines with the privatisation of state industries and the weakening of workers' rights. This has been beneficial not only for overseas investors, but also for Greek capital itself. In the words of Philip Mirowski, 'never let a good crisis go to waste'. For its part, the Troika successfully embedded itself within the institutions of Greek government, with advisors having access to key ministries and government data. In this way, not only did the Troika manage to secure concessions for capital in Greece, but it also managed to avoid the embarrassment that would have been the losses heaped upon the German and French banks had the Greek government defaulted.

Lessons from Marikana? South Africa's sub-imperialism and the rise of Blockadia

If attempts at informal imperialism by supranational organisations have upon occasion been thwarted, Jasper Finkeldey outlines developments which serve to lesson the risks to metropolitan economies seeking to exert imperial power. Whereas much of the literature on informal imperialism examines, with good reason, a metropole-periphery imperial relationship, Finkeldey examines a development that puts a third party into the process. Operating through an intermediary, a form of sub-imperialism as Finkedly characterises it, states can be at one and the same time subject to informal imperialism and a participant in its extension. In part the story is a typical one about collaboration. Elites in South Africa have been responsible for the imposition of neoliberal policy prescriptions upon the South African economy. We see this in, for example, the weakening of labour rights and the opening up to direct foreign investment for the South Africans. But in addition, Finkeldey demonstrates how South Africa has become a channelling point for informal means to be spread through the African continent. Just as Quinn outlines resistance to informal imperialism at governmental level in Brazil, Finkeldey finishes with a popular resistance to informal means in the South African case. As a response to a state-orchestrated massacre at the Marakana mines in North West province in South Africa, itself part of attempts to break workers' power, a popular movement has arisen to resist the weakening of workers' rights and prosperity in the face of extractivist capital.

Chile's trade policies in the context of US contemporary imperialism

In the final chapter of this part, José Miguel Ahumada examines US informal imperialism in Chile in the late twentieth and early twenty-first centuries. Picking up on themes in the preceding two chapters, Ahumada demonstrates that in the search for export markets, Chilean capital brought pressure to bear upon the Chilean government to fully embrace free trade agreements with the United States. Worked out with the assistance of the World Trade Organisation, these free trade agreements provided a template that was later imposed upon other South American countries. Ahumada focuses upon the insistence of the United States on certain patent and intellectual property protections which enabled US capital to operate in Chile without fear of Chilean businesses copying US products, allowing for an easing off of the Chilean economy's dependence upon the United States. This legal architecture has locked Chile into a particular economic relationship with the United States that encourages low value-added industries, and it has also prevented the use of measures traditionally employed by developing economies to industrialise. Indeed, of late, manufacturing as a percentage of Chilean GDP has declined, suggesting that a process of deindustrialisation of what little manufacturing Chile had is taking place.

6 Policy as a tool of economic imperialism?

Martin Quinn

Introduction

This chapter will explore the use of policy interventions as a mechanism through which states, supranational bodies and even multinational corporations (MNCs) have attempted to impose a neoliberal hegemony on the world economy. The ten principals of the Washington Consensus – centred on reducing the state's role in the economy and handing state assets over to the private sector – have seen economic policies imposed on states in return for financial and political support from, amongst others, the United States, EU, World Bank and International Monetary Fund. Thomas Friedman (1999) terms this as a 'golden straitjacket' that locked states into neoliberalism and has effectively produced a single global economic policy.

Here, we examine examples from Latin America and the EU to assess the extent to which Friedman's argument holds water and whether or not policy can be an effective way of imposing governance systems and economic ideas on states without the need for military action. To do this, the chapter uses two strands of policy studies literature to explore this phenomenon – the broad literature on policy transfer (Cairney, 2012; Dolowitz and Marsh, 1996; Rose, 1993) alongside Peck's (2011a, 2011b) and Peck and Theodore's (2015) more recent work on the concepts of fast policy and mobility mutation. In doing so, it assesses the extent to which policy transfer can be forced and the potential pitfalls for metropolitan powers. Here the chapter uses Gallagher and Robinson's original work as a frame – in particular, their analysis of free trade imperialism of the British government, which they characterise by drawing the distinction that 'the usual summing up of the policy of the free trade empire as "trade not rule" should read "trade with informal control if possible; trade with rule when necessary"' (1953: 13).

Set in a more recent policy context, we are led to questions on the extent of influence the leading players in the global economy now have. Can policy be used as a tool to spread neoliberal economic imperialism? Which actors have the power to do this – alongside the state, can the global triads of the EU, UN and non-state actors like the World Bank and even MNCs force states to adopt policy? George H. W. Bush's proposed 'new world order' following the end of the Cold War can be seen to run along the lines of the 'trade not rule' part of Gallagher and Robinson's analysis, whereby states are encouraged to become part of global trading blocs. Regarding the second part of Gallagher and Robinson's analysis – 'trade with rule when necessary' – we must consider what recourse today's global powers have when attempts to informal control have not worked. Overt military action is not as easily deployed as it was in the time of the British Empire (although that is not to say states do not find other ways of doing this), and this chapter will explore what happens in the absence of military force and whether the rules of membership of trade blocs are sufficient to force transfer.

The chapter starts with an outline of the policy transfer literature from policy studies showing that the focus of much of this literature is on the reasons why states choose to transfer policy from another state, but without consideration of the extent to which that is in fact a choice. It then moves on to explore the role of global superpowers, supranational organisations and MNCs in forcing policy transfer through initiatives such as the Washington Consensus and the EU's policy responses to the 2008 financial crash. Finally, the chapter explores examples of transfer without the backup of force and the work of Peck on mobility mutation through examples of conditional cash transfers.

Policy transfer – policy forced?

Within policy studies literature, the policy development process is widely discussed. Cairney's (2012) policy cycle model provides a useful outline of the different stages policy goes through before it is enacted. Within this are several points at which actors other than the government of a state looking to enact policy can become involved in the policy process. Scholars point to a range of actors here, including politicians, businesses, labour unions, professional lobbyists and regional representatives as well as those from outside of the state itself, such as other states, supranational bodies and MNCs. Such interventions create the space for the transfer or imposition of policy ideas from other spaces. Numerous scholars including Cairney (2012), Walker (1969), Grey (1973) and Berry and Berry (2007) have explored how the concept of policy transfer has become a popular and attractive model of policy development for governments looking for ready-made solutions to their societal and economic challenges. Dolowitz and Marsh (1996) outline a number of reasons why policy transfer is an attractive idea. However, much of the literature in this area assumes that the transfer process is a voluntary one where the government implementing a new policy is in full control of that transfer and has chosen to do so. As this edited collection demonstrates, when policy transfer is viewed from a more critical angle we can see that this is not the case. In many instances policy transfer is forced by global superpowers (such as the United States and China), supranational organisations or even MNCs.

Policy transfer and borrowing is an increasingly common phenomenon in policymaking. Dolowitz and Marsh (1996: 344) define policy transfer as 'a process in which knowledge about policies, administrative arrangements and institutions in one time and/or place is used in the development of policies, administrative arrangements and institutions in another time and/or place'. Common examples of policies that have been widely transferred around the world include the principle of privatisation of state assets. Between 1980 and 1992, across 80 countries, 8,500 state-owned enterprises were privatised (Cairney, 2012). And New Public Management has been used as a method to reorganise the public sector, electoral systems and environmental policies as well as systems of welfare, housing, education and health. In most cases transfer involves the copying of successful policy interventions from around the world in an attempt to replicate their impact. However, in others, the transfer is less voluntary and done in exchange for investment from a richer, more developed state or supranational body.

Generally, there are two commonly identified conceptual approaches to understanding policy transfer: market-driven approaches and cultural, or cross-national, approaches. The market-based approach to explaining policy transfer starts from the position that states can enhance their position, and thus gain a competitive advantage, by transferring best practice from another place. There are a number of assumptions within this approach which may be seen as problematic. First, it assumes that best practice is readily identifiable. Rose's (1993) lesson-drawing steps and Cairney's policy cycle both have the potential to take a considerable amount of time to complete – especially if multiple variations of policy exist. This poses two issues for the market-based approach, cost and time pressures, which may negate any competitive advantages that 'best practice' could offer. The market-based approach also assumes that examples of successful policy in one place can actually be transferred. As discussed below, this ignores contextual factors that may also influence transfer, including the policy framework and the extent of outside pressure on transfer.

Crucially for this chapter, we must question the extent to which policy transfer is a voluntary activity by the state or in fact imposed upon states by global forces such as supranational bodies and even multinational corporations. The debate here is concerned with issues of structure and agency and the extent to which the state is free to implement policy as it sees fit in the global economy. Supranational agencies such as the EU, UN and World Bank offer financial and even military backing in exchange for the transfer of policy ideas into developing economies. In the case of the EU this can be seen across a wide range of policy areas such as the monetary union and the common agricultural policy, and in the post-financial crisis era in return for fiscal bailouts in Greece, Italy and the Republic of Ireland. This is not merely a post-2008 phenomenon however. Friedman (1999) tracked the development of what he calls the Washington Consensus, a set of policy prescriptions (or golden handcuffs) that states must sign up to in order to receive development funds from the World Bank or the International Monetary Fund (IMF) or from larger states such as the United States.

The Washington Consensus demands that states in receipt of funds or support adopt a series of neoliberal policy reforms. This ranges from broad commitments to having the private sector as the primary engine of growth in the economy to fiscal policy interventions to ensure the maintenance of low inflation and price stability. In addition, states are encouraged to maintain a balanced budget, eliminate tariffs wherever possible and end protectionism. Finally, pressure is applied to deregulate capital and domestic markets, including the privatisation of national assets such as minerals, oil and transport.

The remainder of this chapter discusses some examples of policy transfer as economic imperialism. Starting with the influence of global superpowers and supranational organisations, the chapter fleshes out the use of the Washington Consensus to force policy transfer, moving on to more recent examples of the growth of China and the response of the EU to the financial crash. We then move to examine the use of aid as a tool of imperialism through the World Bank's Conditional Cash Transfer initiative and participatory budgets. However, we see that there is a fundamental issue insomuch as where policy transfer has failed to achieve its goals for organisations such as the World Bank, they have not had the facility to fall back upon formal imperialism in the way Gallagher and Robinson argue Britain did. Formal imperialism in the light of the failure of supranational organisations has had to come from these organisations' constituent states, and there have been occasions where the will to impose formal imperialism by these states has been lacking. The result is that where informal control by supranational organisations has not worked, more convoluted and aggressive informal methods of economic control have been the only fallback. Where these have failed, so too have some attempts at neoliberal policy transfer.

Global powers and supranational organisations

Global superpowers and supranational organisations are crucial to the contemporary version of policy as informal imperialism, forcing less well-off States into adopting policies in return for financial aid or the promise of military support. Although the United States and China (the latter replacing the role formerly taken by the USSR) are central to this process, it is also important to acknowledge that the move to the supra-state tier has seen the growing influence of non-state actors in economic development. As the global economy has continued to develop in the neoliberal era, the nation state is no longer automatically the most appropriate site for economic policy development. It has, to some extent, been overtaken by supranational organisations such as the UN, the World Bank and the EU. In most cases this is the result of key actors in the world economy transferring powers to these organisations whilst retaining control over them; for example, the United States remains a leading player within the structure of supranational organisations it subscribes to.

Closely related to this is the key triad (Dicken, 2015) of trade blocs based on the principals of free trade (EU, NAFTA, ASEAN[1]) through which most global trade is conducted and which reduce the state's ability to intervene and protect key national industries. The 1973 Oil Crisis saw a sea change in how economic crises were managed, with the recovery being dealt with by the IMF and World Bank rather than individual states. In the United Kingdom the pound was forcibly devalued, and pressure was put on states to liberalise their economies, and especially the money supply, in return for financial support and backing. The decade ended with the election of Thatcher in the United Kingdom followed by Reagan in the United States in 1981; both were fully supportive of the IMF and World Bank and added their political weight to the economic pressure being applied.

Another set of actors who can influence the transfer of free trade principals are multinational corporations. Although many companies have operated on an international scale for several decades, if not centuries, we are perhaps witnessing a return to the scope of influence of private companies not seen since the days of the East India Company and Jardine Matheson at the height of the British Empire. MNCs' ability to move production around their global production networks has seen states compete to introduce the lowest possible rates of corporate tax. Witness the scramble between cities in North America to attract Amazon's new base. Major companies can demand that cities or states alter their tax laws, labour regulations and infrastructure in exchange for moving jobs to that area. However, there is little the state can do to keep those jobs if another country follows their lead with lower taxes or lower wage costs, as the movement of the production of Adidas trainers between Indonesia and Vietnam demonstrates. In addition to this, MNCs are directly benefiting from trade deals between global blocs. The proposed Transatlantic Trade and Investment Partnership (TTIP) deal between the United States and the EU includes clauses that allow companies to sue national governments in the event that a new policy might harm profits and guarantee access to previously nationalised sections of the economy, such as health, for major corporations.

Washington Consensus

As noted above, Freidman (1999) describes the set of policy prescriptions associated with the Washington Consensus as a 'golden straightjacket' for developing economies. The use of this set of policies fits neatly with the era of 'trade without rule' described by Gallagher and Robinson (1953) and enables developed Western states (and especially the United States) to dictate and control the economic policy of developing nations. In exchange for IMF or World Bank support, developing nations are expected to implement policies that can result in the wholesale restructuring of their economy and sale of national assets. States are expected to position their economies so that the private sector is the primary engine of growth, aided by commitment to maintaining low inflation, balanced budgets and price stability. States are encouraged to remove and reduce their bureaucracy and to sell off national assets, often to multinational companies from the West. In order to further support private sector investment, economic policies are changed to end protectionism for domestic industries and deregulate capital and markets as well as lowering or eliminating tariffs to encourage overseas investment. All of these changes of course give huge advantages to global players in the world economy in terms of being able to use these newly developing economies as the assembly points of their global production networks; and as Dicken (2015) points out, little in the way of profit from this exercise remains within the developing economy.

These ideas are not especially new and, indeed, were already in play when Gallagher and Robinson (1953) were writing. What has changed in the intervening period is the extent to which states have been able to back up their wishes with overt military pressure; instead, more covert methods have been used. When Guatemala elected a left-wing government in 1951, led by Jacobo Árbenz, which introduced a policy of reappropriating land from private ownership, one of the biggest losers was the American firm United Fruit. The US government gave United Fruit assistance to begin a propaganda campaign against the Árbenz administration, even going as far as to use the CIA to arm a rebel invasion and support the imposition of a new dictator, friendly to free trade, who reversed the land policy and allowed United Fruit to operate once again. Similarly in Chile, the Allende government's policy of nationalising copper mines and the telephone service brought it into direct conflict with US conglomerates who relied on these industries for significant profits. Again the United States, through the CIA, funded and supported a military coup putting General Pinochet in power and protecting him from international justice in return for implementing a series of neoliberal economic reforms that further opened up the Chilean economy to global organisations.

A further example of forced transfer of policy comes with the EU response to the financial crisis of 2008. This example is important for this chapter for two reasons. First, it demonstrates the extent to which sovereign States such as Greece, Ireland, Portugal and Spain were forced to adopt fiscal policies that their population explicitly rejected at the ballot box. By turning to the example of Iceland, however, we can see that the supranational global governance structure that was in place was unable to force a non-member to comply with these conditions as they had not signed up to the terms of EU membership.

Following the 2008 financial crash, national economies across the globe fell into recession. Within the EU a rescue package was put together to try and assist those worst hit by the crisis, in particular those states whose banking systems were on the verge of complete collapse and who could no longer afford to service their debts to the European Central Bank. The EU response to the financial crisis bares striking resemblance to the Washington Consensus as in exchange for financial support, the bailout of national banks and delays on payment of debts, countries were forced to adopt a series of economic policies designed by the European Central Bank. These included implementing a programme of austerity, resulting in swingeing cuts to public services, and a commitment to quantitative easing. States were expected to guarantee the deposits of individual investors and undertake the nationalisation of toxic arms of banks. Aside from fiscal policies, these states were also expected to implement changes to their social and economic policies. Here states were encouraged to raise the retirement age to keep people in work for longer and save on state pensions and, at the other end of the age spectrum, to increase fees for higher education.

All of this was done despite the success of left-wing parties opposed to austerity and bailouts in both Greece (where Syriza won power and a subsequent referendum on the EU bailouts) and Spain (where Podemos, founded in 2014, became the third-biggest party in the Spanish Parliament). The terms of EU membership meant that in both cases, governments had to accept the bailout conditions imposed by the EU in exchange for much-needed financial support. Spain, Greece and Ireland could not afford to drop out of the Euro and relinquish their membership of the single market, and so they had to accept policy interventions that went against the expressed will of their people. Thus, the EU was able to impose a pan-European response to the financial crisis that maintained the neoliberal stranglehold over policy.

Transfer without legislative force?

Small state theory, through the ideas of alliances or shelter theory (Bailes et al., 2016), tells us that smaller states need the protection of larger supranational bodies such as the EU to survive and thrive in the global economy. Small states such as Ireland ally themselves to larger economies or trade blocs both to gain access to larger markets in times of economic prosperity and to seek shelter in times of economic downturn. However, as discussed above, this can result in the larger partner or trade bloc imposing conditions on the smaller state due to the terms of their membership. Iceland, like Ireland, suffered an economic crash after the 2008 crisis, and both economies were, technically, insolvent. Whilst Ireland was a member of both the EU and the Eurozone, Iceland was independent of both. At the beginning of the crisis Ireland had more access to assistance through the EU and Eurozone than Iceland and looked better placed to recover as a result. However, the stringent policy changes imposed on Ireland have meant that the economic depression continues to this day – especially in terms of the housing market.

By contrast to Ireland, Iceland fell further faster, suffering from an effectively bankrupt economy and collapsed financial system. As a small state that had shied away from membership of both the EU and the euro, Iceland could not fall back on the European Central Bank and the largess of the financial decision makers in Europe to assist its recovery. As a result of this, Iceland was able to make its own policy decisions and chose to ignore pressure from the international community to prop up its failing financial institutions at the expense of its welfare, education and social systems. Instead of implementing austerity, Iceland chose to close its central loss-making bank (something that was not an option for Ireland or Greece) and pursued a policy of criminal charges for leading financiers rather than pumping money back into the finance system. The Icelandic government fed its remaining reserves into stimulating demand in its internal market, and it 'recovered' faster than most if not all of the Eurozone. Other examples of states acting outside of the wishes of the neoliberal majority in the face of financial crisis include Malaysia and Argentina, both of which decided to pursue a Keynesian demand-led recovery. In Dubai, the authorities chose to ignore the trend for bailouts and financial aid from banks and large MNCs when the Dubai World development went into liquidation. Instead, they allowed the project to fail and investors lost money. It is worth noting that those who did act independently of the trend to austerity suffered a loss of trust by the global economy, but that appears to have been a price worth paying at this point in time.

The examples of the Washington Consensus and the fallout of the financial crisis in the Eurozone demonstrate the manner in which supranational organisations can force their member states to alter their governance systems through policy transfer. However, that ability to apply force is limited to members as they do not have the means to apply force to other states. The EU has the ability to produce a pan-European policy that overrides democracy for its member states, but it cannot exert this for non-members. The power to apply force here is based on the legislative force of the triad or supranational organisation rather than the threat of military force by a single state, as with the British Empire.

Mobility mutation

Peck (2011a, 2011b) argues that the pace of policy transfer has sped up to such an extent that the lesson-drawing elements that Rose advocates simply do not happen any more. Almost as soon as a new policy initiative is launched, it will be copied – before any evaluation of its successes or the impact of context. As a result of this, Peck's work shows that policies tend to mutate as they move, often with quite unintended consequences and, in some cases, negating the original intent of the policy. Together with Nick Theodore, Peck adopted a methodology of following policy from place to place to observe those mutations in action (Peck and Theodore, 2015). They focused on two particular policies of the World Bank – conditional cash transfers and participatory budgeting – and found that policies that were originally seen to be restrictive neoliberal initiatives based upon the prescriptions of neoclassical economics came to be used in a more social democratic, almost Keynesian manner. The more democratic policy of participatory budgeting became a vehicle through which cash was moved from the populous to the private sector.

Conditional Cash Transfers are a World Bank policy whereby development funds are made available to states in return for the adaptation of certain policy initiatives, such as education, infrastructure and welfare systems being provided by approved private sector organisations. More than 100 million people worldwide have received funds as a result of this policy initiative, and as Peck and Theodore (2015) show, the outcomes of these projects have been varied both in terms of the impact on the host country and how the policies themselves have evolved and been implemented. In Chile and Mexico, for example, the transfer of policy went as planned by the World Bank, with strict conditions being applied to the families and individuals in receipt of funds. As Peck argues, these are the programmes that feature heavily in the World Bank documentation promoting Compulsory Cash Transfers – there is considerably less information forthcoming about the policy as it played out in Brazil.

In Brazil, the Lula Government used the money from the World Bank to fund the Bolsa Família initiative in the Brazilian *favelas*. More than 50 million people have received financial aid as a result of this programme. However, in the Brazilian version a crucial factor was omitted from the World Bank's initial plans. It did not include any conditions for the use of the cash. Instead the population of the favelas were allowed to spend the money on community initiatives as they saw fit. This neoliberal intervention from the Global North transformed as it moved to the Global South from a prescriptive policy to one that gave the people of Brazil a far greater say in the running of their communities than had been intended, and it has been used as a mechanism to begin to introduce a basic citizen income.

Participatory Budgeting on the other hand started out as an initiative in the Global North to give local communities a greater say in the way in which money was spent in their localities. The original idea was that neighbourhood assemblies would form in which votes would determine how to use funds and which projects to pursue. Peck and Theodore (2015) found that in the case of the Dutch city of Utrecht, what had begun life as a progressive leftist policy become a tool for the private sector to access public funds as they took over the neighbourhood assemblies. Little of the public involvement that was evident in Brazil occurred in the Dutch example, and the policy 'mutated' as it failed to gain the engagement of the local population.

In both these cases, there was little or nothing the World Bank could do to enforce the original intent of their policies. In Brazil the Lula Government simply ignored the pressure from the World Bank to implement the social changes they required in return for the money. With the World Bank having no ability to impose sanctions, the result was that the government in Brazil was able to carry on as it wished.

Conclusions

The chapter has used literature from policy studies on the concept of policy transfer to assess the extent to which policy can be used to 'force' states to adopt neoliberal free trade principals. In doing so, it used the position outlined in Gallagher and Robinson's original paper on the imperialism of free trade – 'trade with informal control if possible; trade with rule when necessary' (1953: 13) – to see if this still applies in the modern global economy. The chapter also demonstrated how in many cases the transfer of policy between states is rarely an entirely voluntary action on the part of the state implementing the policy.

In exploring the roles played by supranational organisations and multinational corporations, the chapter has shown that in a modern context they have little recourse to military force. Overt state-led military pressure is less acceptable, though not ruled out, and so global leaders have to find other methods to force the transfer of policy. Enhanced use of informal means still exists and the concept still applies. But it is more nuanced than overt and has become more sophisticated in its operation. Instead membership of global triads now acts as a key mechanism in forcing the adaptation of neoliberal economic policies and spreading the continuing imperialism of neoliberalism. As shown with the European response to the financial crisis, the evidence from states such as Greece and Spain demonstrate that this can even be achieved in the face of Governments elected specifically to oppose austerity. Where necessary, supranational bodies like the EU and the World Bank can impose austerity and free trade policies on their member states. However, this power is limited to interaction with those member states. Where military or legislative force cannot be applied, policy transfer can 'mutate' (Peck, 2011a) into something the neo-liberal inventors of the policy did not envisage, as the example of conditional cash transfers in Brazil demonstrates, and in the case of States such as Iceland who sit outside of the global trade areas, transfer may not be possible at all.

Note

1 NAFTA refers to the North American Free Trade Agreement; ASEAN refers to the Association of Southeast Asian Nations.

7 The role of the Troika in the Greek economic crisis and its social and political consequences

Costas Eleftheriou and Orestis Papadopoulos

Introduction

This chapter provides an overview of the Troika's role in the Greek economic crisis, delineating the ways through which it intervened in the political, economic and employment spheres of the Greek nation. Despite rhetorical opposition, all Greek governments have implemented harsh reforms at the behest of the Troika and have been supported by dominant sections of Greek capital. We argue that the implementation of Memoranda brought about a tectonic change in the Greek employment and social security systems with dramatic consequences for the working and middle classes. Although some segments of Greek capital also suffered significant losses due to the crisis, the position of this class, and especially of its more dynamic elements, has been strengthened as the result of the reforms.

We view the intervention of the Troika within a dynamic framework that recognises the imposition of reforms on Greece as part of the bailout agreements but without losing sight of the domestic interests served by the introduction and implementation of those reforms. In that way, we can theorise the implemented reforms within a political economy perspective founded on the social divisions of capitalist societies – including Greece – that remain extant and even accelerate in times of crisis. The available data support the view that the handling of the crisis affected in a very diverse way the different classes of Greek society, with the working and middle classes carrying most of the financial burden. The continuous favorable tax rules for sections of capital (shipping) and the resurgence in other sectors (tourism), partly due to labour market reforms, confirm the uneven way that the Troika's intervention manifested in the very class-divided Greek society.

The ideology underpinning the Memoranda

According to the dominant discourse, the Greek crisis was the outcome of the operation of internal factors that were mainly associated with the peculiar nature of the Greek capitalist model. One of the features of Greek capitalism identified by these accounts is the fact that Greek people were consuming more than they were producing and their interest lay not in increasing production but rather in distributing it (Featherstone, 2011). This parasitic form of capitalism was linked to two factors: the cheap money lent to Greece due to its participation in the European Monetary Union and the lost competitiveness of the Greek economy due to corrupt, clientelistic and anticompetitive practices (Mitsopoulos and Pelagidis, 2011).

To sustain these clientelistic networks and political cliques, Greek governments resorted to excessive borrowing and spending, taking advantage of cheap money while at the same time avoiding implementation of necessary structural reforms out of fear of harming the 'vested interests' of their political and electoral friends, including collective organisations such as labour unions (Afonso et al., 2015). According to proponents of this approach, the lack of reforms and the existence of super-regulatory and rigid institutional frameworks gave rise to non-transparent and corrupt practices built upon misusing political power and squandering public money. For this reason, Greek society is deemed responsible for the economic disaster since most of its members enjoyed the excessive benefits and incomes offered by politicians in exchange for electoral support.

The pre-crisis episodes of resistance by the Greek people to welfare and labour market reforms are seen from this perspective as actions triggered by vested interests and adversarial politics tied to clientelism and populism with the aim of maintaining unsustainably high living standards and unfairly earned employment and pension rights (Vasilopoulou et al., 2014; Trantidis, 2016). Despite secondary differences since the beginning of the crisis, most of the accounts associated with this discourse support the implementation of the Memorandum agreements, urging the Greek governments to political resolve and to resist any temptation to retreat from the agreed reform agenda.

The main rationale behind such interventions was that the Greek labour market is rather rigid and inflexible, causing external distortions to the 'normal-market rate of pay' and therefore negatively affecting the entry of young people to the labour market. In addition to that, the positive correlation between deregulation and competitiveness has been regarded as one of the justifying factors for reducing wages for young people and dismantling some of the rights and benefits assigned to them in previous years. Even though this agenda has been portrayed as an outcome of the 'tough line' taken by the international lenders, it is undoubtedly the case that many aspects of the labour market reforms had been core elements of the proposals suggested by employers' organisations (mainly SEV, the Federation of Greek Industries) long before the crisis (Papadopoulos, 2016: 504).

Troika and Greek crisis

The Troika intervention in Greece serves as a model for other, and for future, interventions to other debt-stricken countries in the context of the most severe capitalist crisis of the last four decades. The Troika mechanism inherited the practices of two institutions: first, the EU institutional bodies (European Commission, European Central Bank, Eurogroup), which for decades have been implicated in negotiations with several different countries with the aim of imposing European policies, and which are supported by multifaceted, technocratic and monolithic bureaucracy that defines the content of these policies; and second, the International Monetary Fund (IMF), whose specialised expertise has for many decades been employed in planning, implementing and monitoring austerity programmes, especially in developing countries. The importance of the IMF is manifest in the Greek case since from 2014 it has not participated in the bailout programmes as a lender, but it still retains its position in the Troika and has been utilised as technical advisor during the negotiation between the Troika and the Greek government during the same period. The uniqueness of the Troika stems from the fact that it was 'invented' for the management of the Eurozone crisis.

The trilateral structure of the Troika poses the questions: where is the point of convergence between its three parts, and how is this achieved? When the three parts reach agreement, the Troika can apply direct pressure on a borrowing country. But at the same time, the Troika set-up produced several internal antagonisms that in many cases redefined the content and the implementation methods of austerity programmes, though, of course, always at the expense of the debtors. In that sense we can speak of a single and permanent Troika strategy towards the borrowing countries combined with changing content of policy demands. Last but not least, the Troika expressed, and in one sense defended, the divergences between the European North and the European South, the relationship between which can easily be understood as dependence of the latter upon the former. If we consider that this kind of dependant relationship follows the first steps of the EU project, then we can assume that the Troika mechanism intensifies this unequal relationship. In the case of Greece, the Troika was present at all three bailout programmes, participating in the planning of the programmes and the monitoring of their implementation and, thus, the evaluation of its progress. The functions of planning, monitoring and evaluation of the respective bailout programmes were the Troika's basic means of pressure upon Greek government.

Penetration into the Greek state

The Troika's goals were realised through direct penetration into the Greek state, at least during the first two programmes. The penetration of the Troika into the Greek state bureaucracy, particularly into the bureaucracy of the relevant Greek ministries (Finance, Economy, Labour, Infrastructure, Public Administration), included the establishment of Troika functionaries inside the ministries and the development of formal and informal relations with Greek bureaucrats. This influenced segments of Greek bureaucracy on a pro-austerity basis. Furthermore, the establishment of direct channels of communication between Troika functionaries and the ministers themselves was the most controversial part of the Troika's involvement with the Greek state since it was conducted in public and was perceived extremely negatively by the Greek public. After the January 2015 elections and the advance of Syriza (Coalition of the Radical Left) to government, there was popular pressure to eject Troika functionaries from the ministries and state agencies. Until then, the Troika used the threat of ending negotiations with the Greek government to apply pressure to the latter. Syriza in government opted for a different set of relations with the Troika, first of all by labelling it as 'Institutions' and second by conducting negotiations in the first half of 2015 in non-state locations. This was undoubtedly an act of symbolic value. Nevertheless, the role of the so-called 'Institutions' was more or less the same. Moreover, since the July 2015 acceptance of a new bail-out programme, the European Stability Mechanism (ESM) has been upgraded to become the fourth constituent of the former Troika.

Troika structure

While the composition of the Troika has changed from time to time, at least in Greece it has appeared with the following structure. At the first level there is the 'technical staff', which comprises low-level or mid-level bureaucrats and experts on certain issues. These handle the negotiations with their counterparts in the Greek ministries. The technical staff have their own particular portfolio (e.g. labour relations, taxation, etc.), and they usually negotiate on a previously defined agenda which is restricted and cannot be easily changed during the negotiation process. The negotiators at the technical staff level are not confined to a specific nationality (Greek or other European); on the contrary, they come from all over the world – at least the ones from the IMF – and are recruited according to their specialty and their negotiating ability and experience. Due to the international importance of the Greek crisis and the fact that the Troika mechanism was novel, participation in the Troika technical staff in Greece was, for these officers, an essential stepping stone in their careers.

Inside the 'technical staff' there is another division between the 'specialists', who handle the negotiations issue per issue, and the 'principals', who are responsible for the conclusion of the negotiations. Usually there is one principal from every constituent part of the Troika. The principals along with the heads of the Greek negotiation team (most of the time, they were the ministers) aim to achieve the so-called 'Staff Level Agreement' (SLA) that is considered the prerequisite for the completion of a bailout programme agreement or of an evaluation process. The SLA reaches the EuroWorking Group, which consists of representatives of the Euro area member states (usually the closest associates of the ministers of finance), the Economic and Financial Committee, the European Commission and the European Central Bank. The latter then resolves for the ending of the whole process, either the approval of a bailout programme or the release of a loan instalment. At the same time there is a similar procedure concerning the IMF's contribution to the loan, which feeds in to the IMF's Executive Board for final approval. It is worthwhile to note the central role of the Europe in the management of the crisis, although it holds a semi-formal position between EU institutions. The Schäuble-led Eurogroup became the main locus of final decisions for the development of the negotiations, and Dr Schäuble's hard-line approach on the Greek crisis defined the context and the range of the Troika's intervention.

The structure of the Troika and its *modus operandi* intensifies the rather unequal relationship between it and the borrowing country and jeopardises any negotiation that aims to formulate or even consider an alternative proposal for a bailout agreement. The inequality between the two parties ensures the dominance of the Troika's positions, whenever its three constituents reach a point of agreement. Even if it is feasible for some changes to occur at the political level (discussions between prime ministers or ministers of finance), the content of this 'political' negotiation is confined, or was until November 2017 at least, by the results of the previous technocratic negotiations (it is limited to the withdrawal of some previously agreed measures). In any case, the overall logic of the programme – aiming to impose austerity measures for fiscal adjustment – remains intact.

In addition to this, there is also a *temporal dimension* concerning the working structure of the Troika. The processes of negotiations inside this hierarchic structure tend to be time-consuming, which means that if the fiscal needs of the borrowing country are urgent, it is obliged to meet most of the Troika's suggestions. Whenever there is an impending loan instalment to be released in order to cover either state expenses or the payment of a prior loan (in the case of Greece, three bailout programmes means at least three different loans), the Troika manages to exert decisive pressure on the borrowing country, which otherwise faces bankruptcy. Oftentimes, this tactic has been deployed by the IMF. Nevertheless, this is not something aimed exclusively at the borrowing country but also can function as indirect blackmail on the part of one Troika constituent toward the others (a good example is the ongoing discussion about the sustainability of the Greek debt). Disagreements between the constituent parts produce unexpected delays that prolong uncertainty, usually at the expense of the borrowing country.

Finally, the Troika structure, as in every bureaucracy-style structure, has its own *langue du bois*. The borrowing country needs to endorse this terminology and employ it. For instance, the concept 'programme ownership' is essential in understanding the morals of the Troika's intervention, which are the morals of informal imperialism. The IMF defines the 'ownership' of a programme as

> a willing assumption of responsibility for an agreed program of policies, by officials in a borrowing country who have the responsibility to formulate and carry out those policies, based on an understanding that the program is achievable and is in the country's own interest.(Boughton, 2003: 3)

The borrowing government possesses the sole responsibility for the implementation of the programme; it is the one that needs to legitimise it to its population and manage public unrest caused by it.

Political consequences of the Troika's intervention

The Troika challenged the political situation in Greece. The first signs of the political crisis in Greece originate from the pre-crisis period, and the crisis itself was the catalyst for the acceleration of previously apparent trends (Spourdalakis, 2014). It has affected the functioning of the Greek state; it has contributed to the downgrading of the Greek Parliament; it has paved the way for the advance of anti-system tendencies in party competition and social protest; and it has facilitated the eruption of political cynicism and apathy in Greek society.

The main political outcome of the Troika's intervention, of course, were the results of the critical 2012 elections (May and June), when there was a radical dealignment in the Greek party system. This was marked by the collapse of the social-democratic PASOK (Panhellenic Socialist Movement) and the rise of the radical left Syriza and extreme right Golden Dawn (Voulgaris and Nicolacopoulos, 2014). This dealignment (and subsequent realignment) changed the traditional Greek two-party system to a multiparty system, something that had also occurred in the early 1950s after the end of the Greek Civil War (ibid.).

We will analyze the political effects of Troika intervention in Greece by assessing the threefold political crisis it generated (Eleftheriou, 2016), which clearly affected – and still affects – the quality of democracy in Greece. First, there was an effectiveness crisis, which devalued the technocratic aspect of government and reduced the management capacity of state affairs by the government. This resulted in the substitution of governmental decision makers with Troika functionaries. The Troika's last word on all the critical issues left the political personnel of consecutive governments with the task of implementing a rather harsh and unpopular austerity programme that was always under permanent revisions. This, along with poor economic results and dire social effects, shattered the belief of Greek citizens in the capacity of the Greek political personnel to deal effectively with the crisis. In one sense, this was one of the reasons for the demise of PASOK, since the party had previously been considered by voters to have the most effective and experienced political personnel.

Second, there was a legitimacy crisis, which referred to the contested constitutionality of the proposed austerity measures and the conduct of decision-making processes that comprised mainly decrees and reinforcement of state authoritarianism. This crisis was the direct effect of the urgency pressed upon the government, dictated by the Troika and designed to bypass parliament and implement the austerity measures. Consecutive Greek governments were forced to find ways to tackle parliamentary control, either by using special (presidential or ministerial) decrees or by concentrating all of the imposed measures into one single bill in order to ensure the discipline of parliamentary groups. There were several appeals to the courts concerning the constitutionality of austerity measures, but these were denied on the grounds of preserving the national interest when faced with a disorderly bankruptcy. In that sense, the exceptional austerity measures – that were contradicting certain articles of the Greek constitution – were legitimised as a necessity in the face of the country's financial status and regardless of the subsequent loss of sovereignty (Venizelos, 2016).

Third, the worsening of the long-standing trend of public distrust of political institutions preconditioned the representation crisis, which was the main pillar of the great dealignment in 2012. The fact that the governing parties were tied to the necessity of, and limited by the constraints stemming from, the implementation of the bailout programme created a political gap that was claimed by a variety of old and new political actors. During the years 2010–2012, there was a breakthrough of worker movement activity, consisting of numerous national-level strikes (Papanikolopoulos, 2016). These included the longest strike in Greek democratic history (at the steel factory of 'Halyvourghia'; Bithymitris, 2016), civil disobedience movements, solidarity initiatives at the grass-roots level (free meals, free medical care, etc.) and the 2011 squares movement (Tsakiris and Aranitou, 2012). The latter was a breaking point for the dealignment and realignment of 2012 since it managed the sentiments of political distrust through demands for direct democracy and public transparency combined with anti-austerity claims. The square movement generated mass demonstrations, and its violent suppression in June 2011 symbolised the existence of two blocs in Greek society: one pro-Memorandum, which accepted the bailout agreements as a one-way path for the country; and one anti-Memorandum, which defied this perspective. Of course, these two blocs were internally heterogeneous, including political forces with different and sometimes contradicting ideologies and political identities.

The threefold crisis constituted a broader legitimation crisis which is seen in the electoral losses suffered by the traditional political parties and the reorientation of parts of Greek society to anti-system political practices. Even if the sources of the Greek political crisis date to the contradictory accession of Greece to the EU (1992) and its controversial inclusion in the Eurozone (2001), we cannot understand the timing of the unfolding of the crisis and its form without considering the Troika factor. The Troika's restrictive *modus operandi*, the concept of 'programme ownership' and the urgency of implementing the reforms that will release an impending loan instalment or ensure the continuation of the bailout program constrained the functioning of the Greek polity.

After the 2012 dealignment, the crucial developments in the Greek party system were, on the one hand, a *de facto* prevalence of coalition governments instead of the single-party governments of the past and, on the other hand, the rise of a radical left party as the main opposition party. At the June 2012 elections in particular, there was manifest support of the New Democracy party from European officials, with the latter threatening Greek voters that election of a party with an explicit anti-austerity programme would jeopardise the bailout programme and deteriorate Greece's economic situation. After New Democracy's 'Pyrrhic victory', from 2012 to 2014, Greek party competition was structured across the pro-Memorandum/anti-Memorandum cleavage; Samaras' governments (consisting of the conservative New Democracy party, PASOK and the Democratic Left party until 2013) enjoyed the support of the Troika until the autumn of 2014. It is clear from Samaras' fall that the support of the Troika to a given government is not conditioned by the clear neoliberal orientation of this government or by its undisputed pro-Eurozone views; the only condition is the 'faithful' implementation of the appropriate reforms and the successful completion of the bailout programme.

After the January 2015 elections and Syriza's victory, a confrontation started between the newly elected government and the country's lenders, who were represented by the Troika. A six-month negotiation (January–July 2015) revealed both the limits of an anti-Troika and anti-austerity political programme and the means of pressure that the Troika could employ against a hostile government; for example, the threat of disorderly bankruptcy. The Syriza government started from a position of renegotiating a new bailout programme with the Troika on a 'mutually beneficial' basis and with a different 'mixture of policies', rejecting many of the policy commitments of the previous governments. But gradually it moved to a position of negotiating on a harsh austerity programme, a process that ended with the capitulation of the agreement of 12 July 2015 (Eleftheriou, forthcoming). The referendum on 5 July 2015 was the climax of the anti-austerity movement; for the first time, a European people had the chance to legitimate directly and without mediation a bailout proposal from the Troika. The consequent moderation of Syriza, which became the proprietor of the 2015 bailout programme, was partially a result of Troika intervention.

The 2015 experience showed that the party systems in crisis-stricken countries develop trends of convergence, at least among the governmental parties, which are related to the management of the crisis according to the Troika's objectives and framework. The 'ownership' of the programme by the 'responsible' government and its acceptance by the 'responsible' opposition is a point of convergence that transcends ideological divergences. Thus, the content of 'responsibility' lies in the capability of a given national government to promote in a proper way the necessary reforms. This observed shift of party democracy towards a state of forced convergence between the relevant parties is an essential variation that it will characterise European party systems in the future.

Effects of Memoranda agreements on employment and social conditions of Greek people

The pre-crisis protections provided to Greek workers, either through collective agreements or labour law, have been curtailed and in many cases simply abolished (Koukiadaki and Kokkinou, 2016). More specifically, the dismantling of the pre-crisis employment model was triggered by a series of legislative acts whose common denominator was the creation of a very flexible landscape aiming to reduce labour costs and boost economic growth. This new legislative framework makes specific arrangements for young people, with the more characteristic among these being the reduction of the minimum wage for this age group. The new law (Law 4046/2012), derived from the Second Memorandum, requires the general reduction of minimum wages by 22% for all and by 32% for all workers under 25 regardless of their occupation and sectoral agreement coverage (Ministry of Labour and Social Insurance, 2012).

In addition, a series of legal actions have overhauled basic features of the Greek employment landscape, triggering a significant deterioration of working peoples' rights. Specifically, with the first Memorandum there was an increase in the number of collective dismissals within one month (Article 74(1), Act 3863/2010), promotion of flexible employment contracts with the reduction of part-time pay (Act 3846/2010), extension of short-term and fixed-term work (Act 3846/2010 and Act 3986/2011) and derogation of the company-level agreements at sectoral and collective levels (Act 3845/2010). The conditions attached to the Second Memorandum in 2012 required unemployment benefits to be reduced by 22%, and eligibility criteria were tightened and the duration of benefits reduced (European Commission, 2012).

Even though the Troika has been rather decisive in affecting the direction and content of policies, we should be a bit cautious when interpreting the exact forces behind the social and economic developments that have unfolded since 2010. For instance, a significant part of the implemented reforms in Greece had been on the agenda of some social partners – notably large employers – long before the eruption of the crisis. The constant support that employers have given to these reforms during the 2010–2017 challenges the notion that Greece was just the receiver of policies that contrasted with the will of the entire population. The ideological and political backbone of Memoranda, centred on the reduction of labour costs and social protection expenditure, was underpinned by the strategic interests of large capital in Greece. In that sense we argue that the relationship between Greece and the Troika did expose conflicts between the interests of imperialist organisations and those of an indebted country, but at the same time the relationship was much more complex and dynamic than that assumed by some accounts. Suffice it to say that labour market reforms, the overhaul of the pension system, the privatisation of state-owned enterprises and the reduction of public sector workers and their pay levels had been attempted several times before the crisis by previous governments, but with very limited success (Papadopoulos, 2016).

The effect of austerity and liberal reforms on Greek people has been widely discussed in public debates and scholarly papers. According to Eurostat (2017a) data, 35.6% of Greek people were at risk of poverty in 2017 compared with 27.6% in 2009. But the crisis has affected some social categories more than others, as was expected. For instance, for children, risk of poverty or social exclusion varies significantly depending on the educational attainment of their parents. For those children aged 0–6 with parents on the lowest educational level (levels 0–2), the risk of poverty climbed to 77.4% in 2016 from 49.5% in 2007. In contrast, for children of the same age whose parents possess the highest educational qualifications (levels 5–8), the risk of poverty or social exclusion was 15.2% in 2016 compared with 11.3% in 2007. In a UNICEF report on child poverty in Greece (Papatheodorou and Papanastasiou, 2017), the authors argue that the proportion of children who experience poverty is much higher than is reported in official statistics. They especially stress that the reduction of incomes (median income) has lowered the relative poverty threshold – defined as 60% of the median – thus underestimating the number of children who experience poverty. So according to that report, in 2014, 55.1% of children were experiencing poverty compared to 20.7% in 2009 (Papatheodorou and Papanastasiou, 2017).

In many quality of life indicators, it seems that a significant part of the Greek population fares much worse now than before austerity was introduced, albeit with variations across the population due to social background. For instance, according to data from Eurostat (2017a), the ability of Greek people to keep their homes adequately warm has been significantly deteriorating, with many households being unable to buy enough energy supplies. Almost three out of ten people reside in a household with inadequate heating due to inability to bear the higher energy costs prompted by tax increases. The same applies to other household liabilities like arrears for mortgages and rents and utility bills, with household debt having substantially increased since the crisis, generating public debates on whether these debts will ever be paid off. Harsh austerity has also impacted on the ability of households to face unexpected financial expenses, with one out of two people being unable to do so in 2016, compared to 2010 when only three out of ten found themselves in this position. In a recent study on the expenditure of Greek households on food (Eleftheros typos, 2017), it was reported that the overall revenue generated by supermarkets has dropped by 4 billion euros in a period of seven years (2009–2016), reaching 10 billion euros in 2016. Concomitantly, the average monthly expenditure on food has decreased from 380 euros in 2009 to 250 euros in 2016.

The explanation for the dramatic increase in relative poverty is not surprising considering that welfare and labour market reforms have negatively affected the overall income of most Greek people. The reduction of national minimum wage by 22% for all and 32% for those under 25, as specified in the Second Memorandum, and the suspension of the favourability principle supporting sectoral agreements over company-level ones have altered the labour market context with serious consequences for employees' income. For example, Eurostat (2017a) data shows that for 2016 the medium income (equivalent net income) was 7,500 euros when in 2010 it was 11,496 euros. For those low-skilled workers on the lowest wage scale, earning 9,923 euros, in 2010, the changes have had an even more detrimental impact on their lives – after austerity and labour reforms, they were called upon to survive with just over 5,000 euros (5,300) in 2016. These numbers reflect a labour market in which a significant number of newly hired employees are recruited on flexible contracts.

According to data from the official system (Ergani) of the Ministry of Labour, from January 2017 to July 2017, six out of ten new employees were hired on a flexible contract. The high incidence of part-time work (47.9%) explains then the significant drop in median income, as for part-time workers the average wage has been reduced to 397.67 euros per month. Although there are still sectoral differences in wages, it seems that the deregulation of the labour market has indistinctively affected all sectors, with an average 18.1% wage reduction across the economy as shown in a recent study by INE-GSEE (2017).

We have noted that employment and social prospects of young people have worsened since the eruption of the crisis. This 'lost generation' has been one of the worst affected groups of the population, as frequently illustrated in many academic and non-academic studies. For instance, the households where young people live with low work intensity increased from 6.4% in 2009 to 18% in 2013. The trends in long-term youth unemployment (ages 15–29) exemplify the above statement as for the 2009–2015 period, long-term unemployment (12 months or longer) increased from 6.4% to 26.6%. Furthermore, the change in youth unemployment is depicted by the fact that the youth unemployment ratio has increased from 9.8% in 2009 to 19.7% in 2015, demonstrating that young people represent a much higher proportion of those unemployed than they did before the crisis (Eurostat, 2017b). Even though the rise in youth unemployment is evident at all educational levels, the available data show that for those with lower educational qualifications, unemployment rates are higher. For instance, the unemployment level of those aged 20–29 with upper secondary and post-secondary non-tertiary education has skyrocketed, reaching 40.6% in 2015 compared with 18.6% in 2009 (Eurostat, 2017c). In addition to that, since the eruption of the economic crisis, the number of young people that are neither in employment nor in education or training (NEETs) has increased considerably, especially for some age groups. More specifically, during the 2006–2015 period there was an overall increase of 9.3% in NEETs among the 20–24 age group, with one out of five in this group belonging to the NEETs category in 2015 (Eurostat, 2017d).

Apart from the labour market reforms, successive post-crisis governments have introduced and implemented active labour market measures to tackle youth unemployment by providing work experience to young people. However, there is ample evidence that these policies have failed, mainly because their duration is rather limited and the participants receive very low wages and restricted training. A case in point is the increasing use of active labour market programmes in the form of vocational training to provide some theoretical and practical training to young people with a view to helping them become integrated into the labour market in dynamic fields of the Greek economy. However, a recent study (Bithymitris and Papadopoulos, 2017) on the use of voucher programmes in tourism shows that training opportunities, even in dynamic service sector industries such as tourism, rarely provide viable career paths for the participants and do not contribute to quality job offers, at least not as long as the vocational culture reflects the sector's predisposition towards flexible contracts and flexible skill sets and mindsets. Other studies (Gialis *et al.*, 2015: 4) have noted that active labour market policies, primarily in the form of training programmes introduced to combat unemployment, support the reproduction of 'very atypical' jobs and contribute to – rather than work against – insecurity.

Conclusions

As we have seen, the Troika mechanism was designed to plan, negotiate and eventually impose an austerity programme on behalf of the country's lenders. To implement the measures of the programme, a number of subjugation methods were employed with successive Greek governments. The so-called 'Memorandum' itself could be easily described as a document that prescribes the conditions for radical change in state-society relations in Greece in a neoliberal direction, as evidenced in the preceeding analysis of its social-economic impact on Greek people. Thus, the results of the imperialist interventions in Greece have been catastrophic for Greece not only in economic but also in social and political terms. The crisis period and the imposition of the subsequent bailout programmes intensified certain trends of the pre-crisis period by concluding long-standing reforms that had been blocked by social and political resistance in the past. In this sense, the content of the Troika intervention, which was highly ideological and aimed at total domination of the borrower countries, was in fact a partial vindication for parts of the Greek bourgeoisie and Greek establishment that were in favour of the Memorandum policies. And whilst the social resistance and popular unrest that blossomed during the crisis period created the space for the advance of new parties and the increase of influence for others, nevertheless, the subjugation Troika tactics, the concept of 'programme ownership' and the implementation of reforms by radical left parties like Syriza function as a barrier for the rise and expression of a viable alternative option. This type of intervention by imperialist forces like the Troika shows that there are relations of dependency and subjugation even among developed countries; but at the same time the present crisis, which is after all a capitalist crisis, reinstates the fundamental capital-labour relation as the essential cleavage in the debtor countries in Europe, something that raises several conceptual and political questions that exceed the remit of the present chapter.

8 Lessons from Marikana?

South Africa's sub-imperialism and the rise of Blockadia

Jasper Finkeldey

Introduction

In this chapter I add two elements to the discussion around informal imperialism. First, I suggest that in order to understand current forms of imperialism it is vital to look beyond imperialist hubs such as the United States. Gallagher and Robinson (1953: 10) mention the particular role played by countries such as Brazil and Argentina in sustaining Britain's informal empire and global influence. I will spell out in some detail how contemporary South Africa, as a middle-income country, takes the role of 'deputy sheriff' in a modern inversion of free trade imperialism from the middle (Bond, 2013a). This is partly to update the historical considerations regarding free trade imperialism.

The African National Congress (ANC) government opened South Africa's economy to the world market as apartheid trade sanctions were lifted and World Trade Organization (WTO) standards were zealously embraced. South Africa is now integrated into the world economy in complex ways. Multinational companies with former headquarters in South Africa such as DeBeers, South African Breweries, Old Mutual, and Mondi Paper removed their primary stock listings from South Africa in the 1990s, but nevertheless have primary business interests in the country.

Sub-imperialism is a form of imperialism from the middle in which elites in the Global South are lubricating neoliberalism expansion, chiming nicely with Gallagher and Robinson's examination of collaboration. Synthesising key literatures on sub-imperialism, we see four economic features that characterise it: expansionist economic policy; relative dependency on foreign capital; capital export of state-run industries and lax capital controls; and exploitation of labour (Bond, 2013a, 2004; Samson, 2009; Marini, 1972). These features will be examined more closely in the following discussion of the particular features of South African sub-imperialism. While these features are not exhaustive, they give valuable insights to the functioning of sub-imperialism and help us to reflect further on the role of collaboration in the establishment of informal imperialism.

South Africa's elite strives for the country to become what Saul and Bond call 'the continent's leading bourgeois-aspirant state' (2014: 197). The ANC has not delivered on its promises to remedy excessive levels of inequality, as South

Africa remains among the most unequal countries in the world. While the impoverished masses suffer from record levels of unemployment, only a small elite has transitioned into economic prosperity (Bond, 2014). The political elite appears more and more detached from its liberation ideals, becoming increasingly self-serving. Serious allegations were raised by a former public protector, Thuli Madonsela, who investigated the government's alleged irregular dealings with the Indian Gupta family. Many of these dealings pertained to mining (Madonsela, 2016). Undue influence was allegedly given to the Gupta family through the appointment of government ministers, and it was also alleged that they acquired mines for below market value prices. Although the cases are not ruled on at the time of writing, the Zuma family is known to share business interests with the Gupta family (*Mail & Guardian*, 2013).

Dependency theorists know that global free trade perpetuates the inequality between Western centres and Southern peripheries (e.g. Rodney, 2012). According to this reading, cheap resources flow from the Southern periphery to Western centres, where value is added. While the periphery becomes relatively poorer, the centres gain. However, while South Africa's economy does supply cheap labour, cheap resources and cheap energy for global consumption, this is not its sole activity; it also sits in a position of relative power vis-à-vis its neighbouring countries. With the establishment of the Brazil-Russia-India-China-South Africa bloc (BRICS), free trade imperialism from the middle is further deepening neoliberal trade relations. Sometimes celebrated as an anti-imperialist project, South Africa's admission into the club of emerging powers in 2010 marked the advent of further alignment to the 'corporate agenda' (Bond, 2015: 24). BRICS elites have strengthened their position within international financial institutions such as the International Monetary Fund (IMF), World Bank and WTO, where they tend to further the project of market liberalisation (Bond and Garcia, 2015: 1–2). Indeed, Gallagher and Robinson (1953) show that despite periods of anti-imperialist rhetoric, formal and informal forms of imperialism are often deepened. The BRICS project, despite its anti-imperialist rhetoric, shows continuities with existing forms of free trade imperialism. Bond and Garcia (2015: 3) point out how the 'underlying BRICS project has much in common with the Western status quo regarding the stabilisation of the financial world, in generating additional capacities of "lender of last resort" and in stabilising multilateral governance'.

Gallagher and Robinson describe free trade imperialism as a globally emerging superstructure characterised by 'patterns of overseas trade, investment, migration and culture' (1953: 6). In an update on the Gallagher and Robinson theses, the editors of this volume have pointed out how free trade imperialism is 'an intrinsic facet of modern capitalism' that indeed continues today (Grocott and Grady, 2014: 543). I will argue for Grocott and Grady's addition to integrate elite ideology and neoliberalism into the equation of free trade imperialism. From Gallagher and Robinson's considerations, it does not become sufficiently clear who does imperialism. Rather, they see imperialism as a necessary function of global capitalism. Who the forces behind imperialism are remains relatively opaque. Looking at contemporary forms of sub-imperialism, I will argue that it is vital to look at elites and the way they perpetuate neoliberal ideology, deepening free trade imperialism often despite fierce anti-imperialist rhetoric.

The second element that I will discuss, adding to the emerging literature on sub-imperialism, is the role of resistance to forms of sub-imperial economics. Sub-imperial elites, in collaboration with imperialist elites, engineer and police a framework that ensures financialisation, low wage regimes, limited public spending, and limited workers' rights, among other things. These elite networks impose rigid fiscal obligations set by international monetary institutions such as the World Bank and the IMF as well as rating agencies like Standard and Poor's, Moody's, and Fitch. The consequences of this tight fiscal regime in developing countries is that working classes, and especially the lumpenproletariat, do not get their share of imperial and sub-imperial rents, intensifying pauperisation despite increased gross domestic product (GDP).

In the following, I will first discuss South Africa's gateway position in Africa. I will show that the gateway narrative indeed ties into South Africa as sub-imperial middleman on the continent. In the second section, I will move to an analysis of South Africa's mining sector and, against this backdrop, discuss the four features of sub-imperialism outlined above. I will then discuss the Marikana mining massacre of August 2012, which was the single most lethal event in post-apartheid history. I will show that South Africa's deep integration into the global imperialist architecture indeed contributed to escalation of the situation. Finally, I will discuss the role civil society has played in challenging the extractivist-state nexus more recently and how anti-extractivist movements have restructured their opposition after Marikana. Despite encountering serious threats to their lives, activists stand in line with other 'Blockadia' activists (Klein, 2014).

South Africa – sub-imperialist gateway?

President Jacob Zuma has proudly described his country as a gateway to the African continent (Scholvin and Draper, 2012). South Africa's geostrategic gateway position suggests that the country 'interlinks many other African countries globally' (ibid.: 381). The 'nodal function' (ibid.: 382) of South Africa eases trade in the whole region through the advanced financial and logistic infrastructure available in the country. South Africa's port, airport, and road infrastructure have huge comparative advantages with respect to neighbouring countries. This attracts foreign capital to channel investment in the African continent through South Africa and ensures South Africa's position as regional hegemon.

Multinational companies operating in Southern Africa have their headquarters and regional offices mostly in Johannesburg, with some in Cape Town. Well-connected 'services networks' in Johannesburg and Cape Town, including 'transport, energy, finance and communication', have major advantages over neighbouring countries. South Africa's 'sophisticated' financial markets are seen as especially conducive for businesses (Scholvin and Draper, 2012: 393–394). The financial sector, which contributes around one-fifth of GDP, outperforms other African countries by far. The financial sector has incorporated 'a small black elite', while leaving property relations in the country largely intact (Ashman et al., 2011: 186–187). This incorporation crucially involves 'neither land (other than reallocated mineral rights as opposed to agriculture) nor, in general, productive activity', thus leaving white ownership carried over from apartheid largely unchallenged (ibid.). The financial sector in South Africa has hence allowed for extremely uneven access to capital, reflecting South Africa's position as one of the most unequal countries in the world.

Gateways are characterised by 'the capacity to transport people and goods from one place to another' (Scholvin and Draper, 2012: 383). From a sub-imperialist perspective, it is important to note that this does not happen on a level playing field, but that this exchange is structured to benefit the sub-imperialist hubs. That is, trade relations are organised such that South Africa's sub-imperialist position is strengthened to the detriment of its weaker neighbours. For example, cheap labour is flowing into South Africa from neighbouring countries such as Lesotho, Mozambique and Zimbabwe, crucially lowering prices in mining and agriculture that supply resources for South African goods. Cheap water from the Congo's Inga Dams and Lesotho's Highland Water Project is flowing into water-scarce South Africa.

Sub-imperialist mining?

A crucial question that arises when thinking through South Africa's sub-imperialist gateway position is: what are the particular economic relations both with regards to its economically weaker trading partners in the region and with the core imperialist countries and organisations such as the United States and EU? The mining industry might exemplify better than any other sector South Africa's sub-imperialist location.

The importance of mining in South Africa's history, starting from the discovery of natural resources, cannot be overstated, as '[n]owhere else in the world has a mineral revolution proved so influential in weaving the political, economic and social fabric of a society' (Davenport, 2013: 1). After a rather sluggish one and a half centuries of colonial interference in South Africa, the discovery of mineral resources invigorated British colonialists to start exploiting the country's vast resources. As Humby (2015: 115) shows, since discovery of minerals and metals in the country, elites have called the industry the 'lifeblood' and 'DNA' of the country. From inception, officials' 'psychological dependency on the mining industry seems to extend beyond cost/benefit' (ibid.). At first glance, there are some traits of the industry that warrant the messiah-like characterisation.

South Africa remains the 'world's richest country in commodity wealth' with an estimated US$2.5 trillion in reserves (UK Foreign & Commonwealth Office, 2015). Today, the industry employs over 450,000 people (Chamber of Mines of South Africa, 2017). Mining makes up 38% of merchandise exports in South Africa. In 2015 mining contributed 8% to South Africa's GDP, 17% including indirect benefits (UK Foreign & Commonwealth Office, 2015). Minister of Mineral Resources Molebatsi Zwane announced at the Cape Town

Mining Indaba 2017 that the country is 'looking forward to another 150 years of mining in South Africa' (South African Government, 2017). Indeed, there are diverging views about South Africa's riches: while elites including Zwane characterise it as 'blessing', activists tend to characterise it as 'curse'.

The South African economy lacks the capital to be an imperialist country. The government hence relies on attracting foreign investment to investment-intense industries like mining. In 2015, the mining industry attracted 15.9% of foreign direct investment (FDI) flowing into the country, third to manufacturing and financial and insurance services (Santander, n.d.). The country is the biggest recipient of FDI in Southern Africa, attracting 7% of total FDI into Africa; it is also the African country investing in the highest number of FDI projects on the continent (Klasa and Fingar, 2017). South Africa actively promotes its trade interests on the continent. In the following, I will discuss South Africa's sub-imperialist position considering the mining sector in particular.

The mining industry is dependant on volatile demand for its natural resources, having suffered low commodity prices in recent years. As emphasised by Fine and Rustomjee (1996), the interlinkages between the mining industry and other key industries such as energy are significant. Mining, despite a difficult macro-economic environment, remains crucial to South Africa's economy. The mining sector exercises what Fine and Rustomjee call 'conglomerate power' due to its influence with regard to other economic sectors (1996: 91). Big mining houses are organised in the Energy Intensive Users Group of Southern Africa (EIUG). Through their lobbying, big energy users are only paying a fraction of what average household consumers are asked to pay (Gosling, 2010). According to Bond, the 'minerals-energy complex' remains 'South Africa's economic base' (2014: 15; see also Ashman *et al.*, 2011: 178). Because of its dependency on primary goods revenues, which has historically deepened the extractivist-state nexus, South Africa's economy does particularly well during periods of economic boom, while it suffers harder from busts.

In the introduction, I proposed a four-pronged definition of sub-imperialism. In the following, I will gauge how these apply to the South African case with particular emphasis on the mining industry.

Expansionist economic policy

Sub-imperialism is expansive in that economic activities are undertaken well beyond the country's border. South Africa's companies are very active on the African continent. Of the 20 biggest companies on the continent, 17 are partly or fully South African companies. Measured by annual turnover, 4 of the continent's top 50 companies are South African mining companies (Africa Report, 2015). DeBeers is the biggest diamond-producing company in the world, ranking seventeenth among African companies according to turnover. The company operates mines and carries out exploration in South Africa, Namibia and Botswana as well as in Canada. Its sales operations span across the globe. DeBeers, due to its quasi-monopolistic market position, is able to influence the pricing system in South Africa. There have been serious allegations that by means of improper accounting, the company is not paying its due taxes in South Africa (Bracking and Sharife, 2014). South Africa ranks seventh when looking at illicit financial flows in developing countries worldwide, mainly due to fraudulent trade invoicing (Kar and Spanjers, 2015). Perhaps this is echoing the call of DeBeers founder, Cecil Rhodes, who advocated to 'combine the commercial with the imaginative' to further imperial expansion (Hobson, 2005[1902]: 201–202).

Relative dependency on foreign capital

Sub-imperialist states are highly dependent on foreign capital. Despite its relative economic strength, South Africa aims to attract FDI. This features prominently during State of the Nation addresses. During the 2017 address, President Zuma highlighted that 'mining has always been the backbone of our economy and an important foreign exchange earner' (South African Government, 2017). This was supplemented by a call to public regulators to make it 'easy to do business in South Africa' (ibid.). To 'undo delays' and 'unnecessary red tape' (ibid.) is seen as key to attracting investment.

Business-friendliness has been further ensured through the lowering of corporation tax from close to 37% in 2007 to 34.5% in 2008 and coming down to 28% in 2013. However, the recent downgrade of South Africa's credit rating to 'junk status' by rating agency Standard & Poor's has eroded investors' confidence in the country's stability. Another indication of South Africa's dependency on foreign donors is that 31 projects in South Africa have been funded by the World Bank since the beginning of 2005. Among these funded projects is the biggest ever World Bank loan, of US$3.75 billion, for the construction of the Medupi coal-fired powerstation in Limpopo province. The involvement of international financiers is particularly high in the extractive industries as the sector is highly dependent on capital investment.

Capital export of state-run industries and lax capital control

South Africa's economy has suffered from relisting of companies previously trading on the Johannesburg Stock Exchange (JSE) in post-apartheid South Africa. Anglo American Corporation, DeBeers, Gencor (later BHP Billiton), Old Mutual, and South African Breweries all removed their primary stock listings from Johannesburg in the short period between 1994 and 1998 (Bond, 2014: 21). None of the bigger mining companies operating in South Africa has its primary listings on the JSE. Primary stock market listings and headquarters of the leading mining companies operating in South Africa are in the United Kingdom (Anglo American and Lonmin), Australia (BHP Billiton) or Switzerland (Glencore). All these companies share that they are partnering with black local business partners in fulfilment of their Black Economic Empowerment (BEE) obligations. Mining companies were thus prominent examples of capital flight from South Africa. ANC General Secretary Gwede Mantashe admitted that 'at the time when neoliberalism was on the ascendancy as an ideology, it became fashionable to allow companies to migrate and list in the stock exchanges of developed economies' (quoted in Bond, 2016a).

The BRICS financial architecture, of which South Africa is part, is not in antagonism to the global financial architecture, but rather lubricates it (Bond, 2016b). The contingent reserve of the BRICS Development Bank is directly linked to the IMF. When a BRICS country requests a higher loan, it will be referred to IMF structural adjustment loans (Bond, 2016b: 613). Rather than embodying an alternative to financialised globalisation, the arrangement ties in with existing Washington Consensus-style policies.

Exploitation of labour

In addition to state-subsidised cheap energy and low levels of regulation and taxation, as shown above, labour costs are relatively low. However, wage levels in the mining industry have risen since 2012 as wage disputes intensified across the mining industry. However, this came at high human cost as well as job losses. Discussing labour disputes in 2013, former National Union of Mineworkers (NUM) spokesperson Lesiba Seshoka still characterised the disparity between worker and executive wages as a 'class war' (Steyn, 2013). With mining houses complaining about falling commodity prices, a sustained wage dispute ensued between mining houses and organised labour. While mining houses maintained that there was simply not enough money for pay rises, union movements became increasingly militant in their struggles for better working conditions and wage increases.

Work in the mining sector is precarious and increasingly casualised (Chinguno, 2013). About a third of the labour contracts in the platinum industry are third-party agreements. Contracts that are not signed directly between companies and workers increase precariousness and enhance 'control' (Chinguno, 2013: 640). Chinguno (2013) suggests that worker militancy outside union structures increases with the casualisation of working contracts. Fragmentation is further augmented by the housing situation. There is an increase in informal housing around mines. In post-apartheid South Africa, housing has been marked by an absence in local planning capacity and lack of corporate provision of appropriate accommodation (ibid.: 642). Spatially, workers are increasingly scattered around their places of work.

A tight wage regime in the mining sector results in many miners falling into the hands of 'loan sharks' – locally called '*mashonisas*' – backed by Capitec, African Bank, Nedbank, Standard Bank and First Rand. Interest rates of around 5% monthly plus an initiation fee of up to 15% plus additional surcharges leave miners in an unsustainable debt spiral with loans servicing other loans (Bond, 2013b). Defaulting on *mashonisas* results in confiscation of all personal assets and sometimes even physical assault.

A mining massacre and its aftermath

On 16 August 2012, the small mining town of Marikana in the North West province bordering Africa's financial hub, Gauteng, witnessed an unprecedented post-apartheid atrocity. The mining company Lonmin, that mines the precious metal platinum used for catalysts in cars, colluded with police forces and government to intervene in what ended in the killing of 34 striking miners. The event is important for our understanding of how sub-imperial economics escalates the confrontation between labour exploitation and capital flight on the one hand and social movements demanding economic participation on the other.

This is how the events in Marikana unfolded. Originating in a wage dispute and workers' dissatisfaction with the ANC-linked majority union, the NUM, rock drill operators embarked on an unprotected strike on 10 August, demanding to enter wage negotiation with Lonmin directly. This demand was declined by Lonmin even though the company had previously engaged with wage demands outside unionised structures (Alexander, 2016: 829–830). Striking workers, some of them highly indebted, were calling for a wage increase. In the wake of the massacre, a call for Rand 12,500 (about the equivalent of US$1,420 at the time) was the demand echoing at many mining houses across the North West mining belt.

By 12 August, a joint operation centre had already been established on the premises of Lonmin by the police. The collaboration included the police having access to Lonmin's security cameras as well as informants. After the massacre Lonmin's premises also functioned as a temporary detention centre and conference venue. Alexander (2016: 830) calls the collaboration between Lonmin and police a 'toxic collusion'. Preceding the killings on 16 August 2012, two policemen, two Lonmin security personnel and six workers were killed in clashes between these groups.

On 15 August, the day before the massacre, a meeting was held at which the head of police, having the highest rank, agreed on a 'tactical option' for the following day. The commission of inquiry into the killings suggested that the decision by the police to intervene using military assault rifles allows for the events to be described as premeditated. The official policy to 'disarm and arrest' was soon dropped for the 'tactical option' as debated on the day preceding the killings. At a press conference on the morning of the massacre, Mbombo, the provincial police commissioner, announced that 'today we end this matter', indicating that violence was at least considered an option at this point (quoted in Alexander, 2016: 822).

On the day of killings, no single policeman was injured. Thirty-four miners died. Marinovich (2016), in his meticulous analysis of the events of 16 August, shows that indeed there is much evidence that suggests assassination of fleeing miners. To date none of the policemen or those in charge have been convicted of their actions. To add insult to injury, 270 miners were arrested that day for the 'murder' of their comrades on the basis of 'common purpose' charges carried over from apartheid. Charges were dropped due to public outcry soon after.

Leading government official Cyril Ramaphosa (who became president of the ANC in December 2017 and is likely to become next president of South

Africa) had business interests in Lonmin when the strike broke out. On the day of the first casualties, then Lonmin director Ramaphosa instructed the police minister, Nathi Mthethwa, to reinforce the police contingent (Alexander, 2016: 819). In an email sent to Mining Minister Shabangu the day before the massacre, Ramaphosa described the strikers as 'plainly dastardly criminal' and called for 'concomitant action' (quoted in Marinovich, 2016: 137).

Marikana marks a 'defining moment in the post-apartheid era' (Alexander, 2016: 838). The Marikana massacre showed the ugliest face of the extractivist-state nexus. International capital together with the national ruling elite waged 'class war' against workers (including the working-class policemen who were following orders to shoot striking miners). Some commentators saw the massacre as an assurance to international investors that the state would go a long way to protect capital interests (Bond, 2014; Alexander et al., 2012). Resistance was not confined to Marikana only. Roughly a fifth of South Africa's half a million mineworkers went on strike in 2012 (Bond, 2014: 177). When in 2013 an unprecedented strike wave intensified the tension between capital and unionised workers, the labour struggle was partially successful. However, with the ANC's decision to elevate Ramaphosa to lead the party, there is little hope for progressive social movements and labour to find an ally in the likely new president.

Blockadia: challenging sub-imperialism from below

Half a decade has passed since the Marikana massacre. Lonmin conceded to worker pay rises of between 11% and 22%. This did not amount to the Rand 12,500 the miners asked for (wage demands around Marikana would have amounted to an increase of 200% had the companies given in to the demands; Chinguno, 2013). The wage regime in the South African mining sector remains piecemeal, and unions are far from realising what they have set out to achieve (*Mail & Guardian*, 2015). As presented earlier, the labour regime cannot be seen in isolation.

The strike wave around Marikana took place in a macroeconomic climate showing multiple ills amplified by international recession:

> the rise of unemployment, further property market turmoil, manufacturing stagnation, a severe credit squeeze, and a return to dangerous current account deficits (as the big extractive and financial corporations shipped out funds to London, and as trade slipped into deficit, too).
>
> (Saul and Bond, 2014: 213)

This climate makes the workers' struggle appear like the preverbal fight against windmills. However, new civic alliances are responding to the multiple challenges they face.

The massacre has also resulted in changes to academic thinking on workers' struggles. Critical scholars have emphasised that political opportunities for social movements have broadened with new formations beyond and sometimes even completely outside workers' movements. There has been a shift in emphasis of the research programme from looking at the masculine workers' struggle to exploring community struggles often led by women (Naicker, 2016). Increasingly, workers are portrayed as embedded in wider community circles that, in the past, have all too often been ignored. Sikhala Sonke (We Cry Together) has become a forceful female support group around Marikana, raising awareness about the harsh conditions in the informal settlement they were living in and the unbearable loss of miners shot down by the police. In doing so, 'the women of Marikana also linked their repression to a broad struggle against state repression in South Africa' (ibid.: 163). Well beyond Marikana, new links have been forged that challenge the extractive industries.

After the events at Marikana, civic organisations have challenged the hegemonic story of mining as a development project. These organisations include NGOs, such as the Bench Marks Foundation, GroundWork, Action Aid South Africa, and WoMin (Women in Mining), as well as research clusters, such as the CCS (Centre for Civil Society) and the Centre for Environmental Rights, and grass-roots campaigns, such as the Save our Mfolozi Wilderness Campaign and Frack Free South Africa. Campaigns monitor the corporate footprint of existing mines, holding companies to account through the use of a wide range of methods from legal intervention to forms of direct action. Organisations also challenge exploration applications for extractive projects, trying to prevent mining companies from acquiring mining licences. These ideas are part of a wider solidarity movement that Naomi Klein (2014. 295) describes in the following terms:

> Blockadia is not a specific location on a map but rather a roving transnational conflict zone that is cropping up with increasing frequency and intensity wherever extractive projects are attempting to dig and drill, whether for open-pit mines, or gas fracking, or tar sands oil pipelines. What unites these increasingly interconnected pockets of resistance is … the fact that in their quest for high-priced commodities and higher-risk 'unconventional' fuels, they are pushing relentlessly into countless new territories, regardless of the impact on the local ecology (in particular, local water systems), as well as the fact that many of the industrial activities in question have neither been adequately tested nor regulated, yet have already shown themselves to be extraordinarily accident-prone.

The extractive front in South Africa has built a strong network challenging the extractive industries. There is a growing number of cases indicating how affected citizens are risking their lives to fight off extractivist projects. Examples range from Xolobeni in the Eastern Cape where titanium mining has been stalled to Fuleni in KwaZulu-Natal province where coal mining is contested. In both cases, activists defy threats to their lives and stand up against dangers to their livelihoods. The shooting of anti-mining activist 'Bazooka' Rhadebe at Xolobeni has not yet been resolved. The Fuleni and

Xolobeni communities have been assisted by NGOs providing legal expertise as well as raising awareness in the public domain. In what way does the challenge to the extractive sector from below relate to the preceding remarks about sub-imperial economics?

The extractivist-state nexus has proven that it will close its ranks in the most brutal manner imaginable to defend business interests. There has been no fundamental reversal of public policy in the mining sector. To the contrary, officials have consistently ensured investors that mining remains a safe bet. Inquiries into the relationship between the extractive sector and elite politicians, including the president, suggest deeper convergence between mining and political interests (Leonard, 2016: 331–332; Madonsela, 2016). Following Marikana, the extractive sector has been under close scrutiny by a number of watchdog and environmental justice organisations. Many of these organisations call for an end to the era of fossil fuels. Strategies have adapted to current challenges. In the past, environmental groups have been criticised for their piecemeal or silo-type approaches. Concerns were raised that organisations were too concerned about their own agendas and that their social backgrounds and demands were too heterogeneous (Cock, 2006). Today's anti-extractivist social movements have managed to connect the affected citizenry of different races and classes, conservationists and some environmentally concerned scholars. These movements still fall short of establishing links to labour unions as demands on the shop floor remain workerist at their core (Müller, 2015). However, the National Union of Metalworkers endorses the extension of renewable energy to the national grid (Müller, 2016: 100). Community organisations – often led by women – have shown keen interest in pushing the environmental agenda.

Sub-imperialist economics is characterised by an uneven integration into world trade. Sub-imperialist South Africa is marked by an openness to international trade, offering favourable terms (low corporation taxes, capital flight, incentivising structural reforms via BRICS bank arrangements, World Bank loans). In turn, South Africa attracts imperialist FDI and workers from neighbouring countries willing to work for low wages. Hence sub-imperialist dynamics accelerate contractions between mine-affected communities and elite interests. As seen above, mine-affected communities (including those fighting exploration rights and the issuing of mining licences) have forged new alliances with NGOs and other activist networks. Their activism has been heroic in that they are on the front lines of a battle that has had causalities. Kirsten Youens (2017), an attorney challenging mining applications (often pro bono), suggests that

> In South Africa, defenders of environmental justice and social and political change are threatened, ridiculed, marginalised and punished. There have been many situations in the struggle against coal mining and other intrusive development in rural areas that have resulted in threats, intimidation and death. People's houses and cars are burnt. Many have been murdered and the perpetrators get away unapprehended and unpunished.

Activists are on the front lines of struggles challenging the current extractivist path. The highest echelons of the current political class share interests with the sub-imperialist investors class. As I have shown, there is a new countermovement that has gone well beyond workerist demands to embrace social as well as environmental demands.

9 Chile's trade policies in the context of US contemporary imperialism

The free trade agenda and the loss of national autonomy

José Miguel Ahumada

Introduction: Chile's development and US geopolitics

During the twentieth century, the imperialistic actions of the United States in Latin America in general, and Chile in particular, were considered by most political actors and intellectuals of the region as not only evident, but also key to understanding their underdeveloped condition. In fact, since the mid-nineteenth century, there have been many examples that justify this diagnosis: the US Monroe Doctrine; Manifest Destiny ideology; the invasion of Mexico; and a series of US military interventions, occupations and taking of political control in Central American countries. These clearly showed the imperialistic actions of the United States, designed to control the flow of trade and investment to and from Latin America by any means. During the twentieth century, US imperialism in the region was even clearer. While Latin America was an important area for US investments in services, extractive industries and natural resources (building strong enclave monopolies), the Cold War increased the imposition of direct and indirect pressures by the United States towards Latin American governments. It supported pro-US dictatorships (e.g. Somoza in Nicaragua, Batista in Cuba) and financed/coordinated military coups against national-popular governments (the overthrow of President Arbenz in Guatemala in 1954, President Goulart in Brazil in 1964 and President Allende in Chile in 1973 and the Bay of Pigs invasion in Cuba in 1961) (see Toro Hardy, 2008).

In the case of Chile, the United States had been considered a fundamental actor in determining its development path. Until the mid-1960s, US multinationals controlled Chile's most important economic pillar: the copper industry. The US government permanently supported anti-socialist political coalitions and, through the Alliance for Progress, even financed policies such as land reform and technical support for new industrial projects (in order to maintain the country within the US orbit and distant from the USSR). During the socialist government of Salvador Allende (1970–1973), the United States financed the political opposition and even collaborated with the army to carry out a military coup against its own government. The coup established a dictatorship (1973–1989) that initiated the most radical economic reforms in Chile's history: its path towards neoliberalism.

Since the mid-1980s, Chile's economic growth shifted radically towards exports. This was explained by the fruition of a series of long-lasting industrial policies (running from the 1960s) targeting new areas beyond copper (areas in which Chile had strong comparative advantages, such as forestry, fruits, wine and fishing) plus the market opening since the 1970s (see Ahumada and Sossdorf, 2017). Together with these measures, during the 1980s, export promotion policies and many subsidies were established to support Chile's new exports dynamism. These new sectors were owned by a novel powerful capitalist class built during the dictatorship, a class which became a key political actor in determining Chile's trade policies in the post-dictatorship period (1990 onwards) (see Montero, 1997; Silva, 1996).

Since the 1990s, the new democratic governments have not only deepened the free trade approach with a wave of trade agreements with different countries, but also established certain economic heterodox policies: capital controls to protect the macroeconomy from the flows of speculative capital and the maintenance of subsides for non-traditional exports (see Agosin et al., 2010; Ffrench-Davis, 2014). In this context, and contrary to what happened during the twentieth century, the issue of 'US imperialism' remained unproblematised, disappearing from the realm of public opinion and political discourse and also receiving little attention from academic researchers in the country. 'Imperialism' as a category was considered to be mere Cold War rhetoric.

Is this true? Does this lack of interest in imperialism mean that the United States did not exercise any influence or carry out any imperialistic activity in Chile after its support of the military coup? Is US imperialism a thing of the past in Chile's current trade policies and development? This chapter will indicate that since 1990, US imperialistic actions in Chile have not disappeared and that, moreover, they have become even more successful in restricting Chile's state sovereignty and imposing a free trade agenda upon it. If this is not very easy to detect, it is mainly because, as Gallagher and Robinson (1953) argue, we tend to associate capitalist imperialism with its most violent, direct and formal expressions without considering its goals and the variety of methods available to imperial states. Just as in the case of British imperialism, US imperialism is focused not on territorial conquest for its own sake (as mercantilist and pre-capitalist imperialisms) but in securing their area of influence; creating institutional bases for the free expansion of trade, finance and investments; and ensuring the strict protection of private property. When a country threatens that institutional base, imperialism shows its most direct face (military intervention), but when that is not the case, imperialism acts through a series of informal means: trade agreements, collaboration with internal dominant classes, diplomacy, and so forth (see Grocott and Grady, 2014; Wood, 2005).

Since the 1990s, Chile's trade policies have been led in accordance with the interests of an export capitalist class focused on the exploitation of natural resources (exporting to the United States, Europe and, since the mid-2000s, massively to China), with the main objective of securing stable and common rules in foreign markets for their goods through a wave of bilateral and regional trade agreements (Silva, 2001). The Chilean governments supported their goals in order to obtain their compliance in maintaining the economic stability of the new democracy beginning in 1990.

At the same time, since the negotiations of the Uruguay Round in the mid-1980s, the United States has put pressure on peripheral countries, on the one hand, to adopt a deep free trade agenda (opening up of export markets, financial and foreign direct investment (FDI) deregulation and enforcement of intellectual property rights (IPR)) and, on the other hand, to transform that agenda into a common multilateral constitutional rule. This has been done by two means: the establishment of the World Trade Organization (WTO) and US promotion of a wave of regional (including the North American Free Trade Agreement, NAFTA) and bilateral trade agreements in Latin America that go even beyond the WTO commitments (including restrictions to the use of capital controls, stronger rules on FDI and IPR, etc.) (see Gallagher, 2008).

This chapter will show how the interests of Chile's export capitalist class in securing free trade rules were complementary to US informal imperialism from the 1990s to the end of the 2000s. In this case, imperialism took the form of transaction between two self-interested agents: Chile's power bloc looking for better market access for export capitalists; and the United States looking to implement a deep free trade agenda in Chile and then expand this agenda to the rest of the region. The result in terms of imperialist objectives was, for the first time in US-Chile relations, completely satisfactory: since 2004, Chile has eliminated most of its 'interventionist' and 'protectionist' measures, not only adopting the US free trade agenda, but also accepting it as a formal commitment with the United States and the WTO.

The second section will focus on the US pressures and Chile's loss of economic sovereignty during the WTO and the Chile-US Free Trade Agreement (FTA). It will also show the collaboration of Chile's export capitalist class in accepting and promoting this loss of sovereignty. Finally, the last section will summarise the main ideas of the chapter.

Chile and the United States: the informal rule of US imperialism

US imperialism in the 1990s: informal rule and trade agreements

At the end of the 1980s, the United States considerably changed its geopolitical strategy towards underdeveloped regions – from one which accepted a certain degree of state sovereignty in implementing autonomous policies on industrialisation in peripheral countries in exchange for their commitment to global free trade, to one based on a strong multilateral-regional-bilateral push towards making the peripheral countries adapt their regulatory framework to the US free trade standards settled in the Uruguay Round (see Amsden, 2007).

This was a radical change in US foreign policy that began with the inclusion of peripheral countries into a new global regulatory framework which restricted their national jurisdictions, particularly in regard to FDI, services and intellectual property.[1] This strategy received strong criticism from those countries to which it was applied, but as the agreement that emerged from the Round (the new WTO) was based on the 'single undertaking' clause (a take-it-or-leave-it clause applying to the whole agreement), peripheral countries were left with no option but to accept the agreement in its entirety (see Deere, 2009).

Together with this multilateral pressure, the United States was also developing a series of bilateral and regional strategies: in 1990, President Bush announced the Initiative of the Americas, a long-term programme based upon building a series of trade agreements with different Latin American countries, using the NAFTA agreement (between Canada, Mexico and the United States) as a starting point. This wave implied consolidating not only permanent rules for trade but, as during the Uruguay Round, a series of new norms focusing on increasing the protection of US FDI and financial flows. One of the tools used to pressure countries to sign these agreements was the political use of the Generalised System of Preferences (GSP)[2] as a mechanism for 'economic exchange', with inclusion in the GSP being granted only in exchange for internal reform.

Chile was one of the countries that received the benefits of the GSP. However, as a consequence of the Kennedy Amendment (1976), an important number of Chilean export goods were excluded in 1984 and Chile as a country was excluded in 1987 on the basis of US argument that Chile was in non-compliance of international labour standards (the United States was turning its back on the Chilean military dictatorship). In 1990, the impact of these measures on Chilean exports was estimated to be about US$ 600 million,[3] without including a series of non-tariff protectionist measures imposed by the United States on Chilean exports since the mid-1980s.

In 1990, Chile's exporter capitalists demanded that the government request the United States to re-enter Chile into the GSP and to facilitate this by initiating negotiations for trade agreements that could consolidate permanently both the GSP and rules for trade with the United States.[4] In fact, these demands were in perfect consonance with the United States's regional agenda: Chile immediately accepted the US Initiative of the Americas and, in 1991, signed an agreement with the United States to establish a Council for Trade and Investment. The idea of an FTA was strongly supported by business associations, which considered that it would give a clear sign of the government's commitment to free trade and export-led capitalist accumulation. Signing the FTA with the United States was considered, both by the government and business, to be fundamental for Chile's long-term export consolidation and, in the short run, for its re-entry into the GSP.

However, to accept Chile back into the GSP and to begin the negotiations for the FTA, the United States requested a new measure: not only new labour standards, but also a change in Chile's intellectual property regime. Before 1991, Chile's patent regime did not include the pharmaceutical sector and the duration of patents was only between five and ten years (Law No 958). Such regulation received strong criticism from the US Pharmaceutical Manufacturers' Association, which claimed that Chile's 'weak' patent system had led to a total loss of US$ 94 million for the sector between 1970 and 1990. The Association began lobbying the United States Trade Representative (USTR) at the end of the 1980s. Its basic demand was for Chile to change its IPR regime and to include the pharmaceutical sector into the areas covered by patents, while extending the patent duration to a uniform 15 years (see Jordan, 1994; Durr, 1990). The Chilean government accepted the US demands and incorporated them into a new law (19.039) passed in 1991. The reasons for the government's acceptance of this pressure were clear: being incorporated into the GSP would improve the country's image and mark a step towards signing an FTA with the United States,[5] a clear demand of the business sector.[6] Indeed, Chile was readmitted into the GSP and the negotiations for a FTA started almost immediately.

This negotiation represented the first action of the United States's new imperialist strategy in Chile: imposing an agenda of property protection for US investors (in this case, patent holders) in Chile's national jurisdiction in exchange for inclusion in a 'better market access' scheme for 'internal collaborators' (the export capitalist class). As will be seen next, this has been the typical way that imperialism was expressed in Chile's trade policies since the nineties, as an exchange between self-interested agents (where one was just providing certain tariff reductions and the other was securing the property of foreigners).

The first two attempts for a FTA: Chile's business interests and US internal conflicts

During the 1990s, the new democratic governments were very interested in keeping an alliance with the national capitalist class. The political scenario, according to the new governments, demanded that business associations show their willingness to consolidate the export-led accumulation established during the military dictatorship. This was considered by the new policymakers not only as a necessary concession for maintaining political stability, but also as demonstrating a clear ideological commitment to the free market (see Boeninger, 2014[1997]). In that sense, defending the interests of the extractive export capitalist class in the global market was considered paramount for the new governments. The negotiation of the FTA with the United States in 1991–1992 was, in that context, a key signal for the export class.

However, political conditions in the United States changed in the meantime (environmentalist pressures after the success of the NAFTA negotiation in 1992 and the US election with a victory for the Democrats being two significant developments). This delayed the possibility of a successful FTA (see Direcon, 2009), but it did not mean that Chile stopped its plan to fortify its export-led accumulation. On the contrary, it began to sign a wave of complementary trade agreements (CEAs) with Latin American countries and a series of Bilateral Investment Treaties with developed countries (see Porras, 2003). At the same time, new heterodox measures were implemented such as capital controls, complementing the export promotion policies, in order to subsidise and expand Chile's exports and secure its macroeconomic order from the instabilities of global financial markets (see the chapter introduction).

In 1994, the first step in the US plan for free trade for Latin America was taken: the NAFTA agreement was launched together with the plan for the Free Trade Agreement of the Americas (FTAA). The NAFTA was not based only on tariff liberalisation but, more importantly for US goals, also demanded a complete restructuring of key national economic institutions, such as the elimination of capital controls, strengthening of the intellectual property regime and a radical reduction in the state's ability to implement policies concerning FDI. Besides securing free trade, the NAFTA was a new regional institutional architecture that increased protection for the property owners of patents, FDI and financial assets (the great majority of which had been established in the United States).

The United States' geostrategic idea was to use NAFTA as a platform for 'exporting' its trade rules to the continent (see Weintraub, 2004). In the words of US Commerce Secretary Ron Brown, 'NAFTA is just the first step towards hemispheric trade policy' (quoted in Harding, 1993: 1). This implied two options: to integrate as many countries as possible into the agreement and/or to use NAFTA as the basis for future treaties within the region, both regional and bilateral. In fact, the United States was pursuing different tactics at the same time, simultaneously looking to integrate more Latin American countries into NAFTA, to sign different bilateral trade agreements and/or to unite different existing trade agreements in the region into a single one.

The question then became: with which Latin American country, besides Mexico, would the expansion of the NAFTA begin? The United States wanted to use the invitation as a symbolic gesture, as a way to show other countries the benefit of establishing liberal economic reforms. In this sense, Chile was the perfect candidate. It had a consolidated neoliberal economic model, high economic growth and an established democracy, and both the government and the export capitalist class were actively pursuing any kind of agreement with the United States.[7] In 1994, NAFTA formally offered to make Chile its fourth member.

For the United States, expanding NAFTA, as was shown with Mexico, was not only about increasing trade, but also about expanding a specific regulatory framework to the rest of the continent. Chile was not going to be an exception. In the *Report to the President and the Congress on Significant Market Opening*, in 1994, the USTR accused Chile of: not having an intellectual property regime in line with NAFTA rules; maintaining export subsidies; imposing capital control mechanisms; and maintaining tariff protections for traditional agriculture (see Jordan, 1994).[8] Particularly in the case of IPR, the USTR demanded that Chile lengthen the duration of patents from 15 to 20 years while also imposing a 'pipeline'.[9] In that sense, the United States was, through informal means of trade agreements, expanding its own regulatory framework to peripheral countries.

Indeed, the United States was only willing to integrate Chile into NAFTA if Chile modified, for the second time, its internal economic institutions by expanding patent regulations and eliminating capital controls, subsidies and the tariff protectionist measures towards traditional agriculture (called 'price bands').[10] The capital control mechanism established by Chile in 1990 went against NAFTA rules (art. 1401), and the US Treasury Department quickly presented a report concerning the benefit to US financial capital if Chile's capital controls were eliminated.[11] Just as in the case of the patent law in 1990, Chile was ready to accept US demands. The reason was straightforward: integrating into NAFTA was strongly in the interests of the dominant internal power bloc.

Even though, in terms of tariff reduction, an agreement with NAFTA was not very significant (most of the tariffs went from 0% to 3% under the GSP), the fact that the GSP was constantly being checked and was dependent on the internal decisions of the United States created a sense of uncertainty for Chile's exporters. In addition, particularly in the cases of textiles and certain processed fruits, the tariff jumped up to 30% – a clear detriment to those Chilean exports.

Nevertheless, beyond the small changes in trade that NAFTA would produce, the general perception of Chile's main capitalist business associations (the general association, CPC,[12] the exporters association, ASEXMA,[13] and the industrial association, SOFOFA[14]) was that the central benefit of joining NAFTA lay in the impact it would have on the 'country's image'. The NAFTA agreement would consolidate the country's liberal economic institutions, particularly the trade and investment rules, which would build a sense of certainty, not only in relation to foreign capital (thus increasing FDI and improving Chile's position in the financial markets) but to national capital as well. This sense of certainty would link the economic strategy and its rules to an agreement with the United States, sending a clear signal of the perpetuation of the economic regime. Accepting certain demands from the United States (e.g. fortifying IPR, eliminating capital controls, etc.) was considered, both by the export capitalist class and the government, a low price to pay for the long-term benefits related to the consolidation of their favoured institutions and an improved international image. The export capitalist class would have certainty about the permanence of the economic strategy because of the link between the Chilean trade strategy and the US sphere of influence (see Fazio, 2004).

In this context, the Mexican crisis (1994) changed the perspective of the US Congress on the strategy of 'extending NAFTA' as a way of imposing US hegemony. The high cost for the United States of helping Mexico to overcome the 'Tequila Crisis' was seen as a warning of the dangers of the NAFTA strategy. Thus, after everything, US Congress closed off any possibility of President Clinton including another developing country into the agreement, ending negotiations between the United States and Chile in 1996 (see Rivera, 1995).

With this failure, Chile's business classes found a second-best option: to sign a bilateral FTA with Mexico and Canada in order to facilitate a future agreement with the United States.

From the WTO agreement to the FTA with the United States: losing sovereignty through informal means

As with most of the global periphery, Chile entered into the WTO agreement in 1995. This entrance implied accepting a series of agreements in different areas, such as services (SCM), FDI and financial flows (TRIMS) and intellectual property rights (TRIPS). Thus, Chile had to adapt its own internal regulations to these new global standards promoted by the United States (such as the elimination of a series of export promotion policies that went against the SCM, strengthening of IPR up to TRIPS standards, bringing pro-FDI regimes up to TRIMS standards, reduction of tariffs, etc.). As a result, a series of industrial policies and institutions maintained by Chile were considered counter to the WTO agreements. As can be seen from Table 9.1, policies that were used during the 1980s to promote Chile's export diversification through state support were eliminated or widely restricted by the new agreements.

The government delayed the IPR reform while keeping the price band. However, it had to eliminate or restrict certain export policies. Again, for the Chilean government and the export capitalists, these measures were considered just a small cost compared to the benefits that the integration into the new global standards would generate (i.e. better market access and certainties for the export capitalists). As the export class was already consolidated and had clear comparative advantages in their natural resources, there was no need for continuous state support, at least not for the main export conglomerates.

After these adaptations to the WTO rules, in 2000 President Lagos announced his intention to formally begin negotiations so that Chile could integrate into the MERCOSUR. This decision would have empowered South America vis-à-vis multilateral organisations (WTO) and, of course, the United States. In fact, it would have implied that the United States had to negotiate a FTA and the FTAA agenda not with individual states, but with one powerful actor (Brazil, Argentina, Chile, Uruguay and Paraguay together). One month before President Lagos was supposed to formally begin the negotiations to become a member of MERCOSUR (in November 2000), the United States made a diplomatic move:

Table 9.1 Chile and the WTO: impact on policies

Policies	*Objective*	*Outcome*
Simplified drawbacks	Promotion of non-traditional exports	Widely restricted
Deferred payment for capital imports	Promotion of non-traditional exports	Eliminated
Price bands	Protection of traditional agriculture	Maintained
IPR norms (15-year duration of patents)	Equilibrium between consumers use of technology and patent holders	Temporally maintained

Source: author's own elaboration.

it offered Chile the opportunity to sign a bilateral FTA in order to weaken the MERCOSUR (see Rush, 2000). Chile immediately accepted the US offer and disregarded the MERCOSUR option.

Why did Chile abandon MERCOSUR for the FTA with the United States? The FTA had been a permanent demand of the export capitalists. Chile was in a situation of economic stagnation after the Asian crisis, and a FTA with, at the time, Chile's main trade partner was seen by business associations as an important instrument that would reactivate investment, increase confidence in the government and diversify exports.[15] The government saw in the FTA a possibility to regain the trust of the business class and accepted the US invitation (see Fermandois, 2006).

For the United States, even though Chile represented only 0.01% of its exports at the beginning of the 2000s, it was of key importance for geopolitical reasons. While for the US government the WTO did not advance the agenda of deep integration enough, the EU was increasing its influence in the region (by negotiating an FTA with MERCOSUR at the same time). In this context, the desire of the United States to extend its regulatory framework into the region (particularly in areas that were considered underdeveloped in the WTO and vital for developing US industry, such as intellectual property, investment and financial regulation) led it to establish a new strategy focused on bilateral agreements that would build a WTO-plus regulatory framework (see Gallagher, 2008; Shadlen, 2005).

The FTA with Chile became the first bilateral agreement to follow the US strategy. It served as the template for bilateral agreements that the United States would sign in the coming years with Central America, Peru, Colombia and Panama. The US demands to Chile were the same as in the past: tariffs reduction, elimination of capital controls, strengthening of IPR and deregulation of FDI. The United States offered, in return, elimination of some of its protectionist measures (tariff escalation), permanent integration into the GSP and tariff reduction. For the government and the business associations, the demands of the United States were considered small concessions compared to the benefits. Strong IPR, capital controls or deregulation of FDI did not imply a direct attack to the interests of the extractive export capitalist class; and as their investments were key for Chile's economic recovery, the government allied with business (see Silva, 2001).

Thus, the interests of Chile's export capitalist class and those of the United States were complementary. The former wanted low tariffs and permanent integration into the GSP, while the latter requested internal reforms in key economic areas (see Table 9.2).

Chile signed the agreement in 2003. The United States took the opportunity not only to impose on Chile a new regime on FDI and virtual elimination of capital controls, but also to adapt Chile's IPR regime to the WTO standards. As can be seen in Table 9.3, the final result of both Chile's integration into the WTO and the signing off of the FTA has been a wide reduction in its economic sovereignty in order to adapt to the global institutions for free market promoted by the United States.

In that sense, policies that were key for Chile during the 1980s and 1990s and helped to spark its economic boom (e.g. capital controls and export

Table 9.2 Chile and the United States: interest in signing a FTA

Country	*Demands*	*Objectives*
Chile	• Tariff reduction • Consolidation of the GSP • Elimination of anti-dumping measures • Abolition of escalation tariffs • Dispute settlement	Access to trade: • Increase and diversify exports • Increase the inflow of FDI from the United States • Increase the inflow of financial capital • Reduction in Chilean risk premium
United States	• Tariff reduction • Intellectual property reform • Elimination of capital controls • Elimination of price bands • New rules for investments	Geopolitical/economic consolidation in the region: • Expansion of trade to the region • Present it as the example for the future FTAA negotiations by extending the agreement to non-trade areas (financial, IPR, investment) and imposing WTO-plus rules. • Reduce the power of MERCOSUR

Source: Author's own elaboration.

Table 9.3 State sovereignty after trade agreements

Areas	*Pro-developmental policies*	*Before 1990s*	*WTO*	*FTA Chile-US*
Trade	Export subsidies	✔	✖	✖
FDI	Domestic content	✔	✖	✖
	Technological transfer	✔	✔	✖
	Direct/indirect expropriation	✖	✖	✔
Financial flows	Capital controls	✔	✔	✖
IPR	Patent duration	5–10 years	20 years	20 years

✔: measures accepted;
✖: measures banned.
Source: based on Ahumada (forthcoming).

promotion policies), together with a set of policies traditionally used for productive transformation (e.g. as technological transfer and domestic content measures towards FDI), have been banned or virtually eliminated. IPR became stricter, and measures related to FDI are radically restricted under ambiguous clauses such as 'indirect expropriation'. The final result is a major reduction of Chile's policy space for development given the bilateral and multilateral free trade straightjackets.

The case of Chile was used as a starting point for a series of other FTAs that the United States signed with Latin American countries in order to establish a supranational commitment to free trade and the protection of investor property in the region. After the WTO and the FTA with the United States, Chile consolidated the free trade agenda of the US imperialist strategy with the active support of both the governments and the export capitalist class.

Conclusions: Chile in the imperialist trap

What can be considered the main impact of these reforms on Chile's development strategy? Has this active submission to the US agenda increased its development prospects? During the twentieth century, US imperialism acted in Chile through unilateral pressures, economic boycotts and alliances with dis-establishing national agents as well as through cooperation in economic projects. It has been suggested that since the mid-1980s, and as a part of the new strategy of the United States in Latin America, US imperialism has expressed itself through formal trade agreements between self-interested agents (the United States and the internal power bloc of the government and the export capitalist class). This is considered imperialist not because of the exchange in itself, but because of the objects that were being exchanged: market access for national sovereignty.

This imperialist 'exchange' has resulted in a perpetuation of Chile's peripheral form of economic specialisation: one still based on commodities and manufactures highly dependent on natural resources. In fact, in terms of its export basket with the United States, Chile has maintained its low value added and natural-resource-dependent structure: between 1995–2003, commodities and resource-based manufactures made up 86% of total exports to the United States, while in the period 2012–2016 these jumped to 89%.[16] Also, the free trade agenda built by the export capitalist class and the US imperialist agreements has resulted in a considerable process of premature deindustrialisation of Chile's productive structure: manufacturing dropped from 19% of Chile's GDP in 2001 to 12% in 2016.[17]

Chile's denationalisation of its IPR, FDI and financial regime along with its institutional subordination to the bilateral and multilateral agreements promoted by the United States have resulted in a substantial loss of national autonomy necessary to build alternative pro-development policies – policies that, as Amsden (2007) and Chang (2008) argue, have been traditionally used by peripheries to spark a process of industrialisation and, thus, challenge the imperial powers. In that sense, Chile is an important example of how contemporary US imperialism has succeeded in imposing its free trade agenda and property protection in Latin

America and, more importantly, how it has transformed its agenda into a bilateral-regional-multilateral novel rule order, away from national sovereignty, and locked into a transnational architecture where the United States is, still, at the top of the pyramid.

Notes

1 This change was a clear US strategy developed to confront the emerging threat of the newly industrialised countries (Japan, South Korea, Taiwan and the emerging China) that were gaining competitiveness through flexible IPR rules, increased FDI regulation and strategic trade policies. Such actions were considered 'unfair' and against the spirit of free trade, requiring a radical change in international rules regarding them (see Amsden, 2007; Kwa, 2003; Deere, 2009).

2 The GSP is a unilateral trade preference programme established by the United States in 1974 consisting of eliminating tariffs on many products coming from underdeveloped countries in order to promote their exports.

3 See *Estrategia*, 3 September 1990.

4 See the statement of export business associations in *El Mercurio*, 1 December 1990, B1.

5 See the government's statements in *El Mercurio*, 2 December 1990, D1.

6 In fact, the business sector had been suffering since the 1980s due to a series of protectionist measures established by the United States to protect their own fishing and agricultural sectors, such as marketing order and tariff escalation measures, together with non-tariff measures, such as restrictions on the imports of Chilean grapes after a strange case of a poisoned grape found in an export container in 1989 (see Engel, 1996).

7 In fact, the main Chilean business association (CPC) intensively lobbied the US Congress to accept Chile in the NAFTA while the government was negotiating with the US executive power (see Harding, 1993).

8 Also see *El Mercurio*, 11 December, D19, 1994.

9 Pipeline is a protection for products 'whose patent applications are being evaluated by the national patent office (which can take several years), products that are in the development stage, and products that are not yet sold in countries that are updating their intellectual property law' (Hufbauer and Schott, 1993: 88).

10 As Jordan put it: Chile has made great strides over the last several years, reforming its government, its economy, and its trade policies. They should be rewarded with NAFTA accession, but only if they are willing to comply fully with NAFTA's requirements. Their decision to offer pharmaceutical patent protection reinforced their commitment to enter into a free trade agreement with the United States but their efforts were incomplete. Chile must now be willing to take the final step: offer the full patent protection afforded by NAFTA. This includes a twenty-year pharmaceutical patent and pipeline protection.(1994: 379)

11 See statement in *Diario Estrategia*, 16 January, pp 15–66, 1995.

12 See statement in *El Mercurio*, 10 December, C2, 1994.

13 See statement in *El Mercurio*, 13 December, B1, 1994.

14 See statement in *Diario Estrategia*, 14 December, page 7, 1994.

15 See public statements of the main business association (Confederación de la Producción y el Comercio, CPC), *Estrategia*, 6 December, 2000, p. 6.

16 Data obtained from UNCTAD Stat, by technological content (SITC) under Lall classification.

17 Data obtained from World Development Indicators.

Part IV

The continuing imperialism of free trade

Overview

In this final part we pay attention to the role of finance in pressing informal imperialism. In chapter 10 Higgins, Morino and Iyer bring to bear their professional expertise in tracing funds through tax havens. In doing so, they demonstrate the ways in which funds are funnelled and obscured in order that financial elites can minimise their tax payments. Such arrangements are underpinned by trade-offs and deals between economic and political elites. Higgins *et al.* demonstrate how this plays out at the individual level. Mark Dearn, in chapter 11, demonstrates how economic and political elites have collectively constructed a legal infrastructure that forces peripheral economies to conform to EU standards in order to trade within the zone. While such legal requirements privilege the EU, even if peripheral countries wish to resist they are too greatly dependent upon the EU market to do so. Through force of economic power, the EU therefore continues to press the imperialism of free trade which Gallagher and Robinson analysed in their thesis.

Imperialism, dirty money centres and the financial elite

Building upon their professional expertise, Matthew Higgins, Veronica Morino and Nigel Iyer investigate the ways in which finance capital makes use of 'tax havens', which they characterise as dirty money centres (DMCs), to hide its profits away from various forms of taxation on profits. They examine how systems are in place in DMCs that allow for money to be moved through their banking systems whilst obscuring the money's ownership. Such arrangements are possible in part due to the growing size of financial capital in the global economy, which, by comparison to industrial capital, can easily be moved from jurisdiction to jurisdiction. DMCs allow these transactions to take place for very modest fees and taxes, which benefit the exchequer of the DMC but also ties its policies on financial regulation and taxation to the wishes of investors of money in the DMC. Meanwhile, in metropolitan countries, states lose out on tax revenue from finance capital and so have to find income from elsewhere. However, Higgins, Morino and Iyer argue that this is not a failing of informal imperialism. Rather, it is the point, implicating political elites in the continued evasion of taxation and putting the responsibility of coming up with the missed income on a broader base of the taxpaying population.

Commissioning imperialism: EU trade deals under neoliberalism

We finish with Mark Dearn's examination of the European Union and its role in promoting informal imperialism. Dearn demonstrates that EU officials have on occasion even gone so far as to characterise the global economic reach of the European Union as being an empire without imperialism, which we must surely recognise as a description of informal imperialism. EU trade agreements worldwide are designed, Dearn argues, to help the European Union maintain its global position, particularly as it is threatened by the economic rise of China. By establishing a series of international trade agreements that puts access to markets in the realm of the law, rather than of politics, the European Union has constructed systems that remove political will from the operation of peripheral states' economies. Rather, EU policies focussed around liberal trading agreements, and resembling much of the architecture of the Washington Consensus, provide EU capital with access to peripheral markets and rights to legal action against states that attempt to protect their domestic industries through protectionism. If countries wish to trade with the European Union, then they have little option but to follow the legal frameworks which the EU establishes. The EU market is for many states too significant to be disinvested from.

10 Imperialism, dirty money centres and the financial elite

Matthew Higgins, Veronica Morino and Nigel Iyer

Introduction

In the 1990s, a child of Second World War child refugees, Maria Bjornson, who had grown up in poverty, became famous as Andrew Lloyd Webber's main scenographer and costume designer for the box office hit musical *Phantom of the Opera*. Unlike many rags-to-riches stories, Maria displayed little interest in the massive royalty stream. Instead she dispersed most of her earnings to charities for underprivileged children, arts funds and carers trusts helping the infirm, like her own mother. As Maria was still stateless at the time, she was able, with the help of someone connected to her estranged Norwegian father, to allow all the international royalties from *Phantom* to accumulate in a company in Guernsey. She gave specific instructions that money should be donated to a list of charities she cared for and that any left over was to be given to the Red Cross to help other refugees, just as she and her mother had been.

Maria died unexpectedly in 2002, aged 53, after only a fraction of the money had been distributed to charity. The funds were temporarily frozen, and it was at this point that the fighting began over who was entitled to the hundreds of millions of dollars controlled by the Guernsey trust company and administered by an Anglo-Canadian fund management company (Guernsey Law Reports, 2010). In spite of the efforts of many people to get the money out, some with more generous motives than others, one and a half decades later, the money still languishes in the Guernsey-UK-Canada fund. The president of Norway in the years 2012–2017, who was the friend (and, by the by, her fourth cousin) of Maria who set the company up, has tried repeatedly (arguably with some controversial but still altruistic motives) to get some of the money released (Gallagher, 2015). Even someone with this level of political clout has been met with a wall of legal bureaucracy. The millions earnt legally, placed legally into a Guernsey company, and legally earmarked for charity are in effect 'unmovable'.

Maria's story illustrates how a powerful shadow world of financial and legal organisations impinge on personal arrangements and can envelop individuals and groups without their full knowledge or will. The purpose of the chapter is to outline how imperialism and economic policy continue to work together in the interests of the financial elite through the use of dirty money centres (DMCs), at the expense of wider society. We do so by showcasing real cases and examples (some of which have been anonymised for privacy and legal reasons) which demonstrate how this is achieved in practice, why it must be challenged and how this might be done. Our approach draws upon the skills of two practitioners, Nigel Iyer and Veronica Morino, who over the past 20 years have had the privilege of helping individuals and organisations (both public, listed and private companies) investigate major corporate fraud and corruption, as well as detecting the early warning indicators of wrongdoings and unethical business behaviour. This work has included following money flows in and out of organisations and tracing the ultimate beneficiary owners of complex financial set-ups, which often involved so called 'tax havens' (Shaxon, 2011), or 'dirty money centres' as we are going to call them.

Imperialism and financial elites

At Nelson's Dockyard on the southern coast of Antigua, the egregious face of imperialism is presented for tourists. Despite the presence of covered market stalls selling trinkets and tat to visitors who seek the shade of the market's canopy, this sprawling UNESCO World Heritage site gives only a half-hearted Caribbean nod to Bryman's (2004) 'Disneyization'. The focus on slavery, the control of colonial trade through the Navigation Acts and Horatio Nelson's requited dislike of the people and the place hold the remnants of the sprawling historical buildings together. As the UNESCO descriptor acknowledges, the 'Antigua Naval Dockyard and Related Archaeological Sites' are more than a grouping of naval buildings; they exemplify the human values, relations and technology which enabled the 'development of the British Empire, trade and industrialization' (UNESCO, 2016).

Following the successful re-election of the Antigua Labour Party in 1976, led by former trade unionist Vere C. Bird, Antigua (and Barbuda) achieved independence from the British on 1 November 1981. This marked the end of over 300 years of British colonial rule, incorporating a period that is viewed as the 'Age of Imperialism' (Hodge, 2008), usually characterised by the industrialising countries seeking influence or control over territory beyond their metropolitan area (though we have seen otherwise throughout this volume, particularly in Part I). In the popular imagination, this is the unsavoury but arguably more comfortable face of imperialism. It is an imperialism that is associated with a particular time and place. It is an imperialism located in the past and with particular types of activity. We challenge such a comfortable position and argue that although the frigates of Nelson's day may be resigned to the history books or heritage parks, imperialism is not a historical but a contemporary policy, the beneficiaries of which are quite likely to be residents or visitors in the luxury marinas that surround Nelson's Dockyard. To do this we explore how the processes of innovation and technology which were central to the colonial expansion of the eighteenth century remain important in the commercial and trade relations of contemporary capitalism and how the old militarised forts of Nelson have been replaced by DMCs.

Contrary to traditional Marxist-Leninist perspectives on imperialism, we do not see it as a developmental stage or epoch of capitalist development. Instead, drawing upon Gallagher and Robinson (1953) and Grocott and Grady (2014), we approach imperialism as part of strategic economic relations embedded within capitalism. This provides an approach to the study of imperialism which moves the debate away from a narrow focus on state, empire and land grabbing and looks instead at the interconnection between politics and commerce. Gallagher and Robinson dispute the reliance on territorial occupation as a method to understand imperialism, arguing instead that imperialism need not be solely defined through formal land acquisition and direct rule of its occupants. Territorial occupation was a costly, disruptive and frequently violent means of achieving control, while imperialism can instead be pursued efficiently by 'informal means if possible, or by formal annexations when necessary' (Gallagher and Robinson, 1953: 3). In practice, this involved co-opting local groups, usually through commerce, as the preferred method of exerting control and resorting to more aggressive territorial gains where this failed. One of the key insights from Gallagher and Robinson is that formal and informal imperialism are degrees of difference within political, strategic and commercial relationships. This provides the possibility for centre and periphery relationships to shift between formal and informal imperialism over time, depending on the strength and cohesion of the states and the tensions in the relationship.

To understand the connections between state and financial elite, we need first to introduce the legal concept of a 'trust' before outlining their mutual interests. A trust is a tripartite relationship through which one party (the trustor), transfers property to a second party (the trustee) for the benefit of a third party (the beneficiary). Although it is a tri-partite arrangement, only two entities need to be involved, allowing one party to occupy two positions. Authors such as Avini (1996) outline how the origins of the idea of trust in English law date back to the twelfth century, being a means for the landed elite to protect their property and interests when it was at risk of seizure or when property was not permitted due to religious principles. The Crusades exposed the pilgrims to the Islamic *Waqf*, which was imported back to England to help landed elites protect their assets and interests through trusted third parties. These third parties would manage the interests of the absentee owner. Upon return, many of those who had left their property in trust found that they were unable to reclaim their rights due to existing common law, requiring the crusader to lobby the king to reinstate their rights and giving rise to the idea of equity.

Industrialisation, which figured within the new imperialism of the late eighteenth and nineteenth centuries, has been presented as the displacement of the aristocracy through the growth of a new mercantile financial class and their companies. The emergent nation states shared common interests with industrialists and the financial elites who sought to secure and protect ownership or access to overseas land, markets and trade (Cain and Hopkins, 1987). The financial elite – those merchants, bankers and stockbrokers with their interconnecting directorships (Cassis, 1991) – have lobbied to ensure economic policies and ideologies are conducive to defend and advance their interests. For Harvey (2005) these policies and ideologies have been labelled as neoliberal, with the state responsible for providing an institutional framework that enables, supports and protects market systems within and through which individual human endeavour can be exercised via the accumulation and transfer of private property rights. Crouch (2009) suggests that the neoliberal ideological drive, dominant post 1970, has been supported by overlapping and differing forms of socio-economic models, which have provided an essential lifeline for the neoliberal agenda.

At the core of Crouch's argument is that governments are fearful of the flow of capital that globalisation provides and the consequences on national economies and its citizens should private investment move to new locations. To offset this and to promote market stability, an alignment of democracy, market entrepreneurship and economic models has occurred. The crisis in Keynesianism in the 1970s saw nation states unable to maintain the spending required for a stable economic order, and so governments looked to private capital to take its place. In the United Kingdom and the United States in particular, growth has been possible through the rise of a consumer society and growth in private ownership facilitated through unsecured credit, backed up by the development of service economies, a model Crouch (2009: 390) labels 'privatised Keynesianism'.

Privatised Keynesianism was only possible through ever-increasing private expenditure, and this necessitated the easy availability of unsecured credit. Innovations in the increasingly unregulated financial sectors provided for a ready supply of funds, and access to further funds was also possible through creative management of debt offered by finance houses which traded in risk. The bundling of high- and low-risk debts into derivatives and futures enabled a confidence trick whereby risk was effectively shared across a wide body of investors with minimal transparency about the true nature of the risks involved.

The trading of new debt vehicles opened up new and unregulated markets, furthering profit-making capacity and power (Crouch, 2009). The credit made available through these arrangements fuelled the consumer society, which in turn led to benefits for service providers and goods suppliers. The financial elite needed the various arrangements to enable them to accrue wealth obscured from the nation states which became so dependent on them. These profits accrue from access to raw materials and through the sale of consumer- or state-owned assets. To achieve these goals, tax havens, or dirty money centres play a key and defining role.

Dirty money centres

The precise origins of the tax haven are unclear (Dharmapala, 2008). Raposo and Mourão (2013) suggest that the first instances of tax-free zones can be found in the eastern Mediterranean on the island of Delos around 166 BC. The island's geographical position enabled it to become a trading centre for wheat and spices. In the Middle Ages, 'free towns' adopted a similar principle of releasing traders and buyers from the burden of custom duties and taxation. In the 1920s, countries such as Switzerland and Luxembourg allowed foreigners to discretely deposit capital and, therefore, escape taxation in their own country. Since the 1980s, owing to the liberalisation and deregulation of global financial markets, tax havens have grown exponentially (Chavagneux and Palan, 2007: 28). Raposo and Mourão (2013) assemble the various forms of tax havens into four main groups: historically Western possessions; sovereign nations; countries controlled by cartels; and emerging states. The rationales for labelling jurisdictions as tax havens also vary. Whilst some areas pursue a policy of tax competition to attract inward investment, others accrue cash deposits in local banks for financial security and stability. Some others instead seek overseas investment to fund their financial systems or infrastructure investment. There are of course also those jurisdictions where the tax haven label is used to describe money laundering or political rent-seeking.

For years, commentators have used the phrase 'tax havens' (e.g. Palan et al., 2009) to describe the more advanced and complex forms of tax evasion. This often conjures up images of tropical locations which exist out of the line of sight of tax officials. This label is now arguably quite outdated, because a tax haven is much more than just a hiding place from the tax 'authorities'. Even the name 'offshore' is inappropriate, with many of these 'hiding places' being located very much 'onshore' (Drucker, 2016). Quite possibly, the problem with a name is that it always has associations. So even the term we have chosen to use in this chapter, 'dirty money centres', will soon be under fire for not being descriptive enough.

A DMC, as we define it, is a place where money (or similar assets) can be hidden. But it is not just that it is hidden out of view and inaccessible to all. The money and assets are connected to their rightful owner in a way that is usually legal, but it is virtually impossible to trace who the owner is. Whilst hiding money from the tax authorities may be one objective of these schemes, the key is having a myriad of companies, complex ownership structures and, in the end, money which one can control, move around, use and collect away from the prying eyes of others. Anonymity is key; it is crucial to fraud, corruption and building up and using wealth in subtle ways.

In its simplest form, a DMC is a combination of a safe deposit box and legal privilege. For example, John Doe needs to hide cash and jewellery. A safe deposit firm offers the service, and this firm can be based anywhere in the world. John Doe asks his lawyer (A. Smithee) to open a safe deposit box in A. Smithee's name but with the ultimate owner and beneficiary being John Doe. All instructions and conversations between lawyer and client are confidential and subject to attorney-client privilege, and so through this combination of confidentiality and privilege, A. Smithee cannot be subpoenaed to give evidence in court. The identity of John Doe, the beneficiary, remains private. Other arrangements which are in essence simply progressive iterations of the above include personal bank accounts in a country which permits numbered accounts (e.g. Switzerland) or nominee directors and shareholders who lend their name to a company but which, through a lawyer and client privilege, afford distance between owners and nominees. Complex combinations of numbered accounts, holding companies and nominee directors provide a web of hidden ownership. Although the focus is often on former colonial territories, in reality, far from the likes of Panama, Bermuda and the British Virgin Islands, DMCs exist almost everywhere.

The investigative process common to all is the need to target and track the transactions and analyse the money flows in and out of organisations. By analysing these payments and receipts in conjunction with the registered information about the suppliers and customers which are involved, it is possible to identify shell companies (i.e. companies which have hidden ownership and are possibly just a front) and those financial relationships which indicate that the organisation is actually involved with a DMC. Fraud investigators usually refer to this approach as 'following the money' (Benston et al., 2003).

In the past, DMCs tended to stick out like a sore thumb. They could be as obvious as a company headquartered in the British Virgin Islands, the Cayman Islands or Nevis with clearly no real business address other than a law firm or incorporation agent. Examination of an invoice from the supplier, or a remittance advice, combined with a check online using open-source directories would have revealed, relatively quickly, that the company in question was simply a 'front'. Following the collapse of major corporations through fraud allegations and the press coverage associated with the Panama and Paradise papers, ever more regulations and laws are being drafted and implemented to tackle this issue. This is however a highly innovative area of activity and DMC-related entities are becoming better and better at disguising themselves to look like real companies. This is of course the downside; but at the same time it appears that with improvements in technology, data availability and complex analytical tools, the number of 'footprints' (albeit smaller footprints) are increasing.

The key to detecting harmful business relationships with shell companies and dirty money lies not just in the obvious geographical destinations, of which many still exist, but also in identifying typical patterns associated with how these entities operate today. Given that one has access to an organisation's financial data and money flows, in and out, one could, for instance, undertake a series of reviews to ascertain the likely activity. For example, a typical clue that you have found a DMC is where a constant bank account is linked to regular name changes. Often by identifying supplier or customer bank accounts that are attached to more than one major supplier or customer and combining this with some basic background checks into who these suppliers and customers are, it is possible to flush out potentially criminal organisations which one was unaware one had dealings with. Often, the fact that the supplier or customer domicile is in one jurisdiction and the bank account is in another provides quite a big clue.

A dependent and exclusive relationship between supplier and provider is often another means of establishing if a DMC is involved. The combination of large and regular payments (often round numbers and sometimes in a currency not commensurate with the company's domicile) to a company or person where the so-called 'supplier's own reference number' (i.e. its invoice number) is sequential can often indicate a dependent relationship, and in many cases, also a fraudulent one. In particular, should it be a fraudulent relationship, then the people behind the supplier (which could also be an agent or consultant) would have taken precautionary measures to conceal their identity by building in layers of ownership, in many cases involving one or more DMCs and shell companies. Following the money to its ultimate destination is likely to involve some research into the ownership 'tree', but it is usually worth it (at least in terms of identifying if a DMC is involved).

Tracing the money flows often requires identifying collaborating third parties; for instance, where a credit note is 'paid elsewhere'. One much-used scheme involves identifying sales to third parties on which customers could receive volume discounts or rebates. Should some form of return credit note be issued and the customer wishes that money to be paid 'off book' or to them personally in some form (preferably tax-free too), then the customer will nominate a company and bank account to where this is paid. The supplying company would acquiesce by establishing in its accounts receivable ledgers some form of customer which only received credit notes, thereby registering the name of this company (which, to avoid suspicion, could be similar to the original customer name) but registering it 'elsewhere'. Scratching the surface of this company and its footprint often reveals a hidden DMC.

Finally, investigations often need to look for disguised ownership and hidden (off book) subsidiaries. Shell companies involving DMCs are also detectable in investments, corporate restructuring or joint ventures, possibly to hide ownership, possibly to create a chain whereby prices can be increased or maybe to disguise some other form of criminal behaviour. In many such examples, the footprint can exhibit itself in the form of some minor association with a DMC, such as a payment to a front company or an invoice for fees paid to an offshore incorporation agent or law firm which specialises in establishing (legally, of course, from their perspective) this sort of hidden ownership structure. Often the clue to detecting this sort of major fraud lies in the small details.

Finding dealings with the DMCs has in one way become harder as they are now less obvious. At the same time, because the 'black economy' is growing all the time and because better-quality information is recorded about transactions and open-source information is more easily available, the detection of these relationships has also become easier.

Morality not legality

The release of the Panama Papers in 2016 and the Paradise Papers in 2017 was accompanied by huge media interest. The publication of the papers by an anonymous whistle-blower usurped attorney-client privilege and cast some light on the financial arrangements of individuals and companies and the complex structures used to disguise ownership of assets. The media's reporting was at pains to explain that the vehicles through which this was possible are not illegal. Their focus was, rather, on the purpose these legal vehicles were serving and why those exposed felt the need to hide their identity through such complex vehicles. Moreover, although the Panama and Paradise papers provided reporters with material which could point to individuals, groups and organisations and specific goods or sums of money, these represented only a fraction of a wider problem, especially considering that fraudulent behaviour could not be ascertained.

The concern is that the anonymity afforded by the DMC helps unscrupulous individuals to hide the financial benefits of criminal activities. The issue is not so much what they are; rather, it is what they permit. Examples of 'possible' uses of DMCs include hiding proceeds from criminal activities, embezzlement, bribery and fake bribery, payment of secret bonuses to the 'already wealthy', hiding ownership interests and disguising ownership structures, avoiding taxation, payment of illegal wages, financing of terrorist activities or assassinations, and the laundering of the proceeds of illegal activities.

Although the focus with DMCs is frequently on their deliberate use by individuals or companies for nefarious or criminal reasons, the highly secretive network of organisations which provide the basis for DMCs creates a financial infrastructure which is difficult to detect or evade. Anyone, including the wholly innocent, can get caught up with DMCs without realising it (like we read in the illustrative story with which we opened this chapter). Involvement with DMCs can take multiple forms, ranging from simply buying and paying for goods where the supplier is hiding behind a DMC to receiving money from a customer where the origins of the money are a DMC. Organisations can find themselves involved in a joint venture with partners who hide their identity behind a DMC, and pension funds can invest unwittingly in a DMC-controlled company. The power and spread of DMCs grows with each inadvertent transaction.

Narratives and colonial ties

Postcolonial studies have extensively documented how empires played upon the distance between the domestic and the foreign, with the tension between the exotic and the civilising mission providing fertile space for narratives which connect the colonised with trickery, scams and fraud (Yee, 2016). In serving the interests of the financial elite, DMCs also help to maintain these narratives surrounding countries and peoples previously subjected to colonial power. Despite DMCs being prevalent around the world and being used by a myriad of individuals and companies, the focus on former colonies, especially those in the Caribbean and Africa, portrays those countries as less developed or less 'ethical'. In some instances, the financial elite in the former colonial country have benefited. For example, after emerging from years of civil war Angola opened its potentially massive offshore oil reserves. Deepwater drilling was appealing to the Norwegian oil industry, not only because they could provide valuable support to the fledgling Angolan state-owned oil industry but also because the Norwegian oil companies were keen to expand their horizons from domestic to international, and Angola presented them with a perfect opportunity (OECD/IIEA, 2006).

One of the early transactions was the purchase of a drilling license for a block of sea off the Angolan coast called Block 34. At the time, there was a lot of controversy around how these licenses were obtained because, unlike the more developed countries, the Angolan government levied a flat fee (which they called a 'signature bonus') for exploration licenses, promising that the money would be channelled into the reconstruction and redevelopment of the Angolan economy. The Norwegians, relying on external bodies and NGOs to monitor how the money was used, paid US$58 million directly into a bank account owned ostensibly by the Angolan oil company Sonangol, but in Jersey, not Angola.

It has since then been established in reports by the International Monetary Fund (Reuters, 2012; International Monetary Fund, 2015), with hindsight, that many other Western oil companies have completed similar transactions with Sonangol and very little of this money ever reached the Angolan people; instead, it has been channelled via DMCs, such as the one in the example above, to the ruling elite of Angola. Arguably, the signature bonuses have also been very profitable for the Western oil companies which are now operating widely in Angola with even more sophisticated systems of bribery and money flows in place, also involving Angola's old colonialist owners, Portugal.

Cases where Western companies have exploited the tainted image of former colonial countries rarely surface. In one example, an international industrial company made it their goal to invest in building much-needed factories in Nigeria and Ghana. It was suggested to the board that the best way to do this was to pay out commissions to certain key persons in those countries via a system of accounts in Luxemburg, Bermuda, the Isle of Man, etc. It was generally accepted at the time that this was in fact the only way of doing this business. What was not known was that most of the commissions, instead of ending up in the hands of the influential Africans who were supposed to receive them, were channelled back to some of the company's own management.

In one instance where our investigators followed the money, it had travelled from the industrial company's head office to Luxemburg to an Isle of Man company which was controlled by a member of the management team who distributed the funds to his people. To explain at the company's board level why this investment had not been successful, it was reported that the African leaders had not fulfilled their promises after receiving the commissions. These accusations were refuted widely in Ghana and Nigeria and have been the centre of a lot of media attention. Former Ghanaian president Gerry Rawlings even went on record to say that he had not received any bribes relating to these contracts. But because Africa's credibility in terms of preventing corruption was so low, the African response was largely ignored in the West.

Reframing DMCs

Given the relentless exposure in the media, examples of opposition to DMCs are not difficult to find (Garside, 2017). There is a widespread sense of repugnance at the continuing persistence of DMCs in the global economy and acknowledgement by leading bodies that greater transparency is required. Despite this, leaders of nation states appear unable or unwilling to act on the presence of DMCs. The complicity of the state is of course not a new issue – earlier parallels to piracy (Parker, 2009) could be made here – however, this may overlook the difference in the scale, constituency and reach of DMCs in contemporary global capitalism. Perhaps we need to frame the discussion of DMCs within a broader framework of power and inter-organisational relationships, or to show DMCs for what they are – a system of obfuscation serving the financial elite.

In his thesis on 'risk society', Beck (1992) outlines that the impact of these systems of obfuscations are international in scale and constitute a significant threat to human and environmental well-being. Most of these processes of movement and transformation are concealed from the end user in what has become a complicit deceit which, in itself, is essential for the efficient running of a consumer society. When significant problems in the systems are publicly exposed, as offered by the Panama and Paradise papers, this deceit struggles to continue functioning and the complex nature of contemporary financial systems is subjected to a critical gaze. The response is too frequently to impose even more rules and regulations. For example, after the Panama Papers came out in 2016, companies pressured by their governments felt that they had to show, on paper at least, that they were doing something. In one instance a company was trading oil with another company in London, or rather they thought it was in London until someone pointed out that the company they paid money to was actually in the Cayman Islands. However, to avoid embarrassment, the managing director instructed his people to gather sufficient documentation (some of it from the oil trader itself) and information from other sources such as the trader's new website, which contained an ethics and whistle-blower policy, to satisfy the management and board that this was, at least on paper, a *bona fide* partner with which to do business.

However, new rules and pressure to disclose ownership information simply drives more innovation within the DMC industry and forces the financial criminals to add more layers of image and 'gloss' as well as clean paper trails. For example, a criminal organisation reinvented itself by setting up its head office in an EU country, a fully fledged company with an owner with a clean record. The company even won a business prize for sustainable growth and its contribution to the economy of the region. All of this was of course a front to satisfy the authorities that the company was *bona fide*, but the true owners, with strong criminal connections, had simply built in enough firewalls, including an almost impossibly complex ownership structure, to either satisfy or deter the most ardent of regulators.

As another way of ensuring that everything looked clean, one middleman set up his company in London, but it was registered in the Falkland Islands and ostensibly buying from the United States and selling to none other than Cuba, breaching the trade sanctions which were in place but earning a very large commission at the same time. Hiding in open space and using the United

Kingdom and the Falklands as a 'flag of convenience' is sometimes the best idea. Who would have thought that Cuba, with Argentine-born 'poster-boy' Ernesto 'Che' Guevara, would purchase from the Malvinas, the place British imperialists renamed 'the Falklands'.

Perhaps rather than legislating to seek to stop the behaviour, a more productive approach may be to re-examine how managers construct their realities and manage the 'known' and 'unknown' parties to transactions in the system. For Bauman (1989), the manner in which individuals engage with the 'other' party and the responsibility that comes with this engagement is a site of moral potential. Within the financial system of obfuscation, this encourages us to reflect upon not only those who are party to the transaction but also those who remain hidden, invisible or silent. In the past, it was enough to be able to say that one did not know about something. Today chief executives cannot do that so easily because new laws make them responsible all the same.

Not knowing the facts due to the hidden nature of fraud is more likely than not being familiar with norms and values. When the truth is hidden, individuals can face situations which they find difficult to interpret and judge. According to Latané and Darley (1968), when reality is confusing, individuals have the tendency to postpone reactions, look around for guidance and refer to the behaviour of others. This, together with the tendency to be part of a group and follow the flow (Asch, 1956), could lead to the socio-psychological phenomenon of 'diffusion of responsibility' (Latané and Darley, 1968), which can cause individuals and groups to lose the ability to distinguish between normal and deviant behaviour. Getting the business done is often more of an imperative. In one case, our investigators met one particular 'fixer' (or Mr G.) who had a multitude of shell companies with many DMC faces. Everyone dealt with him and paid his finder's fees … to wherever he demanded they be paid. That was the key to doing business in his country. Rather than taking sole responsibility, a number of chief executives, who sat on each other's boards, decided to collectively ratify Mr G. as a way of giving credence that he was in fact an 'OK guy'.

Perhaps this should not surprise us. Individuals within organisations are bombarded with a multitude of pressures to perform and an ever-increasing intensity of images and actions of others (Gergen, 1991). The result, as neatly encapsulated by Jon Kelly (2017) in his account of the growth of the Isle of Man's stealth financial industry, is 'apathy' amongst employees. The challenge for leadership and managers is to suspend the conventional managerial norms and take a broader perspective. As Cooren (2000: 221) puts it,

> '[t]he art of management … is about seeing employees not only as 'cogs in a machine' … but as multidimensional creatures who cannot be reduced to the role that has been anticipated by organisational schemas'.

Adopting such an approach and acknowledging the fluidity and contextual nature of our relationships may appear a daunting challenge. This requires us to rethink the way we approach accounting and financial systems. Above all, it should discourage us from presenting devices which speak of moral certainties, such as anti-money laundering compliance guidelines, without considering the equivalence within the lived experience. This involves a shift in approach. It is a move from presenting ethics as an administrative act – a concern with compliance and the selection of the right rule for the situation – to a less certain ethics where managers are seen to possess the freedom to carve out space for autonomous consideration of ethical matters. Although the former may be deemed as disempowering for managers by denying their ethical competence, the latter does at least open a space for potential freedoms to be realised and participation to occur, even if it may not necessarily lead to the outcomes desired.

Conclusions

Peter Preston (2011), writing in *The Guardian*, opens his review of Shaxon's (2011) book on international finance and fraud with the following despairing words:

> a chronicle of capitalism's frailty and foulness that digs far beyond its tax haven title and indicts the system that renders such crookedness not merely possible, but entirely predictable. It's not the banks or the hedge funds or the tame solicitors. It's the politicians as well, our politicians. It's not just the Cayman Islanders or the Swiss or the Panamanians. It's London and Washington, the OECD and the World Bank. It's the whole damned thing.

Today, in light of the release of the Panama and Paradise papers, the lid on Pandora's box has been prised further open, and we might well ask of Preston's well-being.

In this chapter, we have taken a step back from the immediate emotional response that the exposure to DMCs brings and have sought to frame the issues within a broader discussion of informal imperialism and capitalism. In doing this, we have presented the historical complicity between financial and political elites and highlighted how a network of obfuscation within financial systems has developed. This network benefits the ruling class at the expense of national reputations and broader social well-being. Through practitioner-derived case studies, we have outlined how attempts at utilising regulations and compliance have simply forced parties within this financial system to adopt ever more inventive and innovative ways of avoiding exposure.

We may recall, however, that at the bottom of Pandora's box one finds Elpsis (or hope). Fraud and corruption needs to be challenged not simply through compliance but through rendering it visible within financial systems and focusing on building individual capability and responsibility within organisations. To do this requires being able to educate individuals about the ever-present danger of fraud and corruption and, crucially, to equip them with the knowledge and confidence to spot and tackle the threats when they appear.

Let us conclude with a final uplifting example. A Western multibillion-dollar energy company discovered it had been purchasing raw materials, worth over US

$100 million, for its power plants from a Cyprus trading company which was in effect set up and controlled by a Russian crime organisation. The virtually bullet-proof ownership structure involved countries like Cyprus, Austria, the British Virgin Islands, Luxemburg, the United Kingdom, Ireland, Switzerland, Estonia and Canada. An in-depth investigation proved beyond all doubt that this was in fact the case, despite the fact that the conglomerate was making significant marketing attempts to show that it were a real company. The managers decided to end 14 years of being supplied by this Russian-crime-owned supplier of raw materials. They did not pull out because some law told them to do so. In fact, the Russian-Cypriot trading company would have fulfilled all the legal and compliance boxes for legitimacy, having today a near-transparent structure, pro forma certificates for the raw materials, a website which contained all the requisite code of conduct documents and ethics policies, even including a whistle-blower policy, and positive media coverage (which they had planted). The Western energy company pulled out of the deal and took the financial hit because they felt it was the right thing to do.

11 Commissioning imperialism

EU trade deals under neoliberalism

Mark Dearn

José Manual Barroso explained his idea of the European Union (EU) to journalists as the Lisbon Treaty negotiations neared completion. His remarks provoked disquiet in EU states uneasy about plans for expanded powers for the EU institutions. A European Commission spokesman clarified Barroso's comments, explaining that 'no one needs to have imperial nightmares' (quoted in Waterfield, 2007). But for periphery states of the Global South negotiating trade deals with the bloc, which they know will destroy nascent industrialisation, European 'imperial nightmares' are the norm. According to Barroso, 'What we have is the first non-imperial empire' (ibid.).

Seen through the lens of Gallagher and Robinson (1953), there is no doubt that the mechanism of 'informal imperialism' is at the heart of the EU's economic expansion. The ambit of the EU's imperialist ambitions has long been visible through its role, alongside Japan and the United States, in a triad (Amin, 2001) controlling the institutions of global neoliberal economic governance, and also through its global web of 'free trade' and investment agreements engineered to incorporate periphery state markets into the expanding EU economic frontier on its terms, resulting in reproduced underdevelopment. The EU trade agenda thus reflects a continuity of purpose much like nineteenth-century British free trade imperialism. And while much has changed, much remains the same.

Then, as now, informal imperialism operated to the same end: as an intrinsic mechanism of capitalism which is 'a sufficient political function of the process of integrating new regions into the expanding economy' (Gallagher and Robinson, 1953: 4). Thus, dominant state – 'metropole' – paramountcy is upheld 'by informal means if possible, or by formal annexations when necessary' (ibid.: 3–5). Then, as now, the 'spatial fix' of capital's geographical expansion is the only viable way to avoid devaluations of capital while maintaining metropole class privileges amidst crises of accumulation (Harvey, 2004). And under neoliberalism, as under liberalism, informal imperialism maintains hegemony through controlling market expansion, the ceaseless extraction of natural resources and the super-exploitation of labour in the periphery (Amin, 2001).

But in marked difference to the nineteenth century, corporations became dominant transnational actors under a US 'autocentric' model which internalised the world market within their organisational domains (Arrighi, 2010: 290).

Financiers are dominant over industrialists, their power increasing as markets are prised open and state regulation is prohibited. Corporations now represent 69 of the world's 100 biggest economies (Global Justice Now, 2017). Their transnational interests are duly reflected in the construction of neoliberal trade policy which is moving beyond a 'North-South' split. In a fundamental challenge to state sovereignty, 200 years after British free trade imperialism mandated extraterritoriality for metropole traders in periphery states, corporations are granted a right to private extraterritorial arbitration. Known as 'investor-state dispute settlement' (ISDS), this arbitration mechanism challenges sovereign acts that harm investment without actually necessitating a relationship with a state, a critical bridgehead in fulfilling the transnational corporate dream of 'absolute non-territoriality' (Arrighi, 2010: 83).

Neoliberal free trade imperialism is still 'kicking away the ladder' (Chang, 2003) to undermine 'protectionist policies that are necessary to first build up a dynamic and competitive economy' (Kiely, 2010: 188), a clearly visible schema in EU relations with the poorest periphery states. But with 80% of world trade situated in the 'global value chains' of transnational corporations and trade in services accounting for more than 40% of global trade, neoliberal trade policy does this and much more besides. In order to meet the needs of the 'trade-investment-services-IP [intellectual property] nexus' (Baldwin, 2013: 24) that sustains transnational corporate trade, it reaches 'behind the border' to remove domestic regulations labelled as 'non-tariff barriers'; locks in the opening of markets, including privatising public services and capturing the commons; and prohibits preferential treatment for domestic industries or regulation of foreign capital. Neoliberal trade policy enforces corporate demands for the withdrawal of state intervention in the economy and for privatisation, deregulation and fully liberalised trade and investment regimes.

The EU, a widely proclaimed 'regulatory superpower' (Keleman, 2016; Webber, 2014; Lipton and Hakim, 2013), is today's paramount global power in the pursuit of neoliberal free trade imperialism. As, against all expectations, the United States steps back from global leadership of neoliberal free trade – rejecting the Trans-Pacific Partnership (TPP), calling for an opt-out from ISDS in the North American Free Trade Agreement (NAFTA) and disagreeing with G20 states over free trade and protectionism – the EU, led by the European Commission, takes its place. As the EU Trade Committee chair outlines, it should 'close the vacuum left by the United States that China would like to fill by itself' (Hoppe, 2017). The EU is the archetypal *constitutionally* neoliberal bloc. It currently leads the global reproduction of neoliberal free trade imperialism, discursively and in practice, against a backdrop of rising 'semi-periphery' powers; EU trade agreements are an imposed externalisation of its internal process of neoliberal constitutionalisation.

EU Economic Partnership Agreements (EPAs) with African, Caribbean and Pacific (ACP) states show the continuing efforts of the EU to enact informal imperialism in a context of '*hierarchical and centre-periphery structures*' (Sepos, 2013: 275), combining 'kicking away the ladder' – ensuring that the colonial pattern of periphery states exporting raw materials while importing manufactured goods continues – with a neoliberal trade and investment agenda.

During EPA negotiations, the Lisbon Treaty introduced constitutional neoliberalism to the EU bloc. The Transatlantic Trade and Investment Partnership (TTIP), which arrived at a critical point in the deepening of this process, establishes a global neoliberal trade template in line with this agenda and in place of failed multilateral efforts, revealing a transatlantic bloc no longer able to dominate (contra Serfati, 2015) the multilateral structures it created. Alongside the EU-Canada Comprehensive Economic and Trade Agreement (CETA) and ongoing efforts to initiate a 'Multilateral Investment Court', TTIP demonstrates the European Commission's self-described 'special responsibility' to ensure survival of the ISDS regime (European Commission, 2015b) and consolidate its role as the new neoliberal informal imperialism hegemon.

The EU: constitutional neoliberalism

After a 1970s crisis of accumulation, neoliberalism was established under US hegemony as a political project to revive capital accumulation and consolidate class power (Harvey, 2005: 19), with a critical role for financialisation; the increasing geographical mobility of capital; the successful coercion of periphery states to adopt neoliberalism; and the global diffusion and influence of neoliberal economic ideology (ibid.: 90–93). 'Regulated capitalism' became anathema to political-economic orthodoxy under political-economic restructuring in metropole and periphery countries, involving forcing open new markets, deregulating existing markets and fully empowering finance capital which had previously been held in check by the state.

Under the triad of the United States, the EU and Japan, in the 1986–1994 Uruguay round of trade talks under the General Agreement on Tariffs and Trade (GATT), corporations wrote provisions covering agriculture and intellectual property rights. The US financial sector heavily influenced the permanent opening of services markets under the GATT (Hilary, 2013), and the European Commission created the European Community Services Group of services exporters to lobby the round. Within the EU, the Commission began a push to control investment liberalisation and protection (Basedaw, 2016: 747–748).

The global neoliberal agenda reached its zenith with the 1995 creation of the World Trade Organization (WTO) to force open global goods and services markets and 'exact tribute' from the periphery (Harvey, 2005: 93). At the same time, metropolitan states sought to use the Organisation for Economic Co-operation and Development to secure a neoliberal trade and investment agenda under the 1995–1998 Multilateral Agreement on Investments, blocked by France after documents leaked to civil society groups. The subsequent failure to secure the same agenda at the WTO – known as the 'Singapore issues' – combined with continued breakdown in talks over metropolitan agricultural protectionism encouraged metropolitan states to look to bilateral and regional alternatives.

Since the 1970s, the Commission has been central to the EU's constitutional adoption of neoliberalism, pursuing a Hayekian internal liberalisation and integration-through-law agenda on a normative-political basis (Scharpf, 2010: 211). Indeed, it is the EU alone which constitutionalised 'end of history' delusions into its treaties, forestalling the ability of states to create socialist or even social-democratic economies within the EU (Guinan and Hanna, 2017: 18–19). The pursuit of this agenda was rarely opposed by member states, which justified liberalisation demands to national publics as being due to EU rules (Bickerton, 2016).

After an attempt to establish a formal EU constitution under the 2004 Treaty Establishing a Constitution for Europe was vetoed by French and Dutch referenda, the Treaty of Lisbon, signed in 2007 before entering into force in 2009, did the same under a different name. Lisbon consolidated the neoliberal shift of successive treaties and agendas – targeting deregulation, state aid for industries, increased privatisation and financialisation, and rules on budget deficits and public debt, among others – from 'embedded liberalism' to an 'embedded neoliberalism' (Bugaric, 2013) which cannot be unpicked without unanimous agreement from member states.

The Commission repeatedly sought the control over EU investment policy it gained under Lisbon, often opposed by states (Basedaw, 2016). However, *contra* Basedaw, while 'Commission entrepreneurship' was decisive to its victory, claims that EU business interests are not central to investment policymaking decisions are spurious. Commission advisory groups have long been dominated by transnational corporate lobbyists, from Jacques Delors's alliance with the European Roundtable of Industrialists, which had a central role in shaping 1980s neoliberal reforms through successive administrations (Corporate Europe Observatory, 2000). Trade Commissioner Leon Brittain worked with the US government and corporations to create the Transatlantic Business Dialogue and the European Services Forum, key lobby groups pushing for TTIP and EPAs respectively. As Brittain told EU chief executives, 'I am in your hands to listen to … your priorities for liberalisation' (quoted in Wesselius, 2003).

Commission collaboration with corporations is matched by a transnational capitalist class 'revolving door' between corporations and top jobs in the EU institutions (Corporate Europe Observatory, 2017; Hilary 2013), exemplified by Barroso's appointment as non-executive director of Goldman Sachs International after a decade as Commission president. The Commission shift towards 'reverse lobbying' (Woll, 2006) of corporations is matched by the number of Brussels lobbyists rising from hundreds to tens of thousands in the course of a few decades.

TTIP arrived at a critical juncture, when EU neoliberal constitutionalism was pre-eminent in ensuring politics could not override free market imperatives. The financial crisis spurred a resurgent ideological drive towards a disciplinary 'austerity' which increasingly removed member state autonomy over redistributive policies (Bugaric, 2013: 25–27), encapsulated by Jean-Claude Juncker's response to Syriza winning power in Greece in 2015: 'There can be no democratic choice against the European treaties' (quoted in Hewitt, 2015).

TTIP represents a fundamental expression of the EU externalisation of its internal process of removing politics from economics: as such, the contemporary EU is correctly understood as neoliberal and 'neoliberalising' due to the way in which it incorporates market economy principles into its various agreements with non-EU states (Nicol, 2010: 89). While nominally an agreement between the EU and the United States, TTIP's true agenda is establishing a global neoliberal template for EU informal imperialism, one it had been unable to achieve through multilateral structures or through drawn-out attempts to coerce periphery states in Africa, the Carribean and the Pacific, among others, to accept trade agreements mandating exports of raw materials and imports of manufactured goods while also going beyond WTO demands for liberalisation.

The EU in Africa: 'You must find a way to accept something'

When Henry Stanley secured treaties for the 'advancement of civilization and trade' with the Congo, resulting in formal annexation under the 1885 Berlin Conference, it was for the 'bounty' of one piece of manufactured cloth per month that the chiefs of Ngombi and Mafela gave up all sovereign rights to their territories 'for themselves and their heirs and successors for ever' (Stanley, 2013: 196).

Ensuring periphery dependence on commodity exports while accepting metropole-manufactured imports has always been a fulcrum of free trade imperialism. Dependence, and an inability to add value to production and diversify economies, continues today: a 2016 fall in commodity prices devastated poverty eradication hopes for African states facing the combination of weak productive bases and low export diversification and a resultant need for high imports, which led to debt accumulation and aid dependence (UNCTAD, 2016).

Yet most of today's wealthy countries used tariffs and subsidies, among other protectionist policies, to industrialise and diversify before adopting free trade. As King George I, enunciating Robert Walpole's 1721 policies, said: 'Nothing so much contributes to promote the public wellbeing as the exportation of manufactured goods and the importation of foreign raw materials' (quoted in Chang, 2007: 44). Although denied by the World Bank's *East Asian Miracle* report (1993), East and South East Asian states also adopted, to varying extents, forms of 'developmental states' in the twentieth century. During the 1960s and 1970s when import substitution policies held sway, periphery state growth rates were often more than double those during ensuing decades of neoliberal hegemony; for the very poorest states in sub-Saharan Africa, GDP dropped at a rate of 0.5% per year under neoliberalism (Chang, 2003: 129).

European Commissioner for Trade Cecilia Malmström took office in 2014 as European and African social movements marked ten years of campaigning against EPAs. EPAs were an outcome of the 2000 Cotonou Agreement's mandate to transition EU-ACP trade relations from non-reciprocal preferences granted to periphery states to WTO-aligned reciprocal relations. Four months before, West African heads of state initialled their regional EPA after negotiations spanning the terms of six previous trade commissioners. But six months later, Nigeria and the Gambia had failed to sign. Malmström visited Nigeria in 2017 to speak to an EU-Nigeria business forum, established under Trade Commissioner Peter Mandelson at the recommendation of a Commission negotiator (Corporate Europe Observatory, 2009). Nigeria had recently launched its Industrial Revolution Plan to diversify away from oil export dependency: it aimed to accelerate industrial growth through manufacturing and processing and to promote local patronage of 'Made in Nigeria' products. Correspondingly, Malmström's Lagos speech was entitled 'The EPA as a pathway to diversification'. And in a remarkable bastardisation, Malmström poached anti-colonial novelist Chinua Achebe's words to suggest imported EU goods and capital would make Nigeria 'whole' (Malmström, 2015: 4, 5):

> Imports – like foreign investment – also transmit ideas and innovation. … As the great Nigerian writer Chinua Achebe has written, 'Whatever you are is never enough; you must find a way to accept something – however small – from the other to make you whole'.

The plea failed. As a Nigerian negotiator explained, other states signed EPAs through the 'back door', unaware of the 'real dangers' (Babatunde and Alli, 2016). The president of the Manufacturers Association of Nigeria said the EPA would flood Nigeria with cheap EU products, leading to the destruction of what few industries were surviving in the region (ibid.). Nigeria's impact assessment predicted a 42% loss of total tariff revenue – when tariff revenues accounted for 39% of the country's non-oil revenue (Nwoke, 2008).

Before Cotonou, the Lomé Convention of 1975 – influenced by periphery state positions under 'New International Economic Order' proposals which sought a radical reappraisal of the international political-economic system – secured non-reciprocal market opening for African states. It marked a potential shift in EU relations from Kwamé Nkrumah's labelling of the 1957 Treaty of Rome as 'the advent of neo-colonialism in Africa' (quoted in Martin, 1982: 229). Neoliberal 'development' policy swiftly reversed this position: Cotonou required EPAs to incorporate WTO diktats on reciprocal market opening between regional trading partners – a position supported by the Commission in the 1990s despite objections from ACP states (Hurt et al., 2013: 72).

But EPAs became a Commission vehicle for enforcing deeper liberalisation than that agreed under the WTO. At the 2003 WTO Cancun meeting, three of four of the Singapore issues proposed by metropole states – competition policy, transparency in government procurement and national treatment for foreign investors – were dismissed by a coalition of periphery states, severely embarrassing the EU, which had led the drive for their inclusion (Hilary, 2013: 43). The Commission instead sought to include the 'issues' in EPAs, against the demands of African states (Christian Aid et al., 2006). But while Mandelson spoke of 'solidarity' with the ACP, claiming he had 'no European business leaders … demanding greater access to ACP markets' (Mandelson, 2004: 1, 3), subsequent correspondence with the European Services Forum lobby showed his desire to appease corporate interests (Cronin, 2013: 146).

In July 2016, a similar fate befell the East African EPA as Tanzania's foreign affairs secretary explained it would destroy local industries. Adding value to natural resources was a critical issue for Tanzania; for the EU, a net importer of fuel and non-ferrous metals and the world's biggest net importer of natural resources (Küblböck, 2013), raw materials and natural resources are also a paramount concern – one deepened by the increasing push by semi-periphery states, including China, Brazil and India, to secure resources.

Under the 2008 Raw Materials Initiative (European Commission, 2008), a central plank of the ongoing European imperialist drive for unabated resource transfer from periphery to metropole, the Commission targets trade-'distorting' government measures including 'export taxes and quotas … subsidies … and restrictive investment rules' that 'disadvantage' the EU. This was despite the Initiative recognising that periphery states pursue 'industrial strategies aimed at protecting their resource base' (ibid.). In 2010, the Commission nonetheless confirmed it would 'use current trade rules to the maximum' to achieve an 'undistorted supply of raw materials and energy' (European Commission, 2010).

This was a particular concern in the context of EPA negotiations, given that African states host 30% of global extractive resources while foreign investment in the sector has grown alongside an anticipated increase in metals production (Küblböck, 2013) and also considering the Commission's push to force ISDS provisions on African states, articulated in its 2015 strategy: 'Protecting investment will be fundamental as the next step to support growth on the continent' (European Commission, 2015b: 33). As an NGO report outlines, removing export restrictions and regulations on foreign investment would harm local industry, government revenues and environmental protection while boosting European companies, resulting in 'unprecedented access to developing country markets, notably natural resources, on the same or even better terms as local businesses' (Curtis, 2009: 8).

In August 2016, Tanzania introduced a ban – prohibited under the EPA but permitted under the WTO – on transporting mineral sands from gold mines for smelting outside the country. Expressing surprise that investors airlift mineral sands out of Tanzania, President John Magufuli said, 'They must now build processing plants right here in Tanzania to purify the mineral sands … because when they export the sands, the government loses some revenue' (quoted in Ibengwe and Malanga, 2016).

Two months before, the Commission had already prepared its response: sign by October 2016 or face the withdrawal of preferential access to EU markets (Kasirye, 2014; Seattle to Brussels Network, 2016). Soon after, the secretary general of the ACP group of states warned that refusal to sign could result in withdrawal of EU aid. In the latest of a series of attempts to force signing of the EPA, the Commission would coerce recalcitrant African states to be made 'whole'. But through the negotiation of TTIP, the EU and the United States planned new terms of trade which African states would either have to accept or face being unable to export to the bloc at all.

TTIP: setting a new template for free trade imperialism

Months after Barack Obama's 2013 announcement of TTIP, then Commissioner Karel De Gucht met Exxon Mobil. In a secret meeting revealed by an access to information request (Neslen, 2016b), the Commission made clear to Exxon its strategic vision for TTIP to 'set a precedent' enabling the world's biggest corporations to access and shape markets and regulations outside the transatlantic bloc. In particular, TTIP could set a crucial precedent for the inclusion of ISDS in subsequent agreements, including EPAs.

A Commission briefing paper for the meeting backed the Raw Materials Initiative aim of using trade rules to the maximum to secure resources:

> TTIP is perhaps more relevant as setting a precedent vis-à-vis third countries than governing trade and investment bilaterally. … [T]his third country element is in the interest of the energy sector. … [C]ompanies like Shell or Exxon Mobil face the same trade barriers when doing business in Africa, in Russia or in South America.(Quoted in Nelsen, 2016a)

In similar meetings, BP called for TTIP to address planned EU rules on tar sands – subsequently altered during CETA negotiations after heavy lobbying from corporations, Canada and the United Kingdom (Dearn, 2017) – Chevron supported the inclusion of ISDS as a 'deterrent' for governments, and BP hailed TTIP as '*the* opportunity to discuss energy and competitiveness in an international context' (Neslen, 2016a, emphasis added).

Through transnational capitalist class structures such as the Transatlantic Business Dialogue and the TTIP-specific Business Alliance for a Transatlantic Trade and Investment Partnership, both jointly established by the Commission and the US Department of Commerce, corporations have been central to long-term efforts to create TTIP. Alongside reverse lobbying of groups including BusinessEurope and the US Chamber of Commerce, the Commission also held 119 secret pre-TTIP meetings with corporate lobbies, 93% of its total outreach: a stark rebuttal to its claimed 'transparent and accountable trade policy based on consultations with all parts of European civil society' (Corporate Europe Observatory, 2013).

With the United States and EU together accounting for 50% of global GDP and 30% of world trade – and the EU bloc the world's leading source of foreign direct investment (FDI) – the European Commission sees TTIP as its most ambitious trade negotiation so far (European Commission, 2015b). Civil society groups frame the deal with three pillars corresponding to a reiteration of neoliberal trade policy: deregulation, privatisation and investor rights (War on Want, 2015). Through this lens, TTIP is an unabashed attempt to open and deregulate markets on behalf of transnational corporations (Hilary, 2015).

This is undertaken through a conjoined deregulatory and investor rights agenda, alongside forcing open markets and 'padlocking' already opened markets; a process deepened by CETA's 'negative listing' approach wherein services are automatically included for liberalisation unless specifically excluded by governments. Led by corporations, and with no input from states outside the transatlantic bloc, TTIP imposes a global economic governance template through rules for trade in goods – covering tariffs and non-tariff barriers – services, investment and intellectual property rights. ISDS, recognised as unnecessary between the United States and EU (Kleinheisterkamp, 2014) – which are already each other's largest sources of FDI – links all these areas, acting as a *de facto* and *de jure* corporate treaty enforcement mechanism providing a means to circumvent domestic law and international law obligations. It highlights the shift in agents and beneficiaries from liberal to neoliberal free trade imperialism, and the paramount role of the EU and its member states in externalising the EU internal process of removing political control over economic policies through law (Bickerton, 2016).

But rather than being indicative of a 'dominant transatlantic bloc' (Serfati, 2015), TTIP reveals the waning power of the EU and the United States. It is a strategic, defensive attempt to set a global free trade imperialism template outside the increasingly competitive confines of the WTO (Estevez, 2017; O'Donoghue and Tzouvala, 2017), with the intention of sidestepping opposition by subsequently importing the template into the WTO. As the Commission argues, a more contested global order requires using smaller coalitions to secure its global agenda; EU trade agreements are thus 'a laboratory for global trade liberalisation' (European Commission, 2015b: 29).

A 'special responsibility' to reform global investment

Metropole states first tried to introduce co-opted international governance for investment protection alongside the Bretton Woods institutions. States subsequently pioneered Bilateral Investment Treaties (BITs) incorporating ISDS at the end of the 1950s, with the German model a recognised template ever since (Poulsen, 2015: 50–52). EU member state BITs account for nearly 1,200 out of a global total of nearly 3,000 – alongside 373 global trade 'treaties with investment provisions' (UNCTAD, 2017). The Commission seeks to use ISDS to ensure 'the progressive abolition of restrictions on foreign direct investment' (European Commission, 2014c) through 'new-generation' treaties incorporating investment alongside trade with states including South Korea, Singapore, Vietnam, Peru and Colombia – in addition to the United States and Canada.

Vaguely defined substantive provisions allow ISDS cases to be launched for breach of treaty – without exhausting domestic law remedies – whenever state policies affect the value of an investment: under 'discrimination' principles, no foreign investor can be treated differently to a domestic business; under 'fair and equitable treatment' (European Commission, 2014), regulatory changes must not breach an investor's broadly defined 'legitimate expectations' (ibid.: 48); under 'indirect expropriation', investors can sue when public policies affect investments (ibid.: 331); and when investment is defined to include 'the expectation of gain or profit' (ibid.: 39; European Commission, 2015c: 1), the lost future value of an investment can be compensated. As a letter signed by

101 EU law academics argues, ISDS 'establishes privileges for foreign investors based on vague substantive standards; threatens regulation in the public interest, democratic change and state budgets; is systemically biased and lacks rule of law safeguards' (Client Earth, 2016).

Thus, as Poulsen (2015) asks, why do periphery states sign up to treaties? One answer is that much as 'collaboration' from local ruling classes dependent on trade for their prosperity sustained nineteenth-century British informal imperialism, metropole coercion and periphery collaboration continue under the ongoing hierarchical core-periphery power relations of neoliberalism. But consent is also manufactured through international agents operating as a mechanism of hegemony, metropole discourses of development and vague treaties (ibid.: 19) masking their real intent.

Metropole state dissembling was reinforced by supranational agents including the World Bank, the IMF – which incorporated investment measures into structural adjustment packages – and UNCTAD. UNCTAD in particular became 'the sine qua non in spreading support for BITs in the latter half of the 1990s and early 2000s' after recognising that its survival depended on alignment with neoliberal policies; it promoted BITs as necessary for FDI, while downplaying studies suggesting the opposite, and offered capacity-building to and facilitated BIT signings for periphery states (ibid.: 98).

But it is only recently that the global web of BITs transformed into a global register of known ISDS cases, rising from 3 in 1995 to 767 by the end of 2016, at an average cost of US$8 million for claimants (European Commission, 2015a); 1998 was the first year in which as many as 10 ISDS cases were recorded, while since 2004 there have been more than 40 known cases per year, rising to more than 50 by 2011. After a series of high-profile dystopian cases, increasingly funded by third parties from the financial sector (Trade Justice Movement, 2017), periphery states are now increasingly aware of and opposed to the mechanism, while UNCTAD (2015: 125) now highlights that BITs can 'bite' with 'huge costs to the state' while limiting 'the regulatory space of contracting parties'.

As a recent analysis of ISDS cases shows, claims increasingly use indirect expropriation to target regulations in 'democratic states' – as opposed to direct expropriation in 'low rule of law countries' (Pelc, 2016). But periphery states with lower regulatory baselines are the most vulnerable to such actions and may be least willing to run the risk of litigation, even when the claim has little legal merit (ibid.). Thus, while ISDS now locks in neoliberalism in metropole states – which has been critical to its exposure, accompanying resistance and ongoing 'reform' agenda – it remains pivotal to the imperialist mission of expanding metropole economic frontiers in periphery states, externally reflecting the EU's constitutionalised internal agenda of using 'law as a mask for politics' (Burley and Mattli, quoted in Sharpf, 2009: 8).

Latin America is the most targeted region under ISDS, a result of abundant natural resources and progressive governments undertaking public and environmental interest legislation combined with a high number of trade and investment agreements. The EU is the region's leading investor; correspondingly, investors from – or with subsidiaries in – ten EU states have sued Latin American states 101 times, with 70% of cases taking place since 2005 (UNCTAD, 2017). While Venezuela is alongside Mexico and Ecuador as among the ten most frequent respondents in the world, Argentina is the most targeted state in the world, facing 60 suits, almost 10% of all known cases.

Periphery and 'semi-periphery' states, including India, Brazil, Morocco and Nigeria, are pioneering alternatives to ISDS which seek to better protect states and increase investor responsibilities. Indonesia, Bolivia and South Africa are cancelling or phasing out ISDS agreements. But it was only in response to EU public outcry that the Commission removed ISDS from TTIP negotiations, replacing it with a 'reformed' version further elaborated in CETA's proposed Investor Court System. In line with its belief that 'the EU is best placed – and has a special responsibility – to lead the reform of the global investment regime, as its founder and main actor' (European Commission, 2015b: 21), the Commission is now attempting to globally institutionalise ISDS under its Multilateral Investment Court proposal.

However, EU reforms to date have failed to address substantive ISDS provisions or the lack of a legal basis for granting a special group of litigants their own court system (Deutsche Richterbund, 2016). As Van Harten (2016: 5) explains, in spite of reforms, ISDS can still 'attack state decisions in areas of agriculture, consumer protection, culture, energy, environment, financial security, intellectual property, land use, mining, public health, taxation, or transportation' while imposing 'vast and uncapped amounts of public compensation for foreign investors in any of these areas'.

'They obey the rules, or they do not export'

The core content of TTIP's wide-ranging deregulatory agenda is also achieved through the removal or 'mutual recognition' of regulations in negotiations and through a 'regulatory cooperation body' (RCB) empowered to change EU and US legislation after TTIP's ratification. TTIP thus follows the 'uncritical acceptance' that 'a wide array of domestic policies are in fact non-tariff barriers'; it is an unequivocal attempt to 'guard the market from political interference' (De Ville and Siles-Brügge, 2016: 64), aligning to a trajectory of accelerating EU deregulation. Under Barroso, regulation was 'a *problem* to be solved', the definition of 'red tape' was expanded and 'methodological alignment' with the United States was sought under the 2007 Transatlantic Economic Council which laid the foundations for TTIP; under Juncker, two months after a Commission TTIP proposal for 'regulatory cooperation', EU deregulation was 'reinforced' by a push towards a US regulatory model (Bartl, 2017).

Composed mainly of officials from both sides of the Atlantic who see the world 'as being composed of barriers and red tape impeding efficient market functioning' (ibid.: 35), the RCB provides updates on planned regulation ahead of formal rule-making procedures in the United States and EU (European Commission, 2016). Thus, before metropole parliamentarians or publics are aware of new regulations, RCB 'stakeholders' have an institutionalised channel for lobbying against them. As trade economist Richard Baldwin explained to a UK Parliament hearing, TTIP regulations directly impact periphery states:

> the problem for developing countries is that we get this US transatlantic [TTIP], transpacific [TPP] set of high-standard rules—but are they the right rules for developing countries? They will not have a choice. They obey those rules or they do not export, just like Switzerland [in the context of the EU].(House of Lords, 2014: 25).

While much attention focuses on TTIP paring down EU regulations, the Commission has pushed for financial services to be included in negotiations, against US wishes; under the Basel III banking regulation framework, the EU is 'materially non-compliant' while the United States, where financial regulation is highly fragmented, is 'largely compliant' due to the 2010 Dodd-Frank Act. A Dodd-Frank architect explained that industry pushed for TTIP because '[t]rade talks would merely serve as a one-way ratchet to pull back from reforms' (Barr, 2013).

As UK financial lobby group, TheCityUK, revealed that the EU's proposal 'reflected so closely the approach of TheCityUK that a bystander would have thought it came straight out of our brochure on TTIP' (Corporate Europe Observatory, 2015). The Commission, with the UK voice the 'loudest' in the room (House of Lords, 2017), pushed for including financial services and financial sector investors alongside applying ISDS to financial regulation, arguing that 'inconsistencies' in financial regulation are 'barriers to trade and investment' which 'undermine … global financial stability' (European Commission, 2014b: 2). Under market access provisions, rules prohibit parliaments from targeting excessive speculation through limiting the total value of a financial institution's operations (SOMO, 2014).

EU financial deregulation – reaching back to the Commission-led 1985 creation of a single market for financial services – reveals the ongoing role of the bloc in empowering global financial flows. As UNCTAD (2015) argues, in the absence of domestic or international financial regulation, excessive financial flows limit fiscal policy, resulting in 'structural fragilities' in productive investment and discouraging the deepening of periphery state productive capacity.

Conclusion: a unique supranational agent of informal imperialism

During a 2014 hearing into TTIP, Peter Mandelson described it as 'a fairly clear policy or approach of encirclement of China' (House of Lords, 2014: 23). As East Asia supersedes the United States as the most dynamic centre of capital accumulation (Arrighi, 2010), TTIP is a response to a rising 'semi-periphery' power breaking open markets and accessing resources that the EU and United States want for themselves.

EU actors resort to 'yellow peril' rhetoric – stoking fears of China 'making the rules' – in direct response to China's threat to the EU's 'regulatory superpower' status. But China stands alongside Japan, the EU and – dependent upon future policy choices – the United States in using bilateral and 'mega-regional' agreements to integrate new regions into the expanding economy, while reifying corporate extraterritoriality: the mechanism of informal imperialism and its drivers remain the same under neoliberalism, but what 'free trade' means, who enacts it and benefits from it have changed.

China established a G20 Trade and Investment Working Group in 2016 – when its capital exports first exceeded imports. It is pushing for the new-generation Regional Comprehensive Economic Partnership, and it too has adopted 'negative listing' to automatically open up all economic sectors in negotiations for a BIT with the United States. It stands apart from major 'emerging economies' including India, South Africa, Indonesia and Brazil in its support for the ISDS system.

However, despite these differences and despite offering alternative models of engagement with periphery states (Brautigam, 2011), BRICS states and emerging economies have legitimated structures of neoliberal global economic governance by bailing out the IMF (Hilary, 2013; Bond, 2014). Little has changed for peripheral states suffering resource theft and systematic super-exploitation under a veil of discourses of development. But the dramatic rise of emerging economy corporations and state-owned enterprises, accompanied by pursuit of the 'spatial fix' of neoliberal free trade, throws into doubt the relevance of North-South framings 'for analysis and for action' (Hilary, 2013: 25–26).

With a trade agenda that is 'by far the most ambitious … in the world today' (European Commission, 2015b: 9), the European Commission is a unique supranational agent of informal imperialism, externalising the EU bloc process of achieving economic integration through 'scaling back political control over economic life' and transforming the balance between public and private sectors from a political debate into a 'legal dispute' (Bickerton, 2016: 79). Given the constitutional underpinnings of Lisbon, the scheduled departure of the United Kingdom from the bloc will do nothing to change this.

While the future trajectories of the United States and China will determine whether and when there is a 'change of guard' in the control of the capitalist world economy (Arrighi, 2010: 343–351), informal imperialism today goes beyond rival states competing for hegemony through the inter-state system. International law is a fundamental conduit for the advancement of the interests of an increasingly transnational dominant class which has found a fertile breeding ground in the EU bloc, where the European Roundtable of Industrialists and the EU-US Transatlantic Business Dialogue sit alongside 'triad' forums and increasingly global groupings including the World Economic Forum and the 'Business 20' (Hilary, 2013). While the state remains diagnostic to informal imperialism, fundamental shifts under neoliberalism suggest that just as British free trade imperialism superseded the Westphalia system (Arrighi, 2010: 56) so too may neoliberal informal imperialism profoundly impact the extant nation state system (ibid.: 82–83).

But the forces of transnational capital continue to be met by transnational resistance to free trade from below. The Commission's efforts to reproduce neoliberal informal imperialism face opposition from social movements and civil society groups at home and abroad, casting doubt on its ability to maintain and expand its informal empire. From the 1999 'Battle of Seattle' to European and African resistance to EPAs and the successful pan-European movement against TTIP, social movements continue to confront free trade imperialism with political action, aware that an EU trade policy 'change of tack' (De Ville and Siles-Brügge, 2016: 138) is far removed from the structural change required to overcome neoliberal capitalism and the informal imperialism it produces.

References

Afonso, A., Zartaloudis, S., and Papadopoulos, Y. (2015). How party linkages shape austerity politics: Clientelism and fiscal adjustment in Greece and Portugal during the eurozone crisis. *Journal of European Public Policy*, 22(3): 315–334.

Africa Report. (2015). Top 500 Companies in Africa 2015. Available at: www.theafricareport.com/Top-500-Companies/top-500-companies-in-africa-2015.html [accessed 2 September 2017].

Agosin, M., Larraín, C., and Grau, N. (2010). *Industrial Policy in Chile*. IDB Working Paper, No 170. Washington, DC: Inter-American Development Bank.

Aguilar, L. E. (1998). Cuba c. 1860-c.1930, in Bethell, L. (ed.), *Cuba: A Short History*. Cambridge: Cambridge University Press, pp. 21–56.

Ahumada, J. M. (forthcoming). Contemporary Globalisation and the Shrinking of the Policy Space for Development: The Case of Chile. Article submitted for publication.

Ahumada, J. M., and Sossdorf, F. (2017). Equidad social y transformación de la estructura productiva en Chile, in Carmona, F. (ed.), *Ensayos para un modelo de desarrollo sostenible*. Santiago: Ical.

Akram-Lodhi, A. H., and Kay, C. (2010). Surveying the Agrarian Question (Part 2): Current Debates and Beyond. *Journal of Peasant Studies*, 37(2): 255–284.

Alexander, P. (2016). Marikana Commission of Inquiry: From Narratives to History. *Journal of Southern African Studies*, 42(5): 815–839.

Alexander, P., Lekgowa, T., Mmope, B., Sinwell, L., and Xezwi, B. (2012). *Marikana. A View from the Mountain and a Case to Answer*. Johannesburg: Jacana.

Amin, S. (2001). Imperialism and Globalization. *Monthly Review*, 53(2).

Amsden, A. (2007). *Escape from Empire*. Cambridge, MA: MIT Press.

Anon. (1879). *Catalogue of the Library at Chatsworth House, Vol. 2*. London: Chiswick Press.

Anon. (1885). *Suakin, 1885: Being a Sketch of the Campaign this Year*. London: Kegan Paul, Trench, and Co.

Arrighi, G. (2010). *The Long Twentieth Century: Money Power and the Origins of Our Time*. London: Verso.

Asch, S. E. (1956). Studies of Independence and Conformity; I. A Minority of One Against Unanimous Majority. *Psychological Monograph*, 70(9): 1–70.

Ashman, S., Fine, B., and Newman, S. (2011). The Crisis in South Africa: Neoliberalism, Financialization and Uneven and Combined Development. *Socialist Register*, 47 (1): 174–195.

Avini, A. (1996). Origins of the Modern English Trust Revisited. *Tulane Law Review*, 70 (4): 1139–1164.

Babatunde, A., and Alli, F. (2016). EPA: $8.94bn development package tears ECOWAS apart. *Vanguard*. 4 January. Available at: https://www.vanguardngr.com/2016/01/epa-8-94bn-development-package-tears-ecowas-apart/ [accessed 15 July 2017].

Bailes, A. J. K., Thayer, B. A., and Thorhallsson, B. (2016). Alliance Theory and Alliance 'Shelter': The Complexities of Small State Alliance Behaviour. *Third World Thematics*, 1 (1): 9–26.

Baldwin, R. (2013). Global Supply Chains: Why They Emerged, Why They Matter, and Where They are Going, in Elms, D., and Low, P., *Global Value Chains in a Changing World*. Geneva: WTO Publications, pp. 13–60.

Balfour, S., and Preston, P. (eds) (1999). *Spain and the Great Powers in the Twentieth Century*. London: Routledge.

Barr, M. (2013). Keep Financial Regulations Out of US-EU Trade Talks. *Brookings Institution*. 30 July. Available at: https://www.brookings.edu/opinions/keep-financial-regulation-out-of-u-s-eu-trade-talks/ [accessed: 19 August 2017].

Bartl, M. (2017). Making Transnational Markets: The Institutional Politics Behind the TTIP. *Europe and the World: A Law Review*. doi:10.14324/111.444.ewlj.2017.01

Basedaw, R. (2016). A Legal History of the EU's International Investment Policy. *The Journal of World Investment and Trade*, 17(5): 743–772.

Bauman, Z. (1989). *Modernity and the Holocaust*. Cambridge: Polity Press.

BBC News (2003). Stevens Inquiry: Key people, 17 April. http://news.bbc.co.uk/1/hi/northern_ireland/2956161.stm [accessed 27 September 2013].

Beck, U. (1992). *Risk Society: Towards a New Modernity*. London: Sage.

Beeler, J. F. (2004). Colomb, Sir John Charles Ready (1838–1909). *Oxford Dictionary of National Biography*. Oxford: Oxford University Press.

Benston, G., Bromwich, M., Litan, R. E., and Wagenhofer, A. (2003). *Following the Money: The Enron Failure and the State of Corporate Disclosure*. Washington, DC: Brookings Institution Press andAEI.

Berend, I., and Rankí, G. (1982) *The European Periphery and Industrialisation 1780–1914*. Cambridge: Cambridge University Press.

Bernell, D. (1994). The Curious Case of Cuba in American Foreign Policy. *Journal of Inter-American Studies & World Affairs*, 36(2): 65–103.

Berry, F., and Berry, W. (2007). Innovation and Diffusion Models in Policy Research, in Sabatier, P. (ed.), *Theories of the Policy Process*. Cambridge, MA: Westview, pp. 223–260.

Bickerton, C. (2016). *The European Union: A Citizen's Guide*. London: Penguin Random House.

Bithymitris, G. (2016). Union Militancy During Economic Hardship: The Strike at the Greek Steel Company 'Hellenic Halyvourgia'. *Employee Relations*, 38(3): 373–389.

Bithymitris, G., and Papadopoulos, O. (2017). Learning Liminality: A Training Voucher Case in the Tourism Sector, in Karakioulafi, C., and Spyridakis, M. (eds), *Society, Unemployment and Social Reproduction*. Athens: Gutenberg [in Greek].

Boeninger, E. (2014[1997]). Democracia en Chile, in Boeninger, E. (ed.), *Gobernabilidad*. Santiago: Uqbar Editions.

Bond, P. (2004). Bankrupt Africa: Imperialism, Sup-Imperialism and the Politics of Finance. *Historical Materialism*, 12(4): 145–172.

Bond, P. (2013a). Sub-imperialism as Lubricant of Neoliberalism: South African 'Deputy Sheriff' Duty within BRICS. *Third World Quarterly*, 34(2): 251–270.

Bond, P. (2013b). Debt, Uneven Development and Capitalist Crisis in South Africa: From Moody's Macroeconomic Monitoring to Marikana Microfinance Mashonisas. *Third World Quarterly*, 34(4): 569–592.

Bond, P. (2014a). BRICS and the Tendency to Sub-imperialism. *Pambazuka News*. 10 April. Available at: https://www.pambazuka.org/governance/brics-and-tendency-sub-imperialism [accessed: 2 September 2017].

Bond, P. (2014b). *Elite Transition*. London: Pluto.

Bond, P. (2015). BRICS and the Sub-imperialist Location, in Bond, P., and Garica, A. (eds), *BRICS: An Anti-Capitalist Critique*. London: Pluto Press, pp. 15–26.

Bond, P. (2016a). Flight of Corporate Profits Poses Biggest Threat to South Africa's Economy. *The Conversation*, 22 June. Available from: https://theconversation.com/flight-of-corporate-profits-poses-biggest-threat-to-south-africas-economy-61337 [accessed 3 September 2017].

Bond, P. (2016b). BRICS Banking and the Debate over Sub-imperialism. *Third World Quarterly*, 37(4): 611–629.

Bond, P., and Garcia, A. (eds). (2015). *BRICS: An Anti-Capitalist Critique*. London: Pluto Press.

Borras, S. M., Jr. (2009). Agrarian Change and Peasant Studies: Changes, Continuities and Challenges – An Introduction. *Journal of Peasant Studies*, 36(1): 5–31.

Boughton, J. (2003). *Who's in Charge? Ownership and Conditionality in IMF-Supported Programs*. IMF Working Paper 03/191. Washington, DC: IMF.

Bracking, S., and Sharife, K. (2014). *Rough and Polished. A Case Study of the Diamond Pricing and Valuation System*. LCSV Working Paper No. 4. Manchester: School of Environment, Education and Development. Available at: http://thestudyofvalue.org/wp-content/uploads/2014/05/WP4-Bracking-Sharife-Rough-and-polished-15May.pdf [accessed 15 September 2017].

Brautigam, D. (2011). *The Dragon's Gift: The Real Story of China in Africa*. Oxford: Oxford University Press.

British Library, India Office Records, IOR/R/20/E/88, W. Wedderburn, Acting Political Secretary, Memorandum on the Red Sea Route, 5 July 1870.

British Library, London. Add.MS 44645, 2nd Earl Granville: Minutes and Memoranda by: 1853–1886. William Gladstone, Personal Minutes of Cabinet Meeting, 8 February 1884.

British Library. London. CM/IOR/026, India Office Records. Lord Hartington to Sir Garnet Wolseley, Telegram, 7 January 1885.

British Library, London. IOR/L/PS/20/MEMO39–43, India Office Records Foreign Office Prints: Correspondence Respecting the Red Sea and Somali Coast. Admiral Sir William Hewett to the Secretary to the Admiralty, Report, 7 January 1884.

British Library, London. IOR/MSS Eur/D604/5–11, India Office Records. Confidential Memorandum on the Insurrection of the False Prophet, 23 November 1883.

British Library, London. IOR/MSS Eur/D604/5–11, India Office Records. Confidential Memorandum on the Insurrection of the False Prophet, February 1884.

British Library, London. IOR/MSS Eur/D604/5–11, India Office Records. Earl Granville to the Earl of Dufferin, Letter, 14 May 1884.

British Library. London, IOR/MSS Eur/D604/5–11, India Office Records. Viscount Lyons to Earl Granville, Letter, 25 April 1884.

British Library, London. IOR/R/20/E, India Office Records. Earl Granville to Musurus Pasha, Letter, 22 August 1884.

Brunt, P. A. (1975). The Administrators of Roman Egypt. *Journal of Roman Studies*, 65: 124–147.

Bryman, A. (2004). *The Disneyization of Society*. London: Sage.

Buckle, G. E. (ed.). (1928). *The Letters of Queen Victoria, Vol. III*. London: John Murray.

Bugaric, B. (2013). *Europe Against the Left? On Legal Limits to Progressive Politics*. LSE 'Europe in Question' Discussion Paper No. 61/2013. London: LEQS.

Burleigh, B. (1884). *Desert Warfare: Being the Chronicle of the Eastern Soudan Campaign*. London: Chapman and Hall.

Burns, A. (2017). *American Imperialism: The Territorial Expansion of the United States, 1783–2013*. Edinburgh: Edinburgh University Press.

Burns, A., and Gallimore, G. (2017). Duplicated Debacles: A Comparison of the 1895–1896 Jameson Raid and the 1961 Bay of Pigs Invasion. *The Historian*: 22–27.

Byres, T. J., Curwen, C., and Shanin, T. (1973). Editorial Statement. *Journal of Peasant Studies*, 1(1): 1–2.

Cadwallader, A. (2013). *Lethal Allies: British Collusion in Ireland*. Cork: Mercier Press.

Cain, P. (1999). British Free Trade, 1850–1914: Economics and Policy. *ReFRESH*, 29: 1–4.

Cain, P., and Hopkins, A. (1987). Gentlemanly Capitalism and British Expansion Overseas II: New Imperialism, 1850–1945. *The Economic History Review*, 40(1): 1–26.

Cairney, P. (2012). *Understanding Public Policy, Theories and Issues*. Basingstoke: Palgrave MacMillan.

Campbell, D. (1984). Victims of the Dirty War. *New Statesman*, 4 May.

Campbell, P. (2017). *Torture and Psychological Effects in Northern Ireland*. Canada: ReMarx Publishing.

Caquet, P. E. (2013). The Napoleonic Legend and the War Scare of 1840. *The International History Review*, 35(4): 702–722.

Carr, R. (1980). *Modern Spain 1875–1980*. Oxford: Oxford University Press.

Cassis, Y. (1991). Financial Elites in Three European Centres: London, Paris, Berlin, 1880s–1930s. *Business History*, 33(3): 53–71.

Castro Mariño, S. M. (2002). U.S.-Cuban Relations during the Clinton Administration. *Latin American Perspectives*, 29(4): 47–76.

Chamber of Mines of South Africa. (2017) *Facts and Figures 2016*. Johanesburg: Chamber of Mines of South Africa.

Chang, H.-J. (2003). *Kicking Away the Ladder: Development Strategy in Historical Perspective*. London: Wimbledon Publishing Company.

Chang, H.-J. (2007). *Bad Samaritans: The Guilty Secrets of Rich Nations and the Threat to Global Prosperity*. London: Random House.

Chang, H.-J. (2008). *Bad Samaritans*. New York: Bloomsbury Press.

Chavagneux, C., and Palan, R. (2007). *Paradis Fiscaux*. Paris: La Découverte.

Chinguno, C. (2013). Marikana: Fragmentation, Precariousness, Strike Violence and Solidarity. *Review of African Political Economy*, 40(138): 639–646.

Chomsky, A. (2011). *A History of the Cuban Revolution*. Malden, MA: Wiley-Blackwell.

Christian Aid, AIPAD Trust, CPDC, ENDA, SEATINI. (2006). *EPAs and Investment*, October. Available at: www.christianaid.org.uk/Images/epas_and_investment.pdf [accessed 15 July 2017].

Client Earth. (2016). 101 Law Professors Say ISDS is Incompatible with EU Law. *Client Earth*. 17 October. Available at: https://www.clientearth.org/101-law-professors-say-isds-is-incompatible-with-eu-law/ [accessed 29 July 2017].

Cobain, I. (2012). *Cruel Britannia: A Secret History of Torture*. London: Portobello Books.

Cobain, I. (2016). *The History Thieves: Secrets, Lies and the Shaping of a Modern Nation*. London: Portobello Books.

Cock, J. (2006). Connecting the Red, Brown and Green: The Environmental Justice Movement in South Africa, in Ballard, R., Habib, A., and Valodia, I. (eds), *Voices of*

Protest. Social Movements in Post-Apartheid South Africa. Scottsville: University of Kwa-Zulu-Natal Press, pp. 203–224.

Cohen, P. A. (1984). *Discovering History in China: American Historical Writing on the Recent Chinese Past*. Columbia University Press: New York.

Colomb, J. (1867). *The Protection of Our Commerce and Distribution of Our Naval Forces Considered*. London: Harrison.

Colvile, H. E. (1996[1889]). *History of the Sudan Campaign 1884–1885*. Nashville: Battery Press.

Connolly, J. (1997[1897]). Shan Van Vocht, in Beresford Ellis, P. (ed.), *James Connolly: Selected Writings*. London: Pluto, pp. 121–124.

Cooren, F. (2000). *The Organising Property of Communication*. Amsterdam: John Benjamin.

Cornell, T., and Matthews, J. F. (1991). *The Roman World*. Stonehenge: London.

Corporate Europe Observatory. (2000). *Europe, Inc.: Dangerous Liaisons Between EU Institutions and Industry*. London: Pluto Press.

Corporate Europe Observatory. (2009). Pulling the Strings of African Business. *Corporate Europe Observatory*. Available at: http://archive.corporateeurope.org/docs/pulling-the-strings-of-african-business.pdf [accessed 15 July 2017].

Corporate Europe Observatory. (2013). European Commission preparing for EU-US trade talks: 119 meetings with industry lobbyists. 4 September. Available at: https://corporateeurope.org/trade/2013/09/european-commission-preparing-eu-us-trade-talks-119-meetings-industry-lobbyists

Corporate Europe Observatory. (2015). TTIP: A Corporate Lobbying Paradise. 14 July. Available at: https://corporateeurope.org/international-trade/2015/07/ttip-corporate-lobbying-paradise [accessed 2 September 2017].

Corporate Europe Observatory. (2017). RevolvingDoorWatch. Available at: https://corporateeurope.org/revolvingdoorwatch [accessed 19 August 2017].

Cronin, D. (2013). *Corporate Europe: How Big Business Sets Policies on Food, Climate and War*. London: Pluto Press.

Crosby, A. (2004). *Ecological Imperialism: The Biological Expansion of Europe, 900–1900*. Cambridge: Cambridge University Press.

Crouch, C. (2009). Privatised Keynesianism: An Unacknowledged Policy Regime. *The British Journal of Politics & International Relations*, 11(3): 382–399.

Curtis, M. (2016). *The New Resource Grab: How EU Policy on Raw Materials is Undermining Development*. Traidcraft Exchange, Oxfam Germany, WEED, AITEC, and Comhlámh.

D'Egville, H. (1913). *Imperial Defence and Closer Union*. London: P. S. King & Son.

Daly, M. W., and Holt, P. M. (2000). *A History of the Sudan: From the Coming of Islam to the Present Day*. 5th Edition. Harlow: Longman Publishing.

Davenport, J. (2013). *Digging Deep: A History of Mining in South Africa*. Johannesburg: Jonathan Ball.

Davenport-Hines, R. (2004). Gordon, Charles George (1833–1885). *Oxford Dictionary of National Biography*. Oxford: Oxford University Press.

De Silva, D. (2012). *Pat Finucane Review: An Independent Review into Any State Involvement in the Murder of Pat Finucane*, 2 vols. London: Stationary Office.

De Ville, F., and Siles-Brügge, G. (2016). *TTIP: The Truth About the Transatlantic Trade and Investment Partnership*. Cambridge: Polity Press.

Dearn, M. (2017). Ecologist Special Report: Impending Vote on the Canada Trade Deal which Forced Tar Sands on Europe. *The Ecologist*. 11 January. Available at:

www.theecologist.org/News/news_analysis/2988514/ecologist_special_report_impending_vote_on_the_canada_trade_deal_which_forced_tar_sands_on_europe.html [accessed 2 September 2017].

Deere, C. (2009). *The Implementation Game*. Oxford: Oxford University Press.

Deutsche Richterbund (DRB). (2016). Opinion on the Establishment of an Investment Tribunal in TTIP: The Proposal from the European Commission on 16.09.2015 and 11.12.2015. February. Available at: https://www.foeeurope.org/sites/default/files/eu-us_trade_deal/2016/english_version_deutsche_richterbund_opinion_ics_feb2016.pdf [accessed 26 August 2017].

Devadoss, S., Aguiar, A. H., Shook, S. R., and Araji, J. (2005). A Spatial Equilibrium Analysis of U.S.-Canadian Disputes on the World Softwood Lumber Market. *Canadian Journal of Agricultural Economics*, 53(2–3): 177–192.

Dharmapala, D. (2008). What Problems and Opportunities are Created by Tax Havens? *Oxford Review of Economic Policy*, 24(4): 661–679.

Dicken, P. (2015). *Global Shift: Mapping the Contours of the World Economy*, 7th edition). London: Sage.

Direcon. (2009). *Chile: 20 años de negociaciones comerciales*. Santiago: Ministry of Foreign Affairs.

Dolowitz, D., and Marsh, D. (1996). Who Learns What from Whom: A Review of the Policy Transfer Literature. *Political Studies*, 44(2): 343–357.

Dominguez, J. (1998). Cuba since 1959, in Bethell, L. (ed.), *Cuba: A Short History*. Cambridge: Cambridge University Press, pp. 95–148.

Drucker, J. (2016). The World's Favorite New Tax Haven Is the United States. *Bloomberg Businessweek*, 27 January. Available at: www.anaford.com/wp-content/uploads/2016/09/Bloomberg-The%20World's%20Favorite%20New%20Tax%20Haven%20Is%20the%20United%20States%20-%20Bloomberg%20Business.pdf [accessed 1 December 2017].

Duménil, G., and Lévy, D. (2004). The Economics of US Imperialism at the Turn of the 21st Century. *Review of International Political Economy*, 11(4): 657–676.

Durr, B. (1990). Chile Surrenders to US Threat on Pharmaceutical Patents. *Financial Times*, 1 February.

Edwards, J. (1979). *The British Government and the Spanish Civil War, 1936–1939*. London: Macmillan.

Eleftheriou, C. (2016). Greek Radical Left Reactions to the Crisis: Three Types of Political Mobilisation, One Winner, in March, L., and Keith, D. (eds), *Europe's Radical Left From Marginality to the Mainstream?* London, New York: Rowman & Littlefield, pp. 289–310.

Eleftheriou, C. (forthcoming). Greece, in March, L., Escalona, F., and Keith, D. (eds), *The Routledge Handbook on Radical Left Parties in Europe*. London: Routledge.

Elliot, G., Sir (1884). Speech to the House of Commons, 10 March, *Hansard Parliamentary Debates*, Commons, vol. 285 (1884), 1075.

Engel, E. (1996). Uvas envenenadas, vacas locas y proteccionismo, in *Documento de Trabajo*. Serie Economía, No. 9. University of Santiago, Chile.

Estevez, I. (2017). *Unpacking Trade and Investment 8: US and EU Trade Strategy Beyond the Doha Round*. Brussels: Rosa Luxemburg Stiftung.

European Commission. (2008). Communication from the Commission to the European Parliament and the Council – The Raw Materials Initiative: Meeting Our Critical Needs for Growth and Jobs in Europe. COM (2008) 0699 final. Brussels: European Commission.

European Commission. (2010). Trade, Growth and World Affairs: Trade Policy as a Core Component of the EU's 2020 Strategy. COM (2010) 612. Brussels: European Commission.

European Commission (2012). *The Second Economic Adjustment Programme for Greece, March*. European Economy Occasional Papers 94. Brussels: European Commission.

European Commission. (2014a). Consolidated CETA Text. September. Available at: http://trade.ec.europa.eu/doclib/docs/2014/september/tradoc_152806.pdf [accessed 26 August 2017].

European Commission. (2014b). EU-US Transatlantic Trade and Investment Partnership: Cooperation on Financial Services Regulation. Available at: http://trade.ec.europa.eu/doclib/docs/2014/january/tradoc_152101.pdf [accessed 2 August 2017].

European Commission. (2014c). Towards a Comprehensive European International Investment Policy. Available at: https://eur-lex.europa.eu/legal-content/en/TXT/?uri=CELEX:52010DC0343

European Commission. (2015a). Investor-to-State Dispute Settlement: Some Facts and Figures. Available at: http://trade.ec.europa.eu/doclib/docs/2015/january/tradoc_153046.pdf [accessed 2 August 2017].

European Commission. (2015b). Trade for All: Towards a More Responsible Trade and Investment Policy. October. Available at: http://trade.ec.europa.eu/doclib/docs/2015/october/tradoc_153846.pdf [accessed 2 August 2017].

European Commission. (2015c). Transatlantic Trade and Investment Partnership, Trade in Services, Investment and E-Commerce, Chapter II – Investment. September. Available at: http://trade.ec.europa.eu/doclib/docs/2015/september/tradoc_153807.pdf [accessed 2 August 2017].

European Commission. (2016). TTIP-EU proposal for Chapter: Regulatory Cooperation. 21 March. Available at: http://trade.ec.europa.eu/doclib/docs/2016/march/tradoc_154377.pdf [accessed 2 August 2017].

Eurostat (2017a). Main Indicator – Europe 2020 target on poverty and social exclusion. Available at: http://ec.europa.eu/eurostat/data/database [accessed: 6 May 2018].

Eurostat (2017b). Database: Population and Social Conditions: Youth. Available at: http://ec.europa. eu/eurostat/web/youth/data/database [accessed 6 May 2018].

Eurostat (2017c). Database: People at Risk of Poverty or Social Exclusion by Most Frequent Activity Status (Population Aged 18 and Over). [accessed 6 May 2018].

Eurostat (2017d). Young People Neither in Employment nor in Education and Training (NEET), by Sex – Quarterly Data. Available at: http://appsso.eurostat.ec.europa.eu/nui/show.do?dataset=lfsi_neet_q&lang=en [accessed 6 May 2018].

Fazio, H. (2004). *TLC: el amarre del modelo*. Santiago: Lom editions.

Featherstone, K. (2011). The JCMS Annual Lecture: The Greek Sovereign Debt Crisis and EMU: A Failing State in a Skewed Regime. *JCMS: Journal of Common Market Studies*, 49(2): 193–217.

Fergusson, J. (1849). *An Essay on the Proposed New System of Fortification: With Hints for its Application to our National Defences*. London: John Weale.

Fermandois, J. (2006). Peace at Home, Turbulence Abroad: The Foreign Policy of the Lagos Administration, in Oppenheim, L., and Borzutzky, S. (eds), *After Pinochet: The Chilean Road to Democracy and the Market*. Gainsville, FL: University Press of Florida, pp. 118–117.

Ffrench-Davis, R. (2014). *Entre el Neoliberalismo y el Crecimiento con Equidad*. Santiago: JC Saez Publisher.

Fieldhouse, D. K. (1999). *The West and the Third World: Trade, Colonialism, Dependence and Development.* London: Wiley- Blackwell.

Fine, B., and Rustomjee, Z. (1996). *The Political Economy of South Africa: From Minerals Energy Complex to Industrialisation.* Boulder, CO: Westview Press.

Fitzmaurice, E., Lord. (1884). Speech to the House of Commons. *Hansard HC Deb.* Vol. 285, 10 March.

Forni, G. (1953). Manio Curio Dentato uomo democratico. *Athenaeum*, 31: 170–240.

Friedman, T. (1999). *The Lexus and the Olive Tree.* London: Harper Collins.

Froude, J. A. (1871). *Short Studies on Great Subjects.* London: Longmans Green, and Co.

Galbraith, J. (1972). *Mackinnon and East Africa 1878–1895.* Cambridge: Cambridge University Press.

Gallagher, J., and Robinson, R. (1953). The Imperialism of Free Trade. *The Economic History Review*, 6(1): 1–15.

Gallagher, K. (2008). Trading Away the Ladder? Trade Politics and Economic Development in the Americas. *New Political Economy*, 13(1): 37–59.

Gallagher, P. (2015). The Phantom of the Opera and a £22m Trust Fund Feud with Norway. *Independent.* 27 March. www.independent.co.uk/news/world/europe/the-phantom-of-the-opera-and-a-22m-trust-fund-feud-with-norway-10140327.html [accessed 19 January 2018].

Gandhi, L. (1998). *Postcolonial Theory: A Critical Reader.* Allen and Unwin: London.

Garcia Sanz, C. (2011). *La Primera Guerra Mundial en el Estrecho de Gibraltar: Economía, Política y Relaciones Internacionales.* Madrid: CSIS.

Garside, J. (2017). The Heat is on: Inaction on Tax Havens will Make May Appear Complicit. *The Guardian.* Available at: https://www.theguardian.com/news/2017/nov/14/paradise-papers-tax-havens-theresa-may-margaret-hodge-transparency [accessed 1 December 2017].

Gerber, J.-F. (2014). The Role of Rural Indebtedness in the Evolution of Capitalism. *Journal of Peasant Studies*, 1–19. doi:10.1080/03066150.2014.921618

Gergen, K. J. (1991). *The Saturated Self: Dilemmas of Identity in Contemporary Life.* New York: Basic Books.

Gerth, H., and Mills, C. W. (1959). *From Max Weber.* London: RKP.

Gialis, S., Tsampra, M., and Leontidou, L. (2015). Atypical Employment in Crisis-hit Greek Regions: Local Production Structures, Flexibilization and Labour Market Re/deregulation. *Economic and Industrial Democracy*, 38(4): 1–21.

Giuliano, M. (1998). The United States' Embargo and Cuba's Foreign Relations: Missed Opportunities for Democratization. *Democratization*, 5(3): 181–199.

Gladstone, W. (1990). *The Gladstone Diaries.* Ed. Matthew, H. C. G. Oxford: Clarendon Press.

Glasgow Herald. (1884). Another Disaster in the Soudan. 6 February.

Global Justice Now. (2017). 10 Biggest Corporations Make More Money than Most Countries in the World Combined. 12 September. www.globaljustice.org.uk/news/2016/sep/12/10-biggest-corporations-make-more-money-most-countries-world-combined

Godfrey, R., Brewis, J., Grady, J., and Grocott, C. (2014). The Private Military Industry and Neoliberalism: Mapping the Terrain. *Organization*, 21(1): 106–125.

Gomez, A. (2016). Fidel Castro to Obama: 'We Don't Need the Empire to Give us Anything'. *USA Today*, 28 March. Available at: https://www.usatoday.com/story/news/2016/03/28/fidel-castro-president-obama-cuba-trip/82347680/ [accessed 31 August 2017].

Gordon, J. (2015). The Invisibility of Human Harm: How Smart Sanctions Consumed All the Oxygen in the Room. *Social Research: An International Quarterly*, 82(4): 863–874.
Gordon, P. (ed.). (2009). *The Political Diaries of the Fourth Earl of Carnarvon, 1857–1890*, Vol. 35. Cambridge: Cambridge University Press.
Gosling, M. (2010). Eskom's Secret Deals Give 138 Companies Cut-price Power. *Cape Times*, 10 March.
Gott, R. (2005). *Cuba: A New History*. New Haven, CT: Yale University Press.
Gott, R. (2012). *Britain's Empire Resistance: Repression and Revolt*. London: Verso.
Greenhut, J. (1984). Sahib and Sepoy: An Inquiry into the Relationship between the British Officers and Native Soldiers of the British Indian Army. *Military Affairs*, 48(1): 15–18.
Grey, V. (1973). Innovation in the States: A Diffusion Study. *American Political Science Review*, 67(4): 1174–1185.
Grocott, C., and Grady, J. (2014). 'Naked Abroad': The Continuing Imperialism of Free Trade. *Capital & Class*, 38(3): 541–562.
Grocott, C., and Stockey, G. (2012). *Gibraltar: A Modern History*. Cardiff: University of Wales Press.
Güell y Ferrer, J. (1880). *Escritos Económicos*. Barcelona: Imp. Barcelonesa.
Guernsey Law Reports 2009–10 GLR 377, International Committee of the Red Cross v. Thommessen and Butterfield Trust (Guernsey) Limited. www.guernseylegalresources.gg/ccm/legal-resources/law-reports/Cases/GLR2009/GLR090377.htm [accessed 28 April 2018].
Guevara, C. (2000). *The African Dream: The Diaries of the Revolutionary War in the Congo*. London: Harville Press.
Guinan, J., and Hanna, T. M. (2017). Forbidden Fruit: The Neglected Political Economy of Lexit. *IPPR Progressive Review*, 24(1): 15–24.
Handy, J. (2009). 'Almost Idiotic Wretchedness': A Long History of Blaming Peasants. *Journal of Peasant Studies*, 36(2): 325–344.
Harcourt, F. (2010). The High Road to India: The P&O Company and the Suez Canal, 1840–1874. *International Journal of Maritime History*, 22(2): 19–72.
Harcourt, W. V. (1873). Our Naval and Military Establishments Regarded with Reference to the Dangers of Invasion. *Journal of the Royal United Services Institute*, 16 (68): 575–607.
Harding, E. (1993). Chile: Private Sector Plans Lobbying Blitz in Washington to Push for Chile-US Free Trade Accord. Latin America Data Base, LADB Article Id: 057706.
Harnetty, P. (1971). Cotton Exports and Indian Agriculture, 1861–1870. *The Economic History Review*, 24(3): 414–429.
Harvey, D. (2004). The 'New' Imperialism: Accumulation by Dispossession. *Socialist Register*, 40: 63–87.
Harvey, D. (2005). *A Brief History of Neoliberalism*. Oxford: Oxford University Press.
Headrick, D. R. (1988). *The Tentacles of Progress: Technology Transfew in the Age of Imperialism, 1850–1940*. Oxford: Oxford University Press.
Hechter, M. (1975). *Internal Colonialism: The Celtic Fringe in British National Development 1536–1936*. London: Routledge and Kegan Paul.
Helwege, A. (1989). Three Socialist Experiences in Latin America: Surviving US Economic Pressure. *Bulletin of Latin American Research*, 8(2): 211–234.
Hewitt, G. (2015). Greece: The Dangerous Game. *BBC News*, 1 February. Available at: www.bbc.co.uk/news/world-europe-31082656 [accessed 2 September 2017].
Hilary, J. (2013). *The Poverty of Capitalism: Economic Meltdown and the Struggle for What Comes Next*. London: Pluto Press.

Hilary, J. (2015). *The Transatlantic Trade and Investment Partnership: A Charter for Deregulation, an Attack on Jobs, an End to Democracy*. Brussels: Rosa Luxembourg Stiftung.

Hilferding, R. (1981[1910]). *Finance Capital: A Study of the Latest Phase of Capitalist Development*. London: Routledge & Kegan Paul.

Hill, R. (1959). *Egypt in the Sudan, 1820–1881*. Oxford: Oxford University Press.

Hobsbawm, E. J. (1973). Peasants and Politics. *Journal of Peasant Studies*, 1(1): 1–15.

Hobson, J. A. (2005[1902]). *Imperialism: A Study*. New York: Cosimo.

Hodge, C. (ed.). (2008). *Encyclopedia of the Age of Imperialism, 1800–1914*. Westport, CT: Greenwood Press.

Hoppe, T. (2017). EU Embraces Nations Spurned by US. *Handelsblatt*. 21 February. Available at: https://global.handelsblatt.com/politics/e-u-embraces-nations-spurned-by-u-s-709260 [accessed 16 July 2017].

House of Lords. (2014). *European Union Committee: 14th Report of Session 2013–14. The Transatlantic Trade and Investment Partnership*. London: The Stationary Office.

Hufbauer, G., and Schott, J. (1993). *NAFTA: An Assessment*. Washington, DC: Institute for International Economics.

Hull, T. A. (1875). The Unsurveyed World, 1874. *Journal of the Royal United Services Institute*, 19(80): 48–73.

Humby, T.-L. (2015). 'One Environmental System': Aligning the Laws on the Environmental Management of Mining in South Africa. *Journal of Energy & Natural Resources Law*, 33(2): 110–130.

Hurt, S., Lee, D., and Lorenz-Carl, U. (2013). The Argumentative Dimension to the EU-Africa EPAs. *International Negotiation*, 18(1): 67–87.

Hyden, G. (1980). *Beyond Ujamaa in Tanzania: Underdevelopment and an Uncaptured Peasantry*. Berkeley, CA: University of California Press.

Ibengwe, S., and Malanga, A. (2016). Tanzania: JPM Imposes Ban On Mineral Sands Export. *AllAfrica.com*, 1 August. Available at: http://allafrica.com/stories/201608010674.html [accessed 15 July 2017].

INE GSEE. (2017). *Interim Report: Greek Economy and Employment*. October [in Greek].

International Monetary Fund. (2015). *Angola Selected Issues*. IMF Country Report No. 15/302. Washington, DC: IMF.

Irish Times. (2010). The Adviser: Selwyn Black's Role. 9 January. Available at: https://www.irishtimes.com/news/the-adviser-selwyn-black-s-role-1.1239784

Jasanoff, M. (2017). *The Dawn Watch: Joseph Conrad in a Global World*. London: Harper Collins.

Jonker, K., and Meehan, W. (2008). Curbing Mission Creep. *Stanford Social Innovation Review*, Winter.

Jordan, K. (1994). Intellectual Property under NAFTA: Is Chile up to the Challenge. *Tulsa Journal of Comparative and International Law*, 2(2): 367–380.

Kampmark, B. (2010). William A. Williams's Tragedy Fifty Years On. *Historical Journal*, 53(3): 783–794.

Kar, D., and Spanjers, J. (2015). *Illicit Financial Flows from Developing Countries: 2004–2013*. Washington DC: Global Financial Integrity.

Karsten, P. (1983). Irish Soldiers in the British Army, 1792–1922: Suborned or Subordinate? *Journal of Social History*, 17(1): 31–64.

Kasirye, S. (2014). Ten Years of the Stop EPA Movement: The Future of Trade Activism. Speech to Free Trade at the Crossroads: Examining the Past Lessons for the Future conference. Rosa Luxembourg Foundation, Germany, 18 November. Available at: http s://www.rosalux.de/fileadmin/rls_uploads/pdfs/Ausland/Afrika/Kasirye_-_10_years_of_the_Stop_EPA_Movement.pdf [accessed online 15 July 2017].

Keleman, D. R. (2016). Regulation in the European Union, in Bignami, F., and Zaring, D. (eds), *Comparative Law and Regulation: Understanding the Global Regulatory Process*. Cheltenham, UK: Edward Elgar Publishing, pp. 73–91.

Kelly, J. (2017). The Island that Swapped Donkey Rides for Offshore Cash. *BBC News*. Available at: www.bbc.co.uk/news/resources/idtsh/the_island_that_swapped_donkey_rides_for_offshore_cash [accessed 25 December 2017].

Kiely, R. (2010). *Rethinking Imperialism*. London: Palgrave Macmillan.

Killingray, D. (1999). Introduction, in Killingray, D., and Omissi, D. (eds), *Guardians of Empire: The Armed Forces of the Colonial Power, c. 1700–1964*. Manchester: Manchester University Press, pp. 1–25.

Killingray, D., and Omissi, D. (eds). (1999). *Guardians of Empire: The Armed Forces of the Colonial Power, c. 1700–1964*. Manchester: Manchester University Press.

Kitson, M., and Michie, J. (2014). *The Deindustrial Revolution: The Rise and Fall of UK Manufacturing, 1870–2010*. CBR Research Programme on Enterprise and Innovation Working Paper No. 459. Cambridge: Centre for Business Research, University of Cambridge.

Klasa, A., and Fingar, C. (eds). (2017). *The Africa Investment Report 2017*. London: The Financial Times Ltd.

Klein, N. (2014). *This Changes Everything*. London: Penguin.

Kleinheisterkamp, J. (2014). Is there a Need for Investor-State Arbitration in the Transatlantic Trade and Investment Partnership (TTIP)? *SSRN Electronic Journal*. 14 February. Available at: https://ssrn.com/abstract=2410188 [accessed 9 August 2017].

Koukiadaki, A., and Kokkinou, C. (2016). Deconstructing the Greek System of Industrial Relations. *European Journal of Industrial Relations*, 22(3): 205–219.

Kramer, P. (2011). Power and Connection: Imperial Histories of the United States and the World. *American Historical Review*, 116(5): 1348–1391.

Küblböck, K. (2013). The EU Raw Materials Initiative – Scope and Critical Assessment. *Austrian Foundation for Development Research*, September. Available at: www.oefse.at/fileadmin/content/Downloads/Publikationen/Briefingpaper/BP8_eu_raw_materials.pdf [accessed 15 July 2017].

Kunović, M. (2017). Five Things You Need to Know about Trump's Cuba Policy – and Who it Will Hurt. *Washington Post*, 22 June. Available at: https://www.washingtonpost.com/news/monkey-cage/wp/2017/06/22/five-things-you-need-to-know-about-trumps-cuba-policy-and-who-it-will-hurt [accessed 31 August 2017].

Kunz, D. B. (2000). The New Empire Redux. *International Studies Review*, 2: 136–137.

Kwa, A. (2003). *Power, Politics and the WTO*. Bangok: Focus on the Global South.

Lambert, A. (2004). Hay, Lord John (1827–1916). *Oxford Dictionary of National Biography*. Oxford: Oxford University Press.

Landau, S. (2009). Finally, Diplomacy with Cuba not Vitiated by Hubris? *Diplomacy & Statecraft*, 20(2): 341–346.

Lane, J. C. (1972). Instrument for Empire: The American Military Government in Cuba, 1899–1902. *Science & Society*, 36(3): 314–330.

Latané, B., and Darley, J. M. (1968). Group Inhibition of Bystander Intervention in Emergencies. *Journal of Personality and Social Psychology*, 10(3): 215–221.

Lattimore, O. (1970). *Britain's Opportunity in Asian Studies*. London: School of Oriental and African Studies.

Lebergott, S. (1980). The Returns of U.S. Imperialism, 1890–1929. *Journal of Economic History*, 40(2): 229–252.

LeoGrande, W. M. (2015). A Policy Long Past Its Expiration Date: US Economic Sanctions Against Cuba. *Social Research: An International Quarterly*, 82(4): 939–966.

Leonard, L. (2016). State Governance, Participation and Mining Development: Lessons Learned from Dullstroom, Mpumalanga. *Politikon*, 44(2): 327–345.

Lipton, E., and Hakim, D. (2013). Lobbying Bonanza as Firms Try to Influence European Union. *New York Times*, 18 October. Available at: www.nytimes.com/2013/10/19/world/europe/lobbying-bonanza-as-firms-try-to-influence-european-union.html?mcubz=3 [accessed 26 August 2017].

Litvin, D. (2003). *Empires of Profit: Commerce, Conquest and Corporate Responsibility*. New York: Texere.

Louis, W. M. (ed.). (1976). *Imperialism: The Robinson and Gallagher Controversy*. New York: New Viewpoints.

Macak, R. (1989). *The CORDS Pacification Program: An Operational Level Campaign Plan in Low Intensity Conflict*. SAMS Monograph. Fort Leavenworth, KS: School of Advanced Military Studies.

Mackay, N. (2000). The Force Research Unit: 'My Unit Conspired in the Murder of Civilians in Ireland'. *Sunday Herald*, 19 November.

Madonsela, T. (2016). *State of Capture Report*. Pretoria: Office of the Public Protector.

Malmström, C. (2015). The EPA as a Pathway to Speech to Diversification. Speech to EU-Nigeria Business Forum, Lagos, 5 November. Available at: http://www.eeas.europa.eu/archives/delegations/nigeria/documents/press_corner/news/20151105-nigeria-eu-nigeria-business-forum-speech-by-eu-commissioner-for-trade_en.pdf [accessed 2 August 2017].

Mandelson, P. (2004). The ACP-EU Relationship in the Global Economy. Speech to ACP-EU Ministerial, Brussels, 1 December. Available at: http://trade.ec.europa.eu/doclib/docs/2005/january/tradoc_120436.pdf [accessed 2 August 2017].

Marini, R. M. (1972). Brazilian Subimperialism. *Monthly Review*, 23(9): 14–24.

Marinovich, G. (2016). *Murder at the Small Koppie*. London: Penguin.

Marquess of Hartington. (1884). Speech to the House of Commons. *Hansard HC Deb*, Vol. 285, 15 March.

Martin, G. (1982). Africa and the Ideology of Eurafrica: Neo-Colonialism or PanAfricanism? *The Journal of Modern African Studies*, 20(2): 221–238.

McDonald, H. (2005). 20 years of Treachery. *The Observer*, 18 December.

McDonald, H. (2015). Two MI5 Surveillance Operations in Northern Ireland Blocked, ISC Reveals. *The Guardian*, 27 July.

McKearney, T. (2011). *The Provisional IRA: From Insurrection to Parliament*. London: Pluto.

Mclaughlin, G., and Baker, S. (2015). *The British Media and Bloody Sunday*. Bristol: Intellect.

Ministry of Labour and Social Insurance. (2012). Circular Number 4601/304/12–3-2012, for the Implementation of Paragraph 6 of Article 1 of the Act 4046/2012. Available at: www.grhotels.gr/GR/BussinessInfo/library/DocLib/egkiklios%204601-yp.ergasias.pdf.

Mitsopoulos, M., and Pelagidis, T. (2011). *Understanding the Crisis in Greece: From Boom to Bust*. London: Palgrave.

Mkandawire, T. (2002). The Terrible Toll of Post-colonial 'Rebel Movements' in Africa: Towards an Explanation of the Violence Against the Peasantry. *Journal of Modern African Studies*, 40(2): 181–215.

Moloney, E., and Mitchell, B. (2013). The Force Research Unit – How It Began. *The Broken Elbow*, 4 January. Available at: https://thebrokenelbow.com/2013/01/04/the-force-research-unit-how-it-began/ [accessed 16 May 2018].

Montero, C. (1997). *La revolución empresarial en chilena*. Santiago: Dolmen Editions.

Morley, M. H. (1984). The United States and the Global Economic Blockade of Cuba: A Study in Political Pressures on America's Allies. *Canadian Journal of Political Science/ Revue canadienne de science politique*, 17(1): 25–48.

Morris, A. (2017). Wanted: Finance Officer to Work for MI5 in Northern Ireland. Must be British – But Finance Qualification Not Essential. *Irish News*, 14 August.

Müller, M. (2015). Das schwierige Verhältnis von sozialen Bewegungen und Gewerkschaften in Südafrika, in Engels, B., Müller, M., and Öhlschläger, R. (eds), *Zwischen Globalisierung und lokalen Kämpfen. Soziale Bewegungungen in Afrika*. Baden-Baden: Nomos, pp. 93–108.

Müller, M. (2016). *Auswirkungen internationaler Konferenzen auf soziale Bewegungen. Das Fallbeispiel der Klimakonferenz in Südafrika*. Wiesbaden: Springer VS.

Nadal, J. (1975). *El fracaso de la Revolución Industrial en España, 1814–1913*. Barcelona: Ariel.

Naicker, C. (2016). Worker Struggle as Community Struggles: The Politics of Protest in Nkaneng, Marikana. *Journal of Asian and African Studies*, 51(2): 157–170.

Nandy, A. (1983). *The Intimate Enemy: Loss and Recovery of Self Under Colonialism*. Oxford University Press: New York.

National Archives, Kew. Ad. WO 33/42, War Office Records. Adjutant-General to the General Officer Commanding in Egypt, Telegram, 12 February 1884.

National Archives, Kew. CAB 129/16/2, Cabinet Papers: Paper from Foreign Secretary, 6 January 1947.

National Archives, Kew. CAB 7/3. Cabinet Office Records. Royal Commission Appointed to Inquire into the Defence of British Possessions and Commerce Abroad, Second Report, 1882.

National Archives, Kew. CAB 37, Cabinet Minutes and Papers, Photographic Copies of Cabinet Letters in the Royal Archives. Lord Northbrook to the Cabinet, Confidential Memorandum, 8 February 1884.

National Archives, Kew, Foreign Office Confidential Records: Correspondence Respecting the Red Sea and Somali Coast, Sir Bartle Frere, Memorandum on the Treaties with the Somalis and other Tribes on the African Coast of the Red Sea and Gulf of Aden.

National Archives, Kew. PRO/30/29/144, Correspondence and Memoranda: Cabinet Opinions. Marquess of Hartington to Lord Granville, Letter, 7 February 1884.

National Archives, Kew. PRO/30/29/144, Correspondence and Memoranda: Cabinet Opinions. Marquess of Hartington to Lord Northbrook, Letter, 14 February 1884. National Library of Scotland, Edinburgh. Acc.11388/60. Lord Northbrook to Lady Louisa Ashburton, Letter, 18 May n.d.

National Maritime Museum, Caird Library & Archives, Goodsall Papers, GDL/6, Logbook of SS Chiltern cable laying in the Red Sea, December 1883–February 1884.

Nehru, J. (1928). *The Nehru Report: The Committee Appointed by the All Parties Conference*. Delhi: Michiko & Panjathan.

Neslen, A. (2016a). EU told ExxonMobil that TTIP Would Aid Global Expansion, Documents Reveal. *The Guardian*, 23 February.

Neslen, A. (2016b). TTIP: Chevron Lobbied for Controversial Legal Right as 'Environmental Deterrent'. *The Guardian*, 26 April.

Nicol, D. (2010). *The Constitutional Protection of Capitalism*. Portland, OR: Hart.

Nkrumah, K. (1965). *Neo-Colonialism: The Last Stage of Imperialism*. New York: International.

Núñez Sarmiento, M. (2014). U.S. Proposals for an Unwanted Transition in Cuba: A Critique. *Latin American Perspectives*, 41(4): 147–163.

Nwoke, C. N. (2008). Nigeria and the Challenge of the EPA. *Trade Negotiations Insights*, 7(9). Available at: https://www.ictsd.org/bridges-news/trade-negotiations-insights/news/nigeria-and-the-challenge-of-the-epa [accessed: 15 July 2017].

O'Donoghue, A., and Tzouvala, N. (2017). TTIP: The Rise of 'Mega-Market' Trade Agreements and its Potential Implications for the Global South. *Trade, Law and Development*, 8(2): 31–65.

O'Dwyer, Bishop (1915). Letter Reproduced in National Unionist Association. *1916 Gleanings and Memoranda*, 46, December: 455.

OECD/IIEA. (2006). *Angola Towards an Energy Strategy*. Paris: International Energy Agency.

Ohrwalder, J. (1892). *Ten Years' Captivity in the Mahdi's Camp, 1882–1892*. London: Low.

Palen, M.-W. (2015). The Imperialism of Economic Nationalism, 1890–1913. *Diplomatic History*, 39(1): 157–185.

Palan, R., Chavagneux, C., and Murphy, R. (2009). *Tax Havens: How Globalization Really Works*. Ithaca, NY: Cornell University Press.

Panitch, L., and Gindin, S. (2012). *The Making of Global Capitalism*. London: Verso.

Papadopoulos, O. (2016). Youth Unemployment Discourses in Greece and Ireland Before and During the Economic Crisis: Moving from Divergence to 'Contingent Convergence'. *Economic and Industrial Democracy*, 37(3): 493–515.

Papanikolopoulos, D. (2016). The Trade-union Dynamics 2010–2015. *Enimerosi*, 232: 2–28 [in Greek].

Papatheodorou, C., and Papanastasiou, S. (2017). *The State of the Children in Greece Report 2017*. Athens: Hellenic National Committee for UNICEF.

Parker, M. (2009). Pirates, Merchants and Anarchists: Representations of International Business. *Management & Organizational History*, 4(2): 167–185.

Partridge, M. S. (1989). *Military Planning for the Defense of the United Kingdom, 1814–1870*. Westport, CT: Greenwood Press.

Paul, H. W. (1905). *The Life of Froude*. London: Sir Isaac Pitman & Sons.

Peck, J. (2011a). Geographies of Policy: From Transfer Diffusion to Mobility Mutation. *Progress in Human Geography*, 35(6): 773–797.

Peck, J. (2011b). Global Policy Models, Globalising Poverty Management: International Convergence or Fast Policy Integration. *Geography Compass*, 5(4): 165–181.

Peck, J., and Theodore, N. (2015). *Fast Policy: Experimental Statecraft at the Thresholds of Neoliberalism*. Minneapolis, MN: University of Minnesota Press.Peers, D. (2013). South Asia, in Black, D. (ed.), *War in the Modern World Since 1815*. London: Routledge, pp. 41–74.

Pelc, K. (2016). *Does the International Investment Regime Induce Frivolous Litigation?* doi:10.2139/ssrn.2778056

Pérez, L. A., Jr (2015). *Cuba: Between Reform and Revolution*. Oxford: Oxford University Press.

Pérez-Stable, M. (1993). *The Cuban Revolution: Origins, Course, and Legacy*. Oxford: Oxford University Press.

Petras, J., and Morley, M. (1996). Clinton's Cuba Policy: Two Steps Backward, One Step Forward. *Third World Quarterly*, 17(2): 269–287.

Pim, Bedford. Speech to the House of Commons. *Hansard HC Deb*, Vol. 233, 19 March 1877.

Platt, D. C. M. (1968). The Imperialism of Free Trade: Some Reservations. *Economic History Review*, 21(2): 296–306.
Porras, J. (2003). *La estrategia chilena de los acuerdos comerciales: un análisis político*. ECLAC, Division of International Trade and Integration, Chile.
Pothier, C. (2003). Propagandist Representation of Vietnamese Women: A Comparative Study. *Review of Vietnamese Studies*, 3(1): 1–20.
Poulsen, L. (2015). *Bounded Rationality and Economic Diplomacy: The Politics of Investment Treaties in Developing Countries*. Cambridge: Cambridge University Press.
Preston, P. (2011). Treasure Islands: Tax Havens and the Men Who Stole the World by Nicholas Shaxson. *The Guardian*, 22 January.
Pugés, M. (1931). *Como triunfó el proteccionismo en España*. Barcelona.
Pye, L. (1962). Introduction, in Pye, L., and Verba, S. (ed.), *Political Culture and Political Development*. Princeton, NJ: Princeton University Press, pp. 3–26.
Quiroga, A., and Ángel del Arco, M. (eds). (2012). *Right Wing Spain in the Civil War*. London: Continuum.
Raaflaub, K. A. (1980). The Political Significance of Augustus's Military Reforms, in Hanson, W., and Keppie, L. (eds), *Roman Frontier Studies*. Oxford: British Archaeological Reports, pp. 1005–1025.
Rabe, S. G. (1988). *Eisenhower and Latin America: The Foreign Policy of Anticommunism*. Chapel Hill, NC: University of North Carolina Press.
RAND. (1967). *John Donnell, Vietcong Recruitment: Why and How Men Join*. Santa Monica, CA: RAND.
Raposo, A., and Mourão, P. (2013). Tax Havens or Tax Hells? A Discussion of the Historical Roots and Present Consequences of Tax Havens. *Financial Theory and Practice*, 37(3): 311–360.
Rayment, S. (2007). Top Secret Army Cell Breaks Terrorists. *The Telegraph*, 4 February.
Rettig, T., and Hack, K. (eds.). (2006). *Colonial Armies in Southeast Asia*. Abingdon: Routledge.
Reuters. (2012). Angola Explains $27.2 Billion of Missing Funds – IMF. Available at: https://www.reuters.com/article/angola-imf/angola-explains-27-2-billion-of-missing-funds-imf-idUSL5E8GAEPJ20120510 [accessed 2 January 2018].
Rich, J. W. (1983). The Supposed Roman Manpower Shortage of the Late Second Century BC. *Historia, Zeitschrift für Alte Geschichte*, 32(3): 287–331.
Rich, J., and Shipley, G. (eds). (1993). *War and Society in the Roman World*. London: Harper Collins.
Rivera, S. (1995). After NAFTA: Western Hemispheric Trade Liberalization and Alternative Paths to Integration. *The Social Science Journal*, 32(4): 389–407.
Roberts, D. (2016). Obama Lands in Cuba as First US President to Visit in Nearly a Century. *The Guardian*, 21 March.
Robinson, R., and Gallagher, J. (1981). *Africa and the Victorians: The Official Mind of Imperialism*. Basingstoke: Palgrave MacMillan.
Rodney, W. (2012). *How Europe Underdeveloped Africa*. Cape Town: Pambazuka Press.
Rodríguez Alonso, M. (1991). *Gran Bretaña y España: Diplomacia, guerra, revolución y comercio, 1833–1839*. Madrid: Actas.
Rose, R. (1993). *Lesson Drawing in Public Policy*. New York: Chatham House.
Rush, C. (2000). Brazil is the Target of Chile-US Trade Accord. *Eire Economics*, 27(50): 4–5.
Said, E. (1991[1978]). *Orientalism*. Harmondsworth: Penguin.
Samson, M. (2009). (Sub)imperial South Africa? Reframing the Debate. *Review of African Political Economy*, 36(119): 93–103.

Sanderson, G. N. (1965). *England, Europe & the Upper Nile: A Study in the Partition of Africa, 1882–1899.* Edinburgh: Edinburgh University Press.

Sandler, S. (2004). *Battleships: An Illustrated History of Their Impact.* Santa Barbara, CA: ABC-CLIO.

Santamarina, J. C. (2000). The Cuba Company and the Expansion of American Business in Cuba, 1898–1915. *Business History Review*, 74(1): 41–83.

Santander (n.d.). South Africa: Foreign Investment. Available at: https://en.portal.santandertrade.com/establish-overseas/south-africa/foreign-investment [accessed 25 January 2018].

Saul, J. S., and Bond, P. (2014). *South Africa – The Present as History. From Mrs Ples to Mandela & Marikana.* Johannesburg: Jacana.

Scharpf, F. W. (2010). The Asymmetry of European Integration, or Why the EU Cannot Be a 'Social Market Economy'. *Socio-Economic Review*, 26 April. Available at: http://www.mpifg.de/pu/mpifg_ja/SER_8_2010_Scharpf.pdf [accessed 22 July 2017].

Scholvin, S., and Draper, P. (2012). The Gateway to Africa? Geography and South Africa's Role as an Economic Hinge Joint between Africa and the World. *South African Journal of International Affairs*, 19(3): 381–400.

Schoultz, L. (2010). Benevolent Domination: The Ideology of U.S. Policy toward Cuba. *Cuban Studies*, 41(1): 1–19.

Schreiber, A. P. (1973). Economic Coercion as an Instrument of Foreign Policy: U.S. Economic Measures Against Cuba and the Dominican Republic. *World Politics*, 25(3): 387–413.

Scott, J. (1976). *The Moral Economy of the Peasant: Rebellion and Subsistence in Southeast Asia.* New Haven, CT: Yale University Press.

Seattle to Brussels Network. (2016). The EU Destabilizes and Blackmails African States to Secure its Economic Interests. *Seattle to Brussels Network*, 15 June. Available at: http://www.s2bnetwork.org/eu-blackmails-african-states/ [accessed 16 July 2017].

Security Service. (2002). *The Intelligence Organisation in Northern Ireland.* 30 September.

Seeley, J. R. (1883). *The Expansion of England: Two Courses of Lectures.* London: Mac-Millan and Co.

Senate House Library. (1888), London. MS903/1B/17, Papers of John Seeley. Lord Brassey to Sir John Seeley, Letter, 11 February.

Senate House Library. (1887), London. MS903/1B/17, Papers of John Seeley. Lord Hartington to Sir John Seeley, Letter, 27 October.

Sepos, A. (2013). Imperial Power Europe? The EU's Relations with the ACP Countries. *Journal of Political Power*, 6(4): 261–287.

Serels, S. (2013). *Starvation and the State: Famine, Slavery, and Power in Sudan, 1883–1956.* New York: Palgrave MacMillan.

Serfati, C. (2015). The Transatlantic Bloc of States and the Political Economy of the Transatlantic Trade and Investment Partnership. *Work Organisation, Labour & Globalisation*, 9(1): 7–37.

Shadlen, K. (2005). Exchanging Development for Market Access? Deep Integration and Industrial Policy under Multilateral and Regional-bilateral Trade Agreements. *Review of International Political Economy*, 12(5): 750–775.

Sharp, A. (2014). Secret Army Unit Credited with Saving THOUSANDS of Civilian Lives Facing Chop. *Mirror*, 9 March.

Sharpf, F. W. (2009). *The Asymmetry of European Integration or Why the EU Cannot Be a 'Social Market Economy'.* KFG Working Paper No. 6. Berlin: Freie Universität Berlin.

Shaxon, N. (2011). *Treasure Islands: Tax Havens and the Men who Stole the World*. London: The Bodley Head.
Silva, E. (1996). *State and Capital in Chile*. Boulder, CO: Westview Press.
Silva, V. (2001). *Estrategia y agenda comercial chilena en los años noventa*. Series Comercio International #11. Santiago: ECLAC.
SOMO. (2014). TTIP Undermines Financial Regulation and Leaves Citizens Unprotected. *Centre for Research on Multinational Corporations*, January. Available at: https://www.somo.nl/wp-content/uploads/2014/01/TTIP-undermines-financial-regulation-and-leaves-citizens-unprotected-SOMO.pdf [accessed 2 August 2017].
South African Government. (2017). President Jacob Zuma: State of the Nation Address. Available at: https://www.gov.za/speeches/president-jacob-zuma-2017-state-nation-address-9-feb-2017-0000 [accessed 19 September 2017].
Speck, M. (2005). Closed-Door Imperialism: The Politics of Cuban-U.S. Trade, 1902–1933. *Hispanic American Historical Review*, 85(3): 449–484.
Spivak, G. C. (1993). *Outside in the Teaching Machine*. New York and London: Routledge.
Spourdalakis, M. (2014). The Miraculous Rise of the 'Phenomenon SYRIZA'. *International Critical Thought*, 4(3): 354–366.
Stanley, H. M. (2013). *The Congo and the Founding of Its Free State: A Story of Work and Exploration*. Cambridge: Cambridge University Press.
Steyn, L. (2013). Mine Bosses Rake in Big Bucks. *The M&G Online*. Available at: https://mg.co.za/article/2013-07-26-00-mine-bosses-rake-in-the-big-bucks [accessed 19 September 2017].
Steil, B. (2013). *The Battle of Bretton Woods*. Princeton, NJ: Princeton University Press. Stille, A. (1996). *Excellent Cadavers*. London: Vintage.
Surrey History Centre, Woking (1884). LM/COR. Major W. Emerson Peck to the Inspector-General of Fortifications, Report, 13 July.
Talhami, G. (1979). *Suakin and Massawa under Egyptian Rule, 1865–1885*. Washington DC: University Press of America.
The New York Times. (1875). The Suez Canal Purchase. 15 December.
The New York Times. (1893). The British Navy. 23 November.Theobald, A. B. (1951). *The Madhiya: A History of the Anglo-Egyptian Sudan, 1881–1899*. London: Longman.
Toro Hardy, A. (2008). *Hegemonía e Imperio*. Colombia: Villega Editores.
Tortella, G. (1977). *Banking, Railroads and Industry in Spain 1829–1874*. London: Arno Press.
Tortella, G. (2000). *The Development of Modern Spain*. Cambridge, MA: Harvard University Press.
Trade Justice Movement. (2017). *Bilateral Investment Treaties: Third Party Funding – The Financialisation of Justice*. London: Trade Justice Movement.Trantidis, A. (2016). Clientelism and Economic Policy: Hybrid Characteristics of Collective Action in Greece. *Journal of European Public Policy*, 23(10): 1460–1480.
Trebilcock, C. (1981). *The Industrialisation of the Continental Powers 1780–1914*. London: Longman.
Tsakiris, A., and Aranitou, V. (2012). 'Under the Weight of the Social': Reactions of the Social Representation System and Antisystemic Challenges During the Era of the Memorandum. Paper presented at the XXIInd World Congress of International Political Science Association (IPSA), Madrid, 8–12 July.
UK Foreign & Commonwealth Office. (2015). *South Africa – Mining Sector: An Update*, 29 January. https://www.gov.uk/government/publications/south-africa-mining-sector-an-update/south-africa-mining-sector-an-update

UNCTAD. (2015). *Trade and Development Report 2015*. Geneva: United Nations Conference on Trade and Development.

UNCTAD. (2016). The Least Developed Countries Report 2016. *United Nations Conference on Trade and Development*, 9 June. Available at: http://unctad.org/en/PublicationsLibrary/ldc2016_en.pdf [accessed 16 July 2017].

UNCTAD. (2017). International Investment Agreements Navigator. *United Nations Conference on Trade and Development*. Available at: http://investmentpolicyhub.unctad.org/IIA [accessed 9 August 2017].

UNESCO. (2016). Antigua Naval Dockyard and Related Archaeological Sites. Available at: http://whc.unesco.org/en/list/1499/documents/ [accessed 1 November 2017].

Urwin, M. (2016). *A State in Denial: The British Government and Loyalist Paramilitaries*. Cork: Mercier Press.

Van de Ploeg, J. D. (2010). The Peasantries of the Twenty-first Century: The Commoditisation Debate Revisited. *Journal of Peasant Studies*, 37(1): 1–30.

Van Harten, G. (2016). Flaws in the European Commission's Proposals for Foreign Investor Protection in the Transatlantic Trade and Investment Partnership. *Foundation for European Progressive Studies*, July. Available at: http://www.feps-europe.eu/assets/6561f22b-2cc3-4595-b000-546f0a230236/van-harten-finalpdf.pdf [accessed 12 August 2017].

Varoufakis, Y. (2017). *Adults in the Room: My Battle with Europe's Deep Establishment*. London: The Bodley Head.

Vasilopoulou, S., Halikiopoulou, D., and Exadaktylos, T. (2014). Greece in Crisis: Austerity, Populism and the Politics of Blame. *JCMS: Journal of Common Market Studies*, 52(2): 388–402.

Venizelos, E. (2016). *Transformations of the State and European Integration*. Athens: Polis [in Greek].

Vetch, R. H. (1901). *Life, Letters, and Diaries of Lieutenant-General Sir Gerald Graham*. Edinburgh: Blackwood and Sons.

Voulgaris, Y., and Nicolacopoulos, E. (2014). The Electoral Earthquake of 2012, in Voulagaris, Y., and Nicolacopoulos, E. (eds), *2012: The Dual Electoral Earthquake*. Athens: Themelio [in Greek].

Walker, J. L. (1969). The Diffusion of Innovations Among the American States. *American Political Science Review*, 63(3): 880–899.

War on Want. (2015). What is TTIP? Available at: www.waronwant.org/what-ttip [accessed 9 August 2017].

Waterfield, B. (2007). Barroso Hails the European 'empire'. *Daily Telegraph*. Available at: www.telegraph.co.uk/news/worldnews/1557143/Barroso-hails-the-European-empire.html [accessed 19 September 2017].

Webber, D. (2014). *Declining Power Europe? The Evolution of the European Union's Power in the Early 21st Century*. Monash University Working Paper Series 2014/1. Available at: http://artsonline.monash.edu.au/wp-content/arts-files/europecentre/Working%20Papers%202014%2001.pdf [accessed 13 August 2017].

Webster, C. (1951). *The Foreign Policy of Palmerston*. London: J. Bell and Sons.

Weintraub, S. (2004). Lessons from Chile and Singapore Free Trade Agreements, in Shott, J. (ed.), *Free Trade Agreements: U.S. Strategies and Priorities*. Washington DC: Institute of International Economics, pp. 79–92.

Wesselius, E. (2003). Driving the GATS Juggernaut. *Red Pepper*, January. Available at: https://www.tni.org/my/node/7197 [accessed 22 July 2017].

Wilder, G. (2015). *Freedom Time: Negritude, Decolonisation and the Future of the World.* Durham, NC: Duke University Press.

Williams, W. A. (1972). *The Tragedy of American Diplomacy.* New York: Delta Books.

Wolfe, P. (1999). *Settler Colonialism and the Transformation of Anthropology.* London: Cassell.

Woll, C. (2006). Trade Policy Lobbying in the European Union: Who Captures Whom? *Max Planck Institute for the Study of Societies*, July. Available at: http://www.mpifg.de/pu/workpap/wp06-7/wp06-7.html [accessed 12 August 2017].

Wolseley, G. (1967). *In Relief of Gordon: Lord Wolseley's Campaign Journal of the Khartoum Relief Expedition 1884–1885.* London: Hutchinson & Co.

Wood, E. M. (2005). *Empire of Capital.* London: Verso.

World Bank. (1993). *The East Asian Miracle: Economic Growth and Public Policy.* Oxford: Oxford University Press.Yee, J. (2016). *The Colonial Comedy: Imperialism in the French Realist Novel.* Oxford: Oxford University Press.

Youens, K. (2017). *Dangers of Being a Defender of Environmental Justice in South Africa: Save our Mfolozi Wilderness Campaign.* Available at: https://saveourwilderness.org/2017/08/30/dangers-of-being-a-defender-of-environmental-justice-in-south-africa/ [accessed 29 September 2017].

Yuen, L. (2018). *The Great Economists: How Their Ideas Can Help Us Today.* London: Viking.

Index

Aden 28, 30, 31
Afghanistan 11
African National Congress 113, 119, 120
Algeria 62
Ali, Khedive Muhammed 24, 25
Allende, Salvador 7, 96, 125
Angola 146–7
Antigua 140–1
Arabi, Colonel Ahemed 24
Árbenz, Jacobo 7, 96, 125
Argentina 97, 113, 132, 162
ATT 7
Attlee, Clement 45
Augustus, Caesar 65
Australasia 23
Australia 12, 13, 62, 118
Austria 151
Austro-Hungarian Empire 9

Bancor 5, 13
Barroso, José Manuel 152, 155, 162
Basel III 163
Batista, Fulgencio 52, 125
berlin blockade 14
Bermuda 9, 144, 147
Bevin, Ernest 45
Bjornson, Maria 139
Blockadia 115, 121–4
Bloody Sunday Massacre (1972) 76, 77, 78, 81
Bolivia 62, 162
Botswana 117
Brazil 88, 98, 99, 113, 125, 132, 162, 164
Bretton Woods 5, 13, 160
BRICS 114, 119, 123, 164
Britain 2, 6, 24, 31, 40, 42, 95, 118, 139, 141–2, 149, 151, 164; and cotton manufacture 10, 35, 36, 37; overseas investment 40
British Empire 1, 6, 12–14, 16, 23, 45, 47, 61, 64, 75, 92, 95, 98, 126, 144, 152; economic strength 29–30, 39; naval defence 28–9, 31, 34
British Virgin Islands 144, 151
Brittain, Leon 155
Bush, George H. W. 55, 91, 128
Bush, George W. 55

Canada 10, 13, 62, 117, 131, 139, 151, 160
Canada-EU Comprehensive Economic and Trade Agreement (CETA) 154, 159
Carlist War 37
Carter, Jimmy 54
Castro, Fidel 21, 47, 48, 52, 53, 54, 55
Castro, Raúl 55, 56
Catalonia 36–8, 40, 41–2
Cayman Islands 142, 148, 150
Chile 6–7, 15, 89, 96, 98, 125, 126; and US informal imperialism 128–36
China 2, 9, 61, 62, 92, 94, 126, 153, 163, 164
Churchill, Winston 44
CIA 7, 53, 96
Clinton, Bill 55
Cobden, Richard 37
collaboration 1, 5, 6, 8, 9, 13, 15, 52, 58
Columbia 132, 160
Congo 59, 67, 156
Crowder, General Enoch 50–1
Cuba 10, 20–1, 34, 47–51, 125, 148, 149; Cuban-American National Foundation (CANF) 55; and Platt Amendment 48, 50, 51; revolution (1953) 10, 19, 47;

and Teller Amendment 50; US blockade 48, 53–6
Cyprus 151

Delors, Jacques 155
Democratic Unionist Party (DUP) 72, 82
Dirty Money Centres (DMCs) 137, 139; business practice reform 150–1; definition 143–5; morality 145–6; origins 142–3; tackling 147–50

East Germany 6
Eastern Telegraph Company 23
Ecuador 162
Egypt 16, 20, 24
Eisenhower, Dwight 52, 60
elites 6, 9, 12, 89, 102, 114, 127, 140–2
Estonia 151
Ethiopia 24
European Central Bank 96, 97, 102, 104
European Union 15, 55, 87, 91, 92, 93, 94, 95, 96, 97, 98, 100, 102, 103, 104, 107, 137, 138, 148, 153; and Africa 156–9; as 'non-imperial empire' 152; *see also* informal imperialism.
Exxon Mobil 159

Falkland Islands 148, 149
financial crisis (2007–8) 92, 96
Finucane, Pat 79
Fitzgerald, Garret 73, 80
Ford, Gerald 54
formal imperialism 1, 5, 8, 9, 20, 24, 43, 57, 87, 94, 142; and United States 47–9, 54, 125
France 6, 9, 14, 24, 34, 35, 39, 45, 62, 68, 75, 88, 154
Franco, Francisco 44, 45
free trade 2, 3, 36, 37, 38, 39, 40, 42, 47, 51, 114, 126, 130, 153; as imperialism *see* informal imperialism; *see also* 'The Imperialism of Free Trade'.
Friedman, Milton 15

Gallagher and Robinson *see* 'The Imperialism of Free Trade'
Gambia 156
Gandhi, Mahatma 60
General Agreement on Tariffs and Trade (GATT) 154
Germany 10–11, 23, 39, 88
Ghana 147
Gibraltar 9
Gladstone, William 25, 26
Goldman Sachs 155
Good Friday Agreement (GFA) 72, 73, 74, 75, 76, 78, 81, 83
Gordon, Major General Charles 26, 27
Greece 15–16, 87, 88, 93, 96, 97, 100, 101, 102; social and economic consequences of Troika bailout 108–11; state and Troika 103–4; political consequences of Troika 105–8
Guatemala 6–7, 15, 96, 125
Güell y Ferrer, Juan 37, 39
Guernsey 139
Guevara, Che 52–3, 67, 68, 149

Hayek, Friedrich 15, 155
Hobson, J. 4
Hong Kong 9, 74

Iceland 96; refusal of EU bailouts 97–8
India 2, 8, 9, 20, 23, 30, 31, 45, 57, 64, 65, 162, 164
Indonesia 95, 162, 164
informal imperialism 1, 3, 5, 8, 12–17, 20, 38, 87, 88, 89, 92, 94, 99–100, 138, 139–40, 141; of Britain 34, 43, 44, 45, 113, 153; of European Union 152, 154–6, 160–5; policy transfer as tool of 94–9; role of finance capital 49; of United States 47–9, 51–2, 53, 57, 89, 126–9, 131–5, 135–6
International Monetary Fund 14, 15, 87, 93, 94, 95, 103, 104, 105, 115, 119, 147, 161
Iran-Iraq war 11
Iraq 8, 11, 57
Ireland, 61, 62, 67, 74; operation of hard and soft power in 72–3, 74, 75–8; Republic of 58, 72, 93, 96, 97, 151; role of Force Research Unit in 79–82; Stevens Inquiry 81
Irish Free State 13
Isle of Man 147
Italy 14–15, 93

Jamaica 62
Japan 62, 68, 152, 154, 164
Jersey 147
Johnson, Lyndon 54
Junker, Jean-Claude 155, 162

Kennedy, John F. 54, 128
Kenya 31

Keynes, John Maynard 5, 14, 16; Keynesianism 98, 142
Korea 8, 11
Kuwait 11

Lenin, Vladimir Ilyich 4, 12, 49, 141
Lisbon Treaty 152, 154, 155
List, Friedrich 37
Luxembourg 143, 147, 151
Luxemburg, R. 4, 12

mafia 14–15
Malaysia 97
Malmström, Cecilia 156, 157
Malta 9, 31
Mandelson, Peter 157, 163
Marikana mining massacre 115, 120–2, 123
Marshall aid 14
Massawa 24
Mexico 10, 98, 125, 131, 162
MI5 73, 74, 76, 77, 79, 81, 82
Monroe doctrine, the 10, 12, 125
Morocco 162; Spanish invasion of 41, 42, 43
Multi National Corporations (MNCs) 91, 92, 95, 98, 115, 125
Mussolini, Benito 43

Namibia 117
Native Americans 10
NATO 11
Nelson, Brian 79
Nelson, Rosemary 79
Neoliberalism 15, 57, 74, 87, 88, 91, 93, 94, 107, 119, 142, 152, 154, 156, 161, 164
Nevis 144
New Democracy Party 107
New Zealand 4, 9, 12, 13
Newfoundland 13
Nigeria 147, 156, 157, 162
Nixon, Richard 52
North American Free Trade Agreement (NAFTA) 94, 126, 127, 129, 130, 131, 153
North American Free Trade Agreement (NATFA) 47
Northern Ireland 57, 58, 72, 73, 75, 82
Norway 146–7

Obama, Barack 56, 159
Oil Crisis (1973) 94
Organisation for Economic Cooperation and Development (OECD) 150
Organisation of American States (OAS) 54

Palmerston, Henry John 35–6, 37
Panama 132, 144, 150
Panama and Paradise Papers 144, 145, 148, 150
Panhellenic Socialist Movement (PASOK) 106, 107
Paraguay 132
Pasha, Khedive Ismail 24
Pasha, Khedive Tewfik 24
peasants and peasantry 57, 58, 60, 70, 71; defined 61–3; military-peasantry complex 60–1; relationship with military 62–7; resistance to occupation 68
Peru 132, 160
Philippines 62
Pinochet, Augusto 7, 96
Podemos 97
Poland 12
Police Service Northern Ireland (PSNI) 73, 74, 76, 77, 78, 79, 80, 81, 82
Portugal 96, 147
Primo de Rivera, Miguel 43; corporativist state of 43–4
privatisation 93, 94
Provisional IRA 76, 79, 80, 81, 82

Rawlings, Gerry 147
Reagan, Ronald 54, 95
Red Cross 139
Ricardo, David 2
Rio Tinto mines 19, 39, 40, 43
Roman Empire 57, 65–6
Royal Navy 28, 30, 31
Royal Ulster Constabulary (RUC) *see* Police Service Northern Ireland (PSNI)
Russian Empire 9, 23
Russian Federation 151

Samaras, Antonis 107
Singapore 160
Sinn Fein 82
Smith, Adam 2, 3
South Africa 13, 23, 30, 89, 113, 114, 115, 162; exploitation of labour in 119–21; influence of foreign capital in 118–19; mining industry 116–17, 118;

as sub-imperialist gateway 115–16, 122–4
South Korea 160
Soviet Union 6, 8, 9, 10, 14, 20, 48, 53, 54, 94, 125
Spain 12, 19, 20, 96, 97, 100; economy of 35–9, 41; industrial unrest 41, 43; industrialisation of 34; mineral resources of 39–40, 43; railway network of 39; Second Republic (1931–9) 44; tariffs 41; *see also* Catalonia
Spanish-American War (1898) 10, 19, 20, 41, 47, 49–50
Statute of Westminster (1930) 13
Suakin 23, 24, 25, 26, 27, 28, 30, 31
Sub-imperialism 89, 113, 115; and South African mining 116–17; *see also* South Africa
Sudan 19, 24, 25, 27
Suez Canal 20, 30, 31, 45
Switzerland 118, 143, 150, 151
Syzria 16, 97, 104, 106, 108, 112, 155

Tanzania 158
tariffs 1
tax havens *see* Dirty Money Centres (DMCs)
Tel-el-Kebir, battle of 24
Thatcher, Margaret 10–11, 95
'The Imperialism of Free Trade' 1–2, 3, 4, 5, 6, 8, 12, 20, 87; and Chile 126; continuity of imperial purpose 4–8; and Dirty Money Centres 141–2; and European Union 91, 92, 94, 95, 96, 99, 152; and South Africa 113, 114; and Spain 34–5, 36, 38, 43, 45; and United States 47, 48–9, 53, 56, 58; Wisconsin School, comparisons with 48–9
Trafalgar, Battle of 28, 35
Trans Atlantic Trade Partnership (TTIP) 95, 154, 155, 156, 158, 165; and informal imperialism 159–60, 162–3
Trans Pacific Partnership 153
Treaty of Rome (1957) 157
Troika 15–16, 88, 101, 102, 103, 111; and 'programme ownership' 107; structure of in Greece 104–5; *see also* Greece
Trump, Donald 56
trusts 141
Turner, Frederick Jackson 10

Ulster Defence Association (UDA) 79
Ulster Defence Regiment 76
United Fruit 7
United Kingdom *see* Britain
United Nations 6, 11, 45, 93, 94
United States 19, 20, 21, 23, 57, 62, 68, 69, 75, 77, 113, 125, 126; and 2003 Iraq War 12, 16–17; and Chilean sovereignty 131–5; Civil War 28, 30; and Cuba 40, 45, 50, 51, 56; and Dirty Money Centres 142, 148; and international trade 152, 153, 154, 156, 158, 159, 160, 163, 164; military-industrial complex 60; and NAFTA expansion 129–31; and policy transfer 91, 92, 93, 94, 95, 96; and Spain 37, 39; and 'The Imperialism of Free Trade' 2, 5, 6, 8, 10, 11, 13, 14, 15; trade agreements in Chile 127–9
Uruguay 132

Varoufakis, Yannis 16
Venezuela 162
Vietnam 8, 57, 59, 62, 68–70, 95, 160

Walpole, Robert 156
Washington Consensus 15, 88, 91, 92, 93, 94, 96, 98
West Germany 6, 10, 14
Wilson, Harold 73, 80
Wilson, Woodrow 50
Wolseley, Garnet 24, 27
World Bank 14, 15, 87, 115, 123, 150, 154, 156, 161; and conditional bank transfers 98–9; role in policy transfer 91, 93, 94, 95, 98, 100
World Trade Organisation (WTO) 55, 89, 113, 126, 127, 128, 131, 132
Wounded Knee, battle of 10

Zuma, Jacob 115

For Product Safety Concerns and Information please contact our EU representative GPSR@taylorandfrancis.com Taylor & Francis Verlag GmbH, Kaufingerstraße 24, 80331 München, Germany